CONTESTING INEQUALITIES

CONTESTING INEQUALITIES

MEDIATED LABOR ACTIVISM AND RURAL MIGRANT WORKERS IN CHINA

Siyuan Yin

STANFORD UNIVERSITY PRESS
Stanford, California

Stanford University Press
Stanford, California

Library of Congress Cataloging-in-Publication Data
Names: Yin, Siyuan (Communications professor) author
Title: Contesting inequalities : mediated labor activism and rural migrant
    workers in China / Siyuan Yin.
Description: Stanford, California : Stanford University Press, 2025. | Includes
    bibliographical references and index.
Identifiers: LCCN 2024040182 (print) | LCCN 2024040183 (ebook)
    | ISBN 9781503642560 paperback | ISBN 9781503642065 cloth |
    ISBN 9781503642553 ebook
Subjects: LCSH: China—Social conditions—2000- | Migrant labor—Political
    activity—China | Equality—China | Rural-urban migration—China | Mass
    media—Social aspects—China | Working class—Political activity—China |
    Migrant labor—China—Social conditions
Classification: LCC HD5856.C6 Y56 2025 (print) | LCC HD5856.C6 (ebook) |
    DDC 331.6/20951—dc23/eng/20241104

LC record available at https://lccn.loc.gov/2024040182
LC ebook record available at https://lccn.loc.gov/2024040183

Cover design: Daniel Benneworth-Gray
Cover photograph: Louise Jiaxi/Unsplash

To my parents, Yuan Ying and Yin Qi,
and grandparents Liu Jingui and Yin Ziqiang.

Contents

Acknowledgments

This book is dedicated to Chinese rural migrant workers, whose suffering, resilience, and struggles have been the greatest inspiration for me to undertake this project. In 2007, as a freshman in college, I visited a rural village in northwest China during a field trip organized by a student association. Having grown up in urban China, I was shocked by the sharp contrast in living conditions in the village: poorly constructed homes, insufficient healthcare services, and limited educational opportunities. Girls and boys dropped out of school at an early age to work in cities at fourteen or fifteen, encountering numerous difficulties. To me, the Chinese state and media discourse celebrating the country's achievements through economic reform became highly ironic.

Since then, the rural-urban divide has been one of my primary concerns as I developed my scholarly interest in social inequalities and resistance. When I spoke with rural migrant workers during my fieldwork in 2016, their stories often reminded me of the village I visited. I felt intense anger toward the inequalities present in contemporary China, and I genuinely admired these workers' courage to resist and fight against them. These individuals merit my highest acknowledgment. I am especially grateful to the activists, scholars, volunteers, and journalists who have generously shared their invaluable thoughts and experiences with me. Their commitment and efforts to advocate for migrant workers' rights have provided me with profound insights.

This book is the culmination of an academic journey, and I am deeply indebted to my advisors and mentors: Martha Fuentes-Bautista, Jonathan Ong, Lisa Henderson, and Cara Wallis. Their rigorous criticisms, steadfast guidance, and resolute support have been crucial in shaping this work. Without their invaluable input and encouragement, the creation of this book would have been unattainable. I would also like to express my sincere gratitude to my teachers at the University of Massachusetts Amherst and the University of Illinois Chicago: Sut Jhally, Mari Castañeda, Emily West, Jarice Hanson, Laura Briggs, Henry Geddes, Claudio Moreira, Ann Ferguson, Briankle Chang, Anne Ciecko, Kevin Barnhurst, Elaine Yuan, and Zizi Papacharissi. Their mentorship has been fundamental in molding my intellectual path, offering vital expertise and direction essential for my advancement and progress across a range of academic endeavors. Special thanks are also due to my undergraduate teachers at Peking University: Yang Boxu, Li Kun, Wu Jing, Tong Xin, and Yang Lihua. It was their thought-provoking classes that stimulated my initial interest in social theories.

I extend my heartfelt appreciation to my colleagues at the School of Communication at Simon Fraser University. In particular, I am grateful to Enda Brophy, Cait McKinney, Sun-Ha Hong, Stuart Poyntz, Sarah Ganter, Zoë Druick, Kirsten McAllister, Daniel Ahadi, Peter Chow-White, Yuezhi Zhao, Milena Droumeva, Shane Gunster, and Ahmed Al-Rawi, whose support and camaraderie have greatly enriched my academic journey. Their critical, interdisciplinary scholarship, insightful discussions, and collaborative spirit have been invaluable in shaping my research and fostering a vibrant intellectual community.

I greatly appreciate Dylan Kyung-lim White, the acquisitions editor at Stanford University Press, for his patience, support, and dedication to this project. I am fortunate to have the opportunity to work with him. Additionally, I am thankful to the two readers for their meticulous and insightful feedback on the book manuscript, which has significantly improved the overall quality of this work.

Throughout the years, I have been fortunate to receive attentive support and considerate concern from many dear friends during the writing of this book. Their continual encouragement and belief in me have provided immense strength and inspiration. I would like to express my wholehearted gratitude to Gong Yuan, Han Xue, Bu Wen, Ren Qunying, Jia Tong, Li Qi, Sun Yu, Liao (Sara) Xueting, Li (Angela) Ke, Gu Mingmin, Zeng Yuan, Gan Yanggu, Guo Jiangtao, Chen Xi, Chen Ziyu, Zhao Zilong, Situ Xuanming, Wang Xiaoyi, Woori Han, Felicitas Baruch, Changwook Kim, Danbi Yoo, Eren Odabasi, Zhang Chunyu, Huang Ying-Fen, Sun Xiaoting, Zhang Chenzi, Chen Rong, Zhou Yajie, Hu Xiaoyu, and Liu Juan.

My deepest gratitude goes to my parents, whose unconditional love, care, and support have been the cornerstone of my journey. Their unwavering devotion to my well-being has always transcended any desire for recognition, as they have consistently prioritized my happiness and fulfillment above all else. They have fostered an environment of respect for my passions and dreams, nurturing my interests and aspirations with boundless encouragement. I am also profoundly thankful for the care and collective love of my extended family—grandparents, aunts, uncles, and cousins—who have enriched my life in countless ways. To my entire family, I owe a tremendous debt of gratitude for shaping the person I am today.

FORMING COUNTERHEGEMONIC FORCES

Resistance Movements and the Possibility of Change

The last four decades of neoliberal transitions have resulted in stark inequalities between elites and working populations across the global North and South. With the increasing trends of marketization, deregulation, privatization, and austerity measures, a small group of elites has consolidated the majority of the world's power and wealth. While politicians, CEOs, bankers, and celebrities in different countries lead extravagant lives, underprivileged and marginalized groups, collectively comprising a global underclass, struggle with unemployment and underemployment, lack of labor protection, inadequate housing, limited access to healthcare and education, and discrimination and social exclusion. Rural-to-urban migrant workers in contemporary China belong to this global underclass. Emerging as a social group in the early 1980s, this migrant population has grown rapidly alongside the acceleration of China's economic reform since the 1990s. By 2022, there were 290 million rural migrant workers in China.[1] They are subject to exploitation of transnational and domestic capital as cheap laborers, the deprivation of political and civic rights by the party-state as secondary citizens, and marginalization and exclusion by mainstream media and culture as inferior and deviant others. The inequality and injustice experienced by rural migrant workers are the manifestations of the intertwined unequal power structures in contemporary China and worldwide.

On one hand, China's enormous and rapid economic growth has often been celebrated in official and popular discourse as the success of a unique Chinese model of development, a socialist market economy under the leadership of a communist party. Deng Xiaoping's famous slogan "Let some people get rich first" has resonated strongly among the political and business elites and the urban middle class, who have been the main beneficiaries of the economic liberalization and uneven distribution of wealth and power in reformist China. Celebratory accounts that champion the power of the market while preserving the state's discursive commitment to socialism have bypassed any substantial critique of China's integration into capitalist globalization as a factory for the world at the expense of rising inequality, disenfranchisement of the rural and urban poor and working class, environmental degradation, and an increasing dependence on transnational capital. Meanwhile, the party-state's sustaining authoritarian power remains intact.

On the other hand, the past two decades have seen a growing number of labor strikes among rural migrant workers, who demand better working conditions, fair wages, and benefits. Most of these have clustered in factories in industrial areas in South China.[2] These protests and strikes belong to the rising waves of workers' collective actions and resistance in the era of neoliberal globalization in different parts of the world, including manufacturing workers' strikes in India, South Korea, and South Africa, and gig and low-income service workers' protests and unionizing in the United Kingdom, Canada, and United States. But workers' resistance encounters varied reactionary forces. For instance, in India and South Korea, workers' protests are often broken up by the repressive governments.[3] In Western liberal democracies, such as Canada and the United States, it is usually the corporations and employers that set obstacles to discourage workers from organizing or participating in collective actions.[4] In China, migrant-worker actions in factories face rather brutal suppression by local governments, including police violence.[5] Due to the Chinese state's extensive control over mainstream-media and social media platforms, labor strikes receive little coverage from mainstream news media and have little presence in social media;

this prevents the broader public awareness of the workers' continuous struggles.

As rural migrant workers in postsocialist China face the formidable powers of the state, the market, and cultural domination, what are the possibilities for them to form resistance movements? Proceeding from that central question, this book explores possibilities of change and social transformation by shedding light on bottom-up, grassroots struggles toward equality and justice. I move beyond conventional interpretations of workers' struggles that see them as focused on substantial rights and against labor exploitation, and that move leads me to ask and address additional questions: How do Chinese rural migrant workers become a new historical subject of change? What forms of collective resistance, other than labor strikes, arise from workers' everyday lives and are more sustainable in authoritarian contexts, like China? To what extent can the formation of workers' collective power build solidarity and alliances with other groups of marginalized people to form a broader base of resistance? These questions respond to the division between labor movements and new social movements since the 1960s, which scholars have criticized.[6] I suggest that only by tying class struggles to resistance efforts against other long-lasting power structures, such as patriarchy and heteronormativity, can an inclusive and transformative counterpower be developed.

In this book, I attend to a range of media, cultural, and communicative practices that rural migrant workers deploy as the main means and sites for their collective resistance efforts. I characterize these practices as mediated labor activism. "Mediated labor activism" refers to the integration of a variety of media, cultural, and communicative practices, such as theater performance, music, cultural production, and uses of digital media, into daily activism for migrant workers' labor rights, equality, and justice. This book investigates diverse social actors and forms of mediated labor activism to demonstrate how mediated labor activism has enabled new possibilities for socioeconomic change in contemporary China. Through multisited and digital ethnography, I explore the experiences of rural migrant workers and engage with varied participants in mediated labor activism, including nongovernmental organizations (NGOs), advocacy groups, activists, scholars, volunteers, and journalists. The research project, carried out between March 2016 and August 2022 in Beijing and Xi'an, diverges from coastal manufacturing hubs. Instead, it concentrates on the construction and service sectors prevalent in northern China, where rural migrant workers constitute the primary workforce.

MEDIA, ACTIVISM, AND RESISTANCE MOVEMENTS

Activists and protesters adopt those communicative and media practices available to them—such as theater, art, video, music, and the internet—in the hopes of appealing to their target audiences. In postcolonial areas, including Africa, South Asia, and Latin America, local people, artists, and activists affect and educate audiences through drama and performance in community-based theaters to advocate for the rights of indigenous people, women, and marginalized groups.[7] In the area of public health communication, storytelling and personal narratives of living with HIV become crucial components in campaigns to change behaviors and perceptions at the individual level and values and norms at the societal level.[8] Artist-activists raise public awareness of inequalities and injustice through various artistic activities. In Japan, for instance, feminist artists challenge the patriarchal gaze upon women's bodies through artistic practices.[9] Musician-activists produce and circulate advocacy songs to foment support for social movements around the world.[10] Labor movements and unions have a long history of creating their own media to promote the ideals of their desired society and to generate discussion among workers.[11] As media scholars Bart Cammaerts, Alice Mattoni, and Patrick McCurdy suggest, a focus on media practices can enable "the embedding of activists' routines and the creative use of diverse media technologies and outlets within the broader set of protest activities"[12]—in other words, workers' theater and activist communication on WeChat (Weixin; 微信) belong to the totality of counterhegemonic struggle just as much as labor walkouts and sit-ins do.[13]

In the mass media age, representation in the mainstream news media has remained one of the most crucial means by which social and labor movements can enhance their public visibility and influence. But the relationship between mainstream media and social and labor movements has been contentious. Media opportunities, together with political opportunities, have become structural forces that shape social movements' ability to reach the general public.[14] Media attention scales the success of the protest, and the relationship between social movements and mass media is far from being a symbiotic one.[15] Radical protests rarely get coverage in mainstream news media.[16] Social movements are often the subject of distorted reports in mass media, which either circumvent their authentic political goals and messages or foster public resentment and hostility.[17] In European news representation of trade unions and labor strikes in Europe, workers' perspectives and voices are almost entirely excluded from reports, and workers are portrayed merely as noisy dissenters.[18]

Activists and movement participants approach and use mass media with one of two broad strategies: resistant and collaborative. Resistant actions include what Dieter Rucht categorizes as "abstention" and "attack."[19] Abstention occurs when, due to negative experiences with mass media, social movements and protest groups stop seeking media coverage. Activists may take verbal and physical actions to prevent media distortion. Examples include student protesters' effort to impede the distribution of Springer newspapers in 1960s Germany, and Greenham women's uses of parody to contest the mainstream media's misrepresentation of their peaceful protest against the siting of US nuclear weapons in the United Kingdom in the 1980s.[20] The collaborative approach occurs when activists, realizing the importance of media visibility, strategically seek attention from the mainstream media. Staging spectacular events, establishing public relations units, and hiring professional journalists are some of the ways various progressive movements have sought to reach mainstream media, often at the expense of some of their political goals.[21] In contemporary China, individual workers often resort to getting media coverage as part of their protest strategies to push employing companies/factories and local governments to address their grievances.[22] But labor strikes and protests as collective actions rarely gain visibility in China's mainstream news media. In this book, I explore how mediated labor activism navigates media opportunities in China to gain visibility and reach a wider public.

Alternative forms of media have been among the most prevalent and significant mediated-activism practices, designed to constitute a counterpower to that of the mainstream media. They are "alternative" in the sense that they intend to supplement, contest, and resist the power of a media system that benefits the elites, largely by establishing independent media outlets for marginalized and silenced groups.[23] Civil society organizations and local communities play a leading role in producing alternative forms of media in various national contexts.[24] In China's media and communication system, the party-state's political regulation and profit-driven commercial forces coexist as dominant powers in the print, broadcasting, and digital media landscape.[25] In response, local communities and NGOs have built alternative forms of media toward specific objectives for social justice and equality. Mainstream media are constitutive of the cultural and social inequality of rural migrant workers, portraying them as degraded others in urban China.[26] My book then examines how migrant workers and labor activists confront their misrepresentation and underrepresentation in mainstream media with their own media practices.

Information-communication technologies (ICTs), such as the internet, mobile technologies, and social media, have greatly expanded the opportunities for activism and resistance movements. Proponents of ICTs' positive roles in facilitating social change mostly follow Manuel Castells's argument that ICTs enable the formation of networks of transnational social movements.[27] W. Lance Bennett builds upon Castells's idea of a network society and claims that the internet fosters the "growth of new global publics" and that "perhaps the next step is a thoroughly personalized information system in which the boundaries of different issues and political approaches become permeable, enabling ordinary citizens to join campaigns, protests, and virtual communities with few ideological or partisan divisions."[28] Bennett and Alexandra Segerberg's concept "connective action" provides a framework to capture a new form of social movements based on individuals sharing content through social media networks.[29] Connective actions are large-scale and deploy inclusive discourse/memes whereby individuals may connect their personalized experiences with those of the movements, and social media play a vital role in the formation process. The transnational flow of MeToo movements is an example of connective action: women and girls, who were previously silenced by the victim-blaming culture, feel empowered by other survivors' stories and actions to speak up and challenge the pervasive sexual violence and harassments.

Contesting the excessive attention to connective actions, Graham Meikle points out that connective action is "the personalization of politics" and argues, "There is no reason to think that the connective has replaced the collective, and the concepts are best understood as complementary."[30] In a similar vein, Paolo Gerbaudo and Emiliano Trere argue that we should avoid overfragmented politics and go back to the collective identity to search for the "we" in social media activism.[31] I contend that in the context of contemporary China, digital media may enable migrant workers to express their voices and share their personal stories, but as an underprivileged and marginalized group, they must build a collective identity and organize collective action to form a truly effective collective counterpower. For social groups who are disenfranchised and lack access to basic rights, forming a collective resistance force is more effective than connective action in contesting material disparities and cultural domination.

We also need to be mindful of the recent scholarly overemphasis on digital technologies in enabling activism and social movements. Drawing upon the cases of the Arab Spring and Occupy Wall Street movements, Christian Fuchs argues that social media do not cause revolutions; instead, it is people facing deep-seated structural problems, such as wealth gaps and political suppression, who make rebellions.[32] Employing a Marxist politico-economic perspective, Fuchs observes that corporate-controlled social media primarily produce commercial and mundane spaces where politics is the exception.[33] In their work on labor movements and digital media, Lina Dencik and Peter Wilkin stress that while digital technologies can be important tools for labor movements, they still should be recognized as an extension of state and corporate power for surveillance, control, and profit making.[34] Maria Rovisco and Jonathan Corpus Ong collect case studies across the global South and North and demonstrate that street protests "are more underpinned by small-scale interpersonal and transnational networks that operate across a range of online and offline environments, rather than by technology-based decentralized networks."[35] Digital and social media such as Facebook and X (formerly, Twitter) are only additive to prevailing conditions and movements.[36] In other words, digital protests do not stand alone as being technology enabled; they are part of the larger body of diverse existing protests.

My approach to mediated labor activism resonates with these critiques. Rather than privileging the role of ICTs in mediated labor activism, I explore how the use of ICTs is embedded in the ongoing struggles and various practices. I suggest a dialectical understanding of ICTs in the context of activism and resistance movements. Digital media carry a significant potential to facilitate activism, but technologies are not a determining factor in advancing resistance and forming collective power. What remains to examine is how activists and advocacy groups adopt ICTs in various ways to build and maintain their offline and online activities, connections, and networks. In considering the Chinese context of heavy state surveillance of the internet and social media, I address how workers and activists navigate these conditions in their collective resistance.

HEGEMONY AND COUNTERHEGEMONIC POWER

I assess the possibility of change through mediated labor activism through the lens of struggles between hegemonic and counterhegemonic powers. Within each historical conjuncture that hegemonic power has asserted its control and domination, there often has emerged a corresponding formation of counterhegemonic forces. These counterhegemonic forces are typically characterized by their opposition to the dominant ideologies, structures, and prevailing norms and narratives and their goal of undermining and transforming the existing order.

Neoliberalism has gained hegemony in the past four decades at a global scale, inflected by local specificities and variations. The Gramscian perspective sees hegemony as being formed through both coercion and consensus. Ruling groups exercise domination through war, military, and police force, while moral leadership and mass support are manufactured by economic and political compromises, such as reforms and granting certain political rights, and cultural and political institutions, including schools, media, and political parties.[37] In our current moment, the expansion of neoliberal globalization has been backed up by the US-led military force and financial domination through institutions like the International Monetary Fund (IMF) and World Bank.[38] Domestically, nation-states set up legal and policy structures to secure the power of corporations and create markets in the industries of real estate, transportation, education, healthcare, and social security. The military-industrial and prison-industrial complexes benefit the state and corporate interests and lead to the mass incarceration and disenfranchisement of Black populations in the Western world.[39] Developing countries, either voluntarily or by coercion, embrace neoliberal reforms to deregulate markets, privatize public resources and services, and suppress local labor struggles.[40] The coercive power of the state and capital consolidates the political and economic systems of neoliberalism.

The consensus of neoliberalism is built through a series of ideological projects to promote free market doctrines and varied conservative and neoconservative values. For instance, in 1980s Britain, to gain popular support for neoliberal reforms and restore the hegemony of capitalism, Margaret Thatcher rebuilt the shared concept of "Englishness" by deploying the discourse of the free market and conservative values of nuclear family and nationalism.[41] Thatcherism presented free markets and the preservation of an English way of life as solutions to address Britain's economic recession and people's fear of the loss of identity; in actuality, it displaced the deep political, economic, and social ruptures that had unsettled British society.[42] In the United States, neoliberal ideology, perpetuated by corporations, media, universities, schools, churches, and professional associations, has simply become common sense. Politicians and dominant media extol individual freedom as the utmost political and cultural value to attain, when, in reality, the discourse of individual achievement camouflages corporate freedom, which helps corporations maximize their profit.[43] In the name of restoring a moral order, cultural nationalism and the discourse of "family values" divide the working class by using xenophobia and prejudice to scapegoat immigrants, women, and racial and sexual minorities.[44] In developing countries, states justify neoliberal reforms by invoking the goals of attracting foreign capital and advancing economic development. Neoliberalism also produces a particular subjective position for individuals to become an entrepreneurial self. In a Foucauldian sense, as Aihwa Ong argues, "neoliberalism is a governmentality that relies on market knowledge and calculations for a politics of subjection and subject-making."[45]

Struggles against neoliberalism take place at different scales and in different places. In the mid-1990s, the Zapatista rebellions resisted the Mexican state's complicity with global capital and demanded rights and autonomy for indigenous people, eventually developing into a national movement against neoliberalism.[46] Elsewhere, cross-national, global justice movements emerged and developed in the late 1990s and early 2000s to protest neoliberal globalization and the unchecked power of multinational corporations.[47] The movements criticized international financial and trade organizations and free trade treaties for exacerbating wealth gaps between rich and poor countries. Shortly after the 2008 financial crisis, the Occupy movement, initiated in the United States, soon spread across the globe to oppose the increasing social inequality and deprivation of a significant portion of the world's working-class population. In Asia, Latin America, and Africa, labor and social movements arose alongside rapid industrialization to fight against neoliberal reforms and its detrimental impacts on workers and marginalized communities; these movements have grown since the 1980s and endured to the present.[48] These examples are not sporadic or unrelated but rather are evidence showing the resilience of counterhegemonic forces despite the formidable challenges posed by the state and capital.

Neoliberalism, as the latest stage of capitalist development, is, of course, by no means the only dominant power structure. Patriarchy, racism and white supremacy, and heteronormativity are systems of oppression that intertwine with capital exploitation and class inequality while retaining distinctive characteristics and effects. Iris M. Young, along with other feminist scholars, rightly reminds us to avoid "the exclusive and oversimplifying effects of reducing all oppressions to class oppressions" and to recognize the "the similarities and overlaps in the oppressions of different groups."[49] Women, racial minorities, lesbian, gay, bisexual, transgender, and queer/questioning (LGBTQ) groups, and people with disabilities constantly encounter sexism, racism, homophobia, and ableism in workplaces and their everyday lives, and systemic violence is produced and reproduced through the institutional powers of the state, the market, education, and media. The historical development of capitalism and the hegemonic formation of neoliberalism adapt to changes in existing power structures. For instance, capitalism intersects with patriarchy to exploit women's productive and reproductive labor.[50] Colonialism fuels the primitive accumulation of capital to extract resources and exploit labor in colonies.[51] The legacy of colonialism lives on in the postcolonial era as a system of power asymmetries that allow for the exploitation and disenfranchisement of racial minorities and immigrants in Western countries and workers in developing countries in the era of neoliberal globalization.

Past and current feminist and racial-justice movements have challenged these systems of oppression. In North America and Europe, the three waves of feminism occurring from the late nineteenth century to the early twenty-first century fought for women's suffrage, access to education, employment, women's reproductive rights and justice, and the rights of LGBTQ people. The US civil rights movement has combated the systemic racism in the United States, while Black feminists have revealed and challenged the interlocking systems of patriarchy, capitalism, colonialism, imperialism, and heteronormativity.[52] In Asia and the Middle East, women's emancipation movements were closely linked with national independence and democratic movements in the early twentieth century.[53] During the Cold War, transnational feminist alliances were formed among feminists from second and third world countries.[54] Throughout the twentieth century, these resistance movements endured at local, national, and global scales. In the past two decades, transnational feminist movements from SlutWalk to MeToo have flourished, with feminists, women, and Progressive men worldwide confronting patriarchal powers that discipline and control women's body and sexuality. The more recent Black Lives Matter movement has revitalized a spirit of collective resistance against systematic racism in Western countries.

Expanding Antonio Gramsci's class-based conception of "hegemony" to consider other systems of social hierarchy, Ernesto Laclau and Chantal Mouffe argue that there is a "need to create a chain of equivalence among the various democratic struggles against different forms of subordination. . . . Struggles against sexism, racism, sexual discrimination, and in the defense of the environment needed to be articulated with those of the workers."[55] In this book, I suggest that workers' struggles must be connected and allied with other collective resistant efforts against hegemonic power and domination. There is no single, universal process by which hegemony forms, but rather the mechanisms and dynamics of hegemony can vary significantly based on specific contexts, historical periods, and social structures. Understanding the constitution of particular hegemonies in particular conjunctures is thus a prerequisite for exploring the potential development of counterhegemonic power. To address the possibilities of forming counterhegemonic forces in contemporary China, it is necessary to first explicate the hegemonic power that currently prevails in the regime.

Structural inequalities in reformist, postsocialist China are sustained through the party-state, which holds unchecked political power through neoliberal globalization that enables transnational and domestic capital to profit from labor exploitation through the urban-rural hierarchy—which produces and sustains the privilege and superiority of the urban population—and through patriarchy—which grants male supremacy and domination over women's bodies and sexuality. These intertwined systemic inequalities particularly affect marginalized and underprivileged groups, including women, sexual minorities, peasants, and the working class. Beginning with Mao Zedong's program of socialism, the party-state's authoritarian control over Chinese politics and society has persisted through the present era of market reform despite economic changes and social transformations.[56] The party-state grants limited political freedoms, imposes restrictions on civil society, and retains centralized control over decision-making. The state-led market reforms facilitate capital investment and foreign trade by privatizing state-owned enterprises and rural collective farms and by marketizing and commodifying essential public resources, including housing, education, and social welfare. China's export-oriented economy relies on the labor exploitation of a significant rural population who become migrant workers employed in offshore manufacturing sites and low-income service work. The authoritarian party-state and capital power constitute the hegemonic bloc of contemporary China, which is defined by David Harvey as "neoliberalism with Chinese characteristics."[57]

Modernization, globalization, and development have become key concepts of the depoliticized ideology that has produced and perpetuated the consensus of hegemony. The party-state's official discourse propagates these concepts, and mainstream media reinforce them, thereby legitimizing China's integration into capitalist globalization and obscuring the increasing inequalities in the country.[58] In postsocialist China, as Lisa Rofel argues, national public culture is the main medium for creating neoliberal subjectivities.[59] The depoliticized and pragmatic approach to promoting economic prosperity is vital in producing neoliberal subjects. The official and popular discourses coordinate to convey a clear message: Chinese people should enhance their skills and capabilities and become self-reliant, competitive participants in the market economy. In doing so, they would contribute to the broader national goals of economic growth and the advancement of the country's position on the world stage. In the cultural and social sphere, an ethos of consumption leads individual to pursue and prioritize material possessions. The flourishing consumerist values, along with the ever-increasing material disparity between the rich and poor, have further marginalized the underprivileged groups, who are deemed to be incapable consumers. The peasants and workers who were once championed as the revolutionary agents of socialist China have become, in the popular media discourse of urban superiority, degraded others and disposable labor.

Patriarchy runs deep throughout Chinese history. Despite the significant success of state-led initiatives for gender equality during the Mao era, male supremacy, misogyny, and feminization of housework have not been fundamentally challenged; nor have the continued dominance of heteronormativity and the pervasive homophobia in Chinese society.[60] Sexist values and norms have been incorporated into the marketization processes of postsocialist China, consolidating patriarchal power in politico-economic and sociocultural domains. Meanwhile, class division among women is conspicuous in reformist China. Whereas middle-class women are desirable consumers in their embrace of so-called modern lifestyles, rural and working-class women have become a cheap labor force used in factories and low-income service sectors.[61]

My book is a scholarly and political project that searches for counterhegemonic potential among the rural migrant workers of China. I begin with an examination of how hegemonic power structures configurate rural migrant workers' lives in postsocialist China and how workers respond collectively to inequalities and injustices. From there, I move on to ask to what extent mediated labor activism may contribute to the formation of counterhegemonic power. Focused specifically on grassroots, bottom-up workers' struggles in China, the book joins the ongoing efforts of scholars and activists who seek to envision and build an alternative world.

TOWARD AN ALTERNATIVE WORLD

Whereas counterhegemonic power often emerges as a response to hegemonic power, there is no guarantee of such formation—the formation of counterhegemonic power is contingent. In this book, I discuss three elements of that contingency, which I suggest as essential elements in forming counterhegemonic power: a new political subject, transformative epistemologies, and informal networks of collective resistance. The first element identifies the importance of defining new ways of being and how individuals or groups perceive their roles in a political landscape. Transformative epistemologies emphasize the need to develop new ways of knowing and understanding the world. Networks and alliances are crucial for mobilizing collective efforts and resources in the pursuit of social change. These elements are interdependent, and they facilitate one another in the processes of change. Through a sustained inquiry into these elements, my book explicates how counterhegemonic power can be formed, maintained, and mobilized in contemporary China.

In considering the relationship between ideology and subject, Louis Althusser argues that "all ideology hails or interpellates concrete individuals as concrete subjects, by the functioning of the category of the subject."[62] According to Althusser, when individuals and their consciousnesses, values, beliefs, and actions are interpellated by ideology, which is an eternal entity, subjects are constituted. The subject thus becomes "a subjected being, stripped of all freedom except that of freely accepting his submission. . . . There are no subjects except by and for their subjection."[63] Michel Foucault's concept of "subjectification" poses a similar critique. "Subjectification" refers to the process through which the subject is constituted and becomes the product of power relations.[64] Although Foucault's critique of power, knowledge, and discourse differs from Althusser's focus on ideology, both philosophers are pessimistic about the possibility of a free, autonomous subjectivity and subject.

While I agree with Althusser's and Foucault's analyses of the effects of constitutive power on individuals, my approach to subject formation aligns more with Kathi Weeks's discussion of the subject since her account suggests possibilities for change. Weeks draws upon Friedrich Nietzsche's account of the subject: "Nietzsche's subject is both autonomous and situated, there is tension, but no necessary contradiction between the fact that we are both always already constituted and at the same time, self-constituting."[65] Weeks suggests two coexisting modes that exist within any subject: a mode of being and a mode of becoming. The mode of being acknowledges the dominant forces that affect individuals, as in Althusser's and Foucault's critiques. The mode of becoming recognizes the subject as an active agent of change. The coexistence of these modes allows the subject to transcend constituted subjectivities and challenge and reshape them.

It is the mode of becoming that opens possibilities to cultivate new subjectivity. English workers of the eighteenth and nineteenth centuries, experiencing the profound impacts of industrialization on their lives, developed working-class consciousness through their everyday lives, rituals of mutuality, community building, and shared radical thoughts.[66] Workers are produced by the dominant powers of state and capital as workers, but they also produce themselves as political subjects with working-class consciousness to realize their subordinated positions in the societal hierarchy and to defend their rights. Consciousness-raising is crucial for women, as they realize their collective experiences of oppression and subordination. [67] Through consciousness-raising, there arises the possibility for a woman to become a feminist subject with feminist consciousness. Here, I use Sandra Lee Bartky's definition of "feminist consciousness"; Bartky conceptualizes "feminist consciousness" as the consciousness of victimization: "The consciousness of victimization is a divided consciousness. To see myself as victim is to know that I have already sustained injury, that I live exposed to injury, that I have been at worst mutilated, at best diminished in my being. But at the same time, feminist consciousness is a joyous consciousness of one's own power, of the possibility of unprecedented personal growth and the release of energy long suppressed. Thus, feminist consciousness is both consciousness of weakness and consciousness of strength."[68] Developing a collective working-class or feminist consciousness enables marginalized individuals to transform themselves from a mode of being into a mode of becoming: overcoming the passive, alienated, and oppressed subjectivities and becoming an antagonist subject against capitalism and patriarchy.

Becoming is not a linear process but one that inevitably involves am-
biguity, complexity, and unpredictability. A woman with a newly developed feminist consciousness may struggle to live a "feminist life."
She may wonder if wearing make-up and getting married are antifem-
inist acts or simply acts of self-expression and individual choice. Some
people may refuse to identify as feminists even though they support
gender equality. Workers may find themselves caught up between the
conflicting maxims that "employers provide jobs" and "employers
profit by exploiting workers." Subordinate groups may find it difficult
to overcome a feeling of inferiority, as the result of what Frantz Fanon
describes as "psychic alienations."[69] These tensions and difficulties can
be attributed to the powerful impact of dominant norms and discourses
that appear as "common sense" in people's lives. Patriarchal culture
compels women to pay extra attention to their appearance and molds
their desire for heterosexual relationships. The stigmatization of feminism and feminist identity dissuades people from embracing the label of
"feminist." Capitalist ideology persuades workers to be grateful to their
bosses for presenting employment opportunities. Sexist, classist, racist,
homophobic, and ableist discrimination perpetuate a culture of inferiority in which marginalized and underprivileged people are systemati-
cally devalued and disenfranchised.

Enabling a mode of becoming thus requires transformative epis-
temological stances to destabilize the established norms, values, and
dominant power that shape people's subjectivities. To challenge the free
market doctrine, Karl Marx and Marxist scholars have revealed labor
exploitation, alienation, and the inherent inequality in capitalist modes
of production. These politico-economic critiques continue to inspire
workers worldwide to organize collective resistance from launching
strikes and protests to forming unions and political parties to staging
revolutions. Gramsci argues, "every revolution has been preceded by an
intense labor of criticism, by the diffusion of culture and the spread of
ideas amongst the masses."[70] He is specifically referring to the spread of
socialist ideas to contest the hegemony of the capitalist system, as En-
lightenment ideas laid the groundwork for the bourgeois rebels against
the feudal monarchs.

If we are to contest the hegemony of intertwined power structures,
we need to employ a variety of critical ideas and approaches: aiming

to expose male domination and patriarchal privilege, feminist scholars and activists encourage women to recognize, problematize, and resist sexism, sexual objectification, disciplinary power and norms, and everyday forms of violence experienced at individual and societal scales. Queer theory deconstructs normative understandings of gender and sexuality and has played a significant role in LGBTQ movements that advocate for the rights and social inclusion of sexual minorities and nonbinary people. Postcolonial theory interrogates the lasting impacts of colonialism and imperialism on people's lives in the global South. The list of transformative epistemologies could certainly extend much further. What they share in common is a goal of disrupting the consensus of hegemonic power within a given context.

Since the 1950s, the world has witnessed a series of social movements that advocate for different yet often-overlapping forms of social justice, including feminist movements, the US civil rights movements, antiwar movements, student protests in western Europe, prodemocracy movements in eastern Europe, LGBTQ movements globally, etc. Responding to various social, political, and economic issues, these movements expand the conventional understanding of conflicts between labor and capital, which drives workers' protests and working-class organizing into unions and parties. These social movements, with varied aims and participants, are often regarded as "new social movements." Donatella della Porta and Mario Diani conceptualize informal networks as a key characteristic of new social movements.[71] "Informal networks" refer to sustained relationships, connections, and interactions among individuals, groups, or organizations involved in a social movement that are not governed by formal structures or institutions. These informal networks often play a crucial role in mobilizing activists, sharing information, coordinating actions, and building solidarity within social movements. They can transcend traditional hierarchical structures and facilitate dynamic grassroots organizing.

Borrowing the concept of the "informal network" from social-movements studies, I suggest that informal networks are also essential to facilitate the formation of counterhegemonic power. Informal networks can foster a sense of solidarity and support among activists and individuals, who may feel marginalized or oppressed by dominant power structures. This emotional and practical support is crucial for the sustainability of collective resistance. Due to their diffuse and decentralized nature, informal networks tend to be more resilient in the face of suppression or resistance from established power structures. Informal networks have important implications for grassroots, bottom-up collective resistance in China's context, as they can enable space for individuals and social groups, without formal affiliations with any advocacy organizations, to collaborate and connect in the process of promoting social change. Such space may reduce the risk of individuals being targeted by authorities and encourage people to participate in the collective efforts of resistance. A recent example is the transnational flow of the MeToo movement in China. The informal networks formed in the process of advancing the MeToo movement create a sense of community and support and inspire a great number of people to break their silence and speak up about sexual harassment and assault. When Feminist Voices (Nü quan zhi sheng; 女权之声)—a high-profile feminist-advocacy organization that played a leading role in facilitating the MeToo movement in China—was disciplined by the government, individuals and social groups connected by informal networks have been able to carry on the movement. [72] Decentralized activism allows people to share their stories, raise awareness, mobilize support, and organize local and community-based initiatives.

Informal networks have also become a vital part of the labor movement, complementing the work of traditional labor unions and expanding the reach of labor-advocacy efforts. Historically, unions have played a pivotal role in mobilizing and organizing workers' strikes, protests, and labor movements. But many established unions have long faced criticism for their hierarchical structures and exclusion of women, racial minorities, and immigrant workers.[73] Legal barriers remain a major obstacle for underprivileged workers around the world who seek to unionize. In a sector of the informal economy, such as domestic service, workers face significant barriers to forming labor unions and collectively organizing in many developed and developing countries.[74] Transnational migrant workers are often prohibited or restricted by law from forming unions. These workers' temporary or irregular status limits their ability to organize collectively with fear of retaliation, such as deportation or visa revocation. New and more flexible forms of labor organizing, such as worker centers, NGOs, and advocacy groups, have emerged to address some of these limitations, providing services and advocating for workers who may not be part of traditional unions. These new actors build connections and collaborations to exchange resources and provide mutual support, which enables a wide range of participants to join in labor advocacy. For instance, in Canada, a sustained network among NGOs, unions, advocacy groups, activists, academics, and migrant workers has formed to demand landed status and labor rights for transnational migrant workers.[75]

In China, where independent labor unions are legally prohibited, labor NGOs have played a vital role in addressing various issues related to rural migrant workers. These NGOs often serve as grassroots forces for advocating labor rights, providing legal advice and assistance, and offering social and cultural services. Recognizing labor NGOs' important presence in rural migrant workers' lives, my book explores the role of labor NGOs in supporting and amplifying the efforts of rural migrant workers in their collective resistance. I address the interconnectedness of civil society, advocacy organizations, and grassroots collective resistance in the pursuit of labor rights and social justice in China.

A MULTIMODAL ETHNOGRAPHIC INQUIRY

This book attends to a variety of social actors and different forms of mediated labor activism, and my research for the book was correspondingly multipronged. Through multisited and digital ethnography, I was able to explore the varieties of rural migrant workers' experiences and engage multiple social actors participating in mediated labor activism, including rural migrant workers, NGOs, advocacy groups, activists, scholars, volunteers, and journalists. Multisited ethnography engages with multiple sites of social worlds and inquires into variously situated subjects in the capitalist world system. Digital ethnography approaches everyday life, culture, and practices that are increasingly mediated by digital technologies, and I adopt a non-digital-centric method to examine how people's digital worlds interact with the "offline" parts of their lives.

I conducted field research in Beijing and Xi'an from March 2016 to August 2022. In contrast to coastal cities in southern China that serve as manufacturing hubs, Beijing, the capital city of China, and Xi'an, a provincial capital in northwestern China, are typical of northern China in that there is no large-scale, labor-intensive manufacturing and rural migrant workers mostly work in the construction and service industries. During fieldwork, I interviewed and had conversations with dozens of rural migrant workers to learn about their experiences, struggles, concerns, and aspirations. These workers belong to the two generations of rural migrants, with ages ranging from twenty to fifty-six years old. The first-generation rural migrants refer to those born in the 1960s and 1970s who moved from rural areas to urban or more developed areas in search of job opportunities. Most of these workers had only finished middle school and carried the financial burden of supporting their families. They usually work in labor-intensive and low-income service sectors, including manufacturing, construction, mining, domestic service, and restaurants. Wage arrears, work injuries, and social exclusion have been common problems faced by the first-generation migrant workers. The second-generation rural migrants are those born in the 1980s and 1990s in rural villages who seek jobs in cities. Compared with their parents, the second generation has attained a relatively higher education level, with high school degrees, and faces less financial burden. They do not need to send money back to their rural hometowns to support family members, as their parents did when they first migrated, and they are also more integrated into urban life. While many second-generation migrants continue to work in factories, an increasing number are finding employment in expanding service industries.

Some scholars attribute the increase in labor strikes in China to greater class consciousness or rights consciousness among second-generation rural migrant workers.[76] My experience with the two generations of migrant workers complicates that interpretation. In actuality, both generations are active participants in mediated labor activism. In addition to talking with workers about their motivations for and experiences of participation in activism, I visited beauty salons and barbershops in Beijing and Xi'an to speak with young migrant workers who were not participants in activism to gain insights into their thinking.

The primary field sites in which I explored mediated labor activism were two labor NGOs, one activist group, and an alternative-media outlet. I chose these four sites because of their dedication to advocacy for migrant workers. These NGOs and advocacy groups represent a new wave of grassroots labor activism that relies on varied media and cultural practices. When I entered the field in March 2016 in Beijing, my primary research sites were two labor NGOs, the Migrant Women's Club (MWC; Dagongmei zhi jia; 打工妹之家) and Migrant Workers' Home (MWH; Gongyou zhi jia; 工友之家). I approached the two NGOs as organizational forces working toward social change and as spaces wherein social actors perform varied types of collective action.

Rural Women Knowing All (RWKA; Nongjia nü baishitong; 农家女百事通), the first NGO for the empowerment of rural women in China, was established in 1993 by Xie Lihua, a retired editor who had previously worked at an official media outlet. In 1996, Xie founded MWC as a branch of RWKA in Beijing, and it is one of the first NGOs to provide service to and advocate for rights for female rural migrant workers. Since its establishment, MWC has maintained a beneficial relationship with the state and has been recognized by scholars as a well-established NGO for female migrant workers.[77] MWC's main work has been to provide services, resources, and skills training to female migrants and policy advocacy with the government. In this book, I specifically analyze MWC's recent advocacy program Didinghua Theater (Didinghua jushe; 地丁花剧社) as part of MWC's broader campaign to demand labor rights for migrant domestic workers.

Migrant Workers' Home was founded by a group of migrant workers and activists in 2002 in Beijing. In contrast with MWC, whose founders and early organizers had relatively high social status, most MWH staff members have been migrant workers themselves. MWH represents the emerging trend of migrant workers organizing their own NGOs; most of them are small-scale and community based. MWH has gradually become one of the most influential grassroots migrant-worker NGOs. MWH's activism focuses on constructing migrant workers' culture and community as the main means to challenge their inequality and injustice.

The two main techniques through which multisited ethnography constructs its objects of study are "follow the people" and "follow the thing"—that is to say, tracking the movement of initial subjects and objects in complex cultural phenomena.[78] I deployed the two techniques to discover the participants and practices of various forms of mediated labor activism. My contact with members of MWH led me to explore activist projects that have grown out of MWH networks. A leading member of MWH told me about the feminist band Jiu Ye when we first met in late April 2016, shortly after the band was formed. Founded by three female activists, Jiu Ye uses its music to advocate gender and class equality for female migrant workers. Jiu Ye represents a typical trend among activist groups in China—namely, that they employ flexible forms of organizing without registering as NGOs.[79]

Jianjiao buluo (尖椒部落; Pepper Community) is an online feminist-advocacy media outlet with a particular focus on female migrant workers. I was introduced to Jianjiao buluo by a migrant-worker participant of MWH who has written for and been a reader of Jianjiao for some time. Several activists founded and registered Jianjiao as an NGO in 2014. In recent years, China has witnessed a growing number of feminist-media NGOs that criticize the unequal power structure rooted in China's patriarchal past and present. These feminist-media NGOs primarily rely on the internet to promote feminist views and analyses to the general public. However, the feminist agenda of these NGOs tends to prioritize gender issues faced by urban middle-class women while largely neglecting working-class politics. In this context, Jianjiao has taken a groundbreaking role in producing feminist nonprofit and advocacy media for migrant workers. I use the cases of Jiu Ye and Jianjiao to discuss how feminist ideas and practices have intervened in the sphere of labor activism and expanded the scope of mediated labor activism.

Over the course of six years of offline and online fieldwork, I adopted the mixed qualitative methods of textual analysis, participant observation, and interviews and have collected archival materials from NGOs, government documents, and news reports. I attended and participated in activities and events, had plentiful discussions with various participants, and conducted a total of fifty-two semistructured interviews with migrant workers, NGO staff members, activists, volunteers, and journalists. I followed the four research sites' public accounts on social media to stay informed and updated about their activities and events and frequently talked with staff members and migrant-worker participants through WeChat. Up to the present, I remain connected with most of the research participants on WeChat.

My access to research sites and participants was largely facilitated by the existing networks among rural migrant workers, labor NGOs, activists, and scholars. I am grateful that these people were willing to, and often enthusiastic about, sharing their experiences, thoughts, and opinions with me. Feminist scholarship challenges the supposed objectivity of existent research methodologies and reveals that subjectivity and subjective relations with research subjects shape the knowledge-production process.[80] I have maintained an awareness that my positionality shapes the power relations and negotiations inherent in any ethnographic research. Growing up in an urban middle-class family in China, I had more class privilege than many rural migrant workers. But this privilege has not prevented me from being highly respectful toward migrant workers, and I continue to admire their resilience. My identity as a woman and a feminist helped me build rapport with female migrant workers and female activists. My academic and professional experience in higher education in China and North America has enabled me to establish connections with a group of domestic and international scholars dedicated to labor advocacy. Fortunately, I was able to build mutual trust with most of the research participants once they recognized our common concern for the well-being of rural migrant workers and other underprivileged and marginalized groups.

STRUCTURE OF THE BOOK

Chapter 1 offers a critical account of Chinese rural migrant workers' inequalities and resistance in the current moment and situates their struggles within the formation of a global working class. The chapter begins by tracing the structural and institutional forces that shape the circumstances of workers in varied national and transnational contexts. Neoliberal transitions have had profound impacts on the well-being of workers across the global North and South. In post-Mao China, the decline of the agricultural economy, the legacy of rural-urban disparity from the Mao era, and the adjusted household-registration policy have driven thousands of millions of rural migrant workers to become cheap laborers in the country's rapid development of a market economy. Mainstream media and culture justify the suffering of migrant workers and become a constitutive force of the unequal social structures of neoliberalism in China and global contexts. The chapter goes on to document how workers respond to precarious employment and inequalities:

informal workers become a leading force in organizing labor strikes at different sites, workplaces, and communities and at different scales— local and national. In reformist China, rural migrant workers are the main force of working-class resistance. Recognizing Chinese rural migrant workers as a new historical subject, I suggest a move beyond structural determinacy toward a path that seeks agents of change.

Chapter 2 embarks on the journey of seeking possibilities of change. Focusing on female migrant workers' participation in the Migrant Women's Club's Didinghua Theater program, I aim to demonstrate how workers begin to see themselves as part of a potential counterhegemony. Middle-aged female rural migrants are the main labor force for paid domestic work in major Chinese cities. Domestic workers lack labor-law protection, employment security, pensions, and other social welfare. The group also faces substantial bias and discrimination. Participants in the performance program cultivate their self-awareness and learn to interrogate the systematic inequalities that limit their lives. Calling for recognition of domestic workers' labor value effectively mobilizes women workers to join in performance as a particular form of mediated labor activism. But at the same time, Didinghua Theater's collective resistance has not extended to forming solidarity with other subordinate groups, as domestic workers' advocacy through theater performance at MWC is primarily focused on their own unique challenges and have not yet connected with the struggles of other marginalized communities.

In search of a more radical advocacy framework, chapter 3 explores how Migrant Workers' Home's labor activism, informed by an explicitly Marxist conception of "class struggle," challenges capitalist and neoliberal ideologies and power in reformist China. MWH's labor activism focuses on facilitating migrant workers' collective cultural production, which becomes a prominent form of mediated labor activism. The construction of a new-worker culture, identity, and community invites migrant workers and other social groups to engage in a range of cultural and media practices and activities, such as music, community newspapers, literary writing, and, among others, questioning class inequality, labor exploitation, consumerist ideologies, and dominant power of mainstream media and culture. In contemporary China, socialism is struggling to maintain its relevance and meaningful engagement with the reality of the country, instead becoming little more than empty words used in the propaganda of the ruling party-state. MWH's labor activism embodies grassroots efforts to revitalize socialist ideas, values, and imaginations by advocating change, cultivating class consciousness, and fostering solidarity. Marxism is deployed in a powerful yet orthodox way. MWH's choice to prioritize class conflict results in the neglect of other dimensions of oppression and inequality, like patriarchy and heteronormativity.

Chapter 4 turns to feminist activists who have intervened into and broadened the scope of labor activism. This chapter examines the intersectional agendas and praxis of two cases of mediated labor activism: Jiu Ye, a feminist band, and Jianjiao buluo, an independent feminist-media platform. I characterize their forms of mediated labor activism as feminist labor activism, emphasizing its focus on intersectionality and commitment to addressing the often-neglected and often-marginalized needs and rights of these groups. In this chapter, I also consider how the lack of antipatriarchy in labor activism and the lack of anticapitalism in grassroots radical feminist activism reveal the unreconciled rifts between feminism and Marxism in contemporary working-class and feminist struggles. Taking the standpoint of working-class women to advocate for both gender *and* class equality, feminist labor-activist projects, such as Jiu Ye and Jianjiao buluo, establish a crucial connection between working-class resistance and feminist activism. The grassroots and inclusive spaces, carved out by feminist labor activism, invite women, migrant workers, LGBTQ groups, and people with disabilities to join in collective resistance, which embraces possibilities to grow into an independent resistance force for transformative changes.

Chapter 5 maps out a range of social-actor participants in the context of mediated labor activism and the offline and online alliances and networks that have been formed. I demonstrate how labor NGOs and activist groups, which play an essential role in mediated labor activism, are constantly negotiating with the political boundary set up by the authoritarian state. Participants in mediated labor activism come from a diverse range of social groups and backgrounds and adopt varied practices. I categorize such diversified participation into four types of counterpublics: (1) subaltern counterpublics, (2) proletariat counterpublics, (3) feminist counterpublics, and (4) nonresistant counterpublics. Along with NGO efforts, the increasing centrality of ICTs in contemporary life has also enabled the formation of various coalitions and informal networks. ICTs sustain the offline activities, practices, and networks while also facilitating the establishment of new connections in the process of mediated labor activism. With the growth and consolidation of these networks, mediated labor activism can gain momentum, broaden its impact, and bring about concrete change in the realm of labor rights and social justice.

The conclusion starts by discussing why mediated activism matters in the contemporary moment and why mediated labor activism serves as a key site of contestations in unequal China. I then move on to assess the main obstacles that prevent mediated labor activism from expanding into a broader, more impactful movement. Looking at social-justice struggles in China and around the globe, I contend that class still matters. While acknowledging the significance of class, I argue that resistance endeavors should not be confined to a traditional Marxist approach exclusively centered on class struggles for liberation. To conclude, I suggest where mediated labor activism needs to go next and how it needs to transcend the state-sanctioned discourse of socialism and embrace democratic socialist and feminist agendas to create broader coalitions to build a more equal, just, and inclusive world.

ONE

ENCOUNTERING UNEQUAL CHINA

Rural Migrant Workers and the Global Working Class

Guo, a fifty-two-year-old rural migrant, has been working as a carpenter for almost ten years in Beijing. Guo works for different contractors and usually receives his entire salary at the end of the year, with few benefits and little job security. Because of the lack of legal protection, Guo, like many other rural migrant workers, is quite often owed back wages. Guo's wife and two children live back in their home village, and he sends most of his salary home to support the family and his children's education. Growing up in a rural village in northern China, Guo went to a nearby town to attend middle school but failed the high school entrance exam. He joined the army and was discharged after four years' service. Obtaining higher education and joining the army are among the very few ways for rural people to pursue social mobility, but the opportunities to do so are rather low. After his military service, Guo returned to his home village and found work in a cement factory in a nearby town. Since then, he has looked for jobs in different cities and towns. Guo has worked in factories, at construction sites, and at craft workshops.

Around 2008, Guo moved to Beijing and started work as a carpenter. To obtain cheaper rents, he has lived in different suburban villages where rural migrant workers and low-income locals live. In metropolitan cities in China, it is almost impossible for rural migrants, like Guo, to afford to rent, not to mention to purchase, a condo in gated communities where middle-class residents live. At the end of our interview, Guo shared his thoughts about migrant workers' situations: "Rural people are forced to migrate to cities and to be separated from their families since there are few job opportunities in the countryside and rural people earn so little money from farming. Migrant workers are treated poorly in the workplace, with low salaries and few benefits. But the government is not doing much to protect us workers."

Guo's experiences are typical among the hundreds of millions of rural migrant workers who serve as the cheap, exploited labor force used for the rapid development of a market economy in post-Mao China. His circumstances epitomize the global trend toward the informalization of labor and precarization of workers across the global North and South in neoliberal capitalism. Lack of access to formal employment, job benefits and security, and social welfare along with unaffordable housing and unequal distribution of educational resources become the common problems underprivileged workers encounter in their daily lives. These workers' hopes for social mobility, better working conditions, and settlement in cities are rarely fulfilled.

Facing inequalities, workers worldwide engage in various protest actions, such as strikes and union and community organizing, in order to demand rights and broader changes. They also cultivate more individualized practices of resilience and resistance. Despite his long working hours, Guo writes almost every day, documenting his life, thoughts, and feelings. He particularly enjoys crafting poems as this written form enables him to see the beauty of life. More than a mere diversion, writing signifies workers' efforts to gather strength to live through their nearly unbearable working conditions. It is also a crucial means of self-expression for underprivileged workers, like Guo, who are often represented in stereotyped images by mainstream media and culture. Guo is an active member of a local NGO, and he attends its activities every weekend. While labor unions still play a pivotal role in protecting workers' rights in many countries, NGOs have become an ever more present force in workers' lives, particularly among migrant workers in China and other countries.

Proceeding from the standpoint of rural migrant workers in reformist China, this chapter looks at both current and historical political actions, as well as scholarly arguments and efforts to begin my search for a new historical subject to confront structural inequalities.[1] I suggest that the inequalities and struggles that Chinese rural migrant workers face should be situated in relation to the formation of a global working class. The chapter asks: What are the structural and institutional forces that shape circumstances of workers in varied national and transnational contexts? How do workers respond to precarious employment and the inequalities that precarity creates? In the context of China, how has market reform affected the lives of rural migrant workers? And how have migrant workers resisted labor structures intended to exploit them? In addressing these questions, I demonstrate why the experiences of rural migrant workers provide a particularly useful prism through which to interrogate social inequalities and practices of resistance in China. By understanding how the Chinese case is both distinct from and similar to the broader politics of global worker struggles, we will be better positioned to identify and locate the potential agents of change.

NEOLIBERAL GLOBALIZATION AND THE DISENFRANCHISEMENT OF RURAL MIGRANT WORKERS IN CHINA

Since the late 1970s, neoliberal transitions across the globe, albeit with local variations, have resulted in disenfranchisement of workers, privatization of public resources, marketization of national economies, and the growing power of transnational corporations.[2] In China, market reform has facilitated the formation of a state-capital nexus, a dramatic rise in the power of transnational and domestic capital, and deepening disparities between rural and urban populations. Among the working population, the four-decade economic reform has consolidated an extremely uneven distribution of income, social welfare, and education resources between urban middle class and rural migrant workers. The latter group becomes an exploitable, cheap labor force in China's integration into neoliberal globalization.

One of the most noticeable consequences of neoliberal transitions is the restructuring of labor forces in the global production chain. Since the 1970s, due to the saturated domestic markets and decreasing profitability of corporations in Western economies and Japan, there has been a shift from Fordist mass production and mass consumption to post-Fordist flexible accumulation.[3] New markets and sites of production are pursued by multinational corporations and neoliberal states. To reduce labor costs and increase profits, corporations have outsourced their production to areas where cheaper labor is available, including China and countries in South and Southeast Asia. As Neils van Doorn observes, the neoliberal reform globally has resulted in "the liberalization of international trade relations and capital circulation, which spurred labor market globalization and the massive 'offshoring' of manufacturing plants to countries with low labor costs."[4] The restructured global market has had a significant impact on the well-being of workers across the global North and South. In North America, Europe, and Japan, the shrinking welfare state and increasing informalization of employment have trapped low-income local workers and immigrants in the precarious gig economy, with rather constrained access to formal employment, job security, and benefits. Contingent labor has expanded in low-income sectors of manufacturing, construction, service, and agriculture.[5] In the United States, an estimated 10 percent of Americans are involved in contingent employment, and 14 percent of gig workers earn less than federal minimum wage.[6]

Among underprivileged populations, migrant workers are particularly vulnerable and susceptible to labor exploitation. In advanced economies, it is often temporary migrant workers and undocumented immigrants who are the main labor force for "3D" (dirty, dangerous, and difficult) jobs. For instance, in Canada, agriculture and food production heavily rely on migrant agricultural workers from Mexico and Central American countries. In the United States, millions of undocumented immigrants work in agriculture and low-paid service sectors. In Europe, domestic workers are migrant women from eastern Europe, Africa, and Latin America. In Singapore, construction workers are mostly migrants from Bangladesh. Without citizenship or permanent residency, migrant workers have to bear severe exploitation and mistreatment, and inadequate labor laws often fail to protect their labor rights. In newly industrializing countries, such as China, India, and South Africa, national policies disenfranchise underprivileged peasants and the urban poor, who are used as a cheap labor force to attract foreign capital. For instance, in India, economic liberalization has intensified the precarity of rural peasants, who are compelled to work low-paid jobs and live in slums in cities.[7] In South Africa, multinational capital flows into the country to extract minerals for profits, and migrant workers, who have little job security and protection, serve as the main labor force in the mining sectors.[8] The nexus of the state and capital, although being structured in varied forms in different countries, secures new paths for profit making through labor exploitation of workers. At the same time, rising material inequalities become the primary condition for the formation of a new global working class amid neoliberal globalization.

Rural migrant workers in China belong to this new global working class. The decline of the agricultural economy, the growing market economy, and extensive disparities between urban and rural lives produced historical and structural conditions that propelled the largest-scale labor migration in world history. The unequal political and economic structures in reformist China have made rural migrant workers an ideal cheap labor force for the global supply chain. Since the early 1990s, despite the continuing rise of agricultural output during the economic reform, the state's tax policy and price scissors policy have left rural households, which rely on farming as their primary source of income, in a rather disadvantageous position.[9] The party-state has advanced labor-intensive and export-oriented industries that demand large numbers of cheap laborers. The special economic zones (SEZs) have been established in the southeast coastal region as an experiment to test the economic reform.[10] Transnational corporations and capital are attracted by China's economic and labor policies to set up factories and take advantage of the cheap labor force. The stagnant agricultural economy, falling living standards in rural areas, and increased job opportunities in cities have become driving forces spurring rural poor to migrate from their villages to urban areas.

The state's adjustment of *hukou* (戶口; household registration), a household-registration policy, is in direct response to the market demand for a cheap labor force.[11] Originally, rural-urban segregation was mandated through the *hukou* policy in Mao's era to forbid rural peasants from working or living in cities. The state's rigid control of population mobility was a crucial way to sustain agricultural production to facilitate the rapid development of the urban industrial economy.[12] It was not until the economic reform of the early 1980s that the policy allowed rural peasants to migrate to and temporarily live and work in urban areas. But *hukou* policy persists to constrain migrant workers' access to basic welfare, such as healthcare and pensions. In Western countries, immigration policy often serves as an institutional force to deprive the political and labor rights of foreign migrant workers, especially the low-income ones, which helps maintain an exploitable workforce. For instance, in Canada, migrant agricultural workers and domestic workers, most of whom are from global South countries, are only granted a closed work permit, which does not allow them to change employers. Due to their precarious immigration status, low-income foreign migrant workers often do those jobs, such as working on farms and care work at private homes, that citizens are unwilling to do. In China, the national household policy preserves the privilege of urban residents and puts rural migrant workers at a disadvantage. While urban residents enjoy access to quality education, housing, healthcare, and pensions, rural migrants become cheap, disposable laborers and secondary citizens in the country's surging market economy.

The drive of capital accumulation, Mao's legacy of creating rural-urban disparities, and the discriminatory policies of the party-state create precarious and exploitative labor conditions for peasants searching for jobs in urban China. Compared with urban residents, most rural migrant workers have relatively low levels of education and skills and much less social capital. Migrant workers take the low-paid, temporary jobs with both heavy workloads and little job security and benefits, which are undesirable to urban residents. The average monthly income is ¥3275 (less than $500). About 55 percent of rural migrants work in the manufacturing and construction industries, and 45 percent are in the service industries: they work in urban construction sites, in factories as assembly-line workers in southern and eastern coastal areas, and in low-end service businesses, like small restaurants or shops.[13] In cities, especially metropolitan ones, such as Beijing, Shanghai, and Shenzhen, where real estate prices and rents are too high for them to afford, migrant workers live in suburban villages to reduce their living expenses. But these villages can only be temporary living places for migrant workers as they are frequently demolished for real estate development or other governmental requisitions.

All the migrant workers I met during my fieldwork came from rural villages or small towns. Due to the severe lack of educational resources in rural areas, very few of them were able to go to college. They dropped out in middle school or high school and then went to cities to seek jobs. Xiaoli, a twenty-six-year-old man, works as an assistant in a hair salon located close to a gated community in Beijing. Xiaoli grew up in a small town in Henan. At the age of seventeen, he went to Zhengzhou, the capital of Henan Province, and worked in a factory. Xiaoli found factory work too boring and isolating. He then worked as a waiter in a restaurant but was not satisfied with the low salary. When Xiaoli turned twenty-one, he wanted to go to Beijing, which in his words is "a really big city with more opportunities."[14] In his five years in Beijing, Xiaoli has worked at one restaurant and three hair salons. When I met him, Xiaoli was working at the third of the three hair salons. He is paid a ¥4000 monthly salary, and to save rent, Xiaoli lives with two other young migrants in a small apartment in a suburban village. The village is 1.5 hours away from the salon where he works. Every day, Xiaoli arrives at the salon around 9:00 a.m. to do cleaning, starts to welcome customers at 10:00 a.m., finishes his work around 10:00 p.m., and then goes home. I asked why he did not rent a place in a nearby community. Xiaoli said, "In those [gated] communities, a two-bedroom apartment costs ¥8000–10000 per month for rent. My salary is not even enough for one room." Concerning his future, Xiaoli plans to get married around thirty and continue to work in the city, though there is little chance that he could eventually afford to buy a condo. He said, "I am not interested in going home. There is much more fun in Beijing. Maybe when I am old, I will go back."

Xiaoli's experiences and views are typical of the second generation of rural migrant workers. Compared with their parents' generation, they are under much less of an obligation to support their families. But their position in the labor market has not changed much. Like the older generation, young migrant workers are trapped in low-income jobs with little security and few benefits. Although young workers find more enjoyment in their urban lives, neither generation has been able to afford housing in cities or send their children to urban schools. In our chats, most of the middle-aged, first-generation migrant workers explained that their children are back in the home village/town with the grandparents. They can only see their children once or twice a year. Jianguo and his wife are such a couple. They work in Xi'an, the capital city of Shaanxi Province, and their fifteen-year-old daughter lives with her grandparents in their home village in Ningxia, a province near Shaanxi. Jianguo is a cook at a medium-sized restaurant, and his wife is a domestic worker. To save money, they live separately. Jianguo stays at the dorm provided by the restaurant with his coworkers, and his wife lives in her employer's home. The couple's biggest hope is that their daughter can be admitted to a good university and get a decent job after graduation. Jianguo said, "I don't mind the hard work. I just wish my daughter can perform well in her studies, but we are too far away and can't take care of her. She doesn't have a Xi'an *hukou* and is not allowed to go to [public] schools in Xi'an."

One of the primary ways that middle-class and elite families seek to achieve and maintain social status is by providing high-quality education to their children. Education is sometimes the only possible means for migrant workers' children to achieve social mobility. Yet their access to quality education is highly limited. As the state gradually privatizes public resources and welfare, the market further subordinates rural migrant workers, which is evident in the unequal distribution of educational resources. In the 1980s and 1990s, lack of an urban *hukou* has prevented migrant workers' children (*liudong ertong*; 流动儿童) from accessing public schools in cities unless their parents pay a fee, which many migrant-worker families cannot afford.[15] Children who stay behind in rural villages and do not go to cities with their parents become "left-behind children" (*liushou ertong*; 留守儿童). Left-behind children live with their grandparents and face many challenges due to the lack of economic and cultural resources in rural communities.[16] A national policy implemented in 2004 prohibits public schools' fee-charging practice, but some schools still manage to charge extra fees from migrant parents.[17] The 2004 policy has not improved the situation, and migrant children still have limited access to public schools due to the fees, bureaucratic requirements, and limited space.[18] Migrant workers cannot afford the elite private schools that rich urban families send their children to. Many migrant children go to schools established specifically for them.[19] Yet there are far fewer of these schools, and they usually cannot provide the quality of education that public and elite private schools do.

The persisting patriarchal power, meanwhile, creates a gendered hierarchy among rural migrants. In factories, female rural migrants take relatively lower-paid and lower-status positions, while male migrants enjoy more and better opportunities. Along with other forms of discrimination, such as racism and xenophobia, gender inequality is a key condition constitutive of the current global working class. Migrant women's labor is devalued and restricted, which remains a vital strategy for global capital accumulation.[20] In the service economy, female migrants work in low-income sectors, as waitresses, janitors, and domestic workers. They often encounter various forms of mistreatment, abuse, and sexual harassment.[21] In marriage and family life, female migrants are constrained by patriarchal norms. For instance, Zhang Li's ethnographic work on affluent migrant families in Wenzhou, a town in southeast China famous for its trading economy, shows that although wives often display strong business skills, their mobility is rather limited in terms of access to spaces that are male dominated, including business and public-entertainment locations.[22]

I met Zhangjie, a fifty-six-year-old female migrant, at a public hospital in Xi'an, where she worked as a janitor. Originally from a rural village in Sichuan Province, Zhangjie had worked in different towns and cities as an assembly-line worker, waitress, and janitor for almost four decades. Every winter during the Spring Festival, Zhangjie returned to her home village, which was the only time of the year she was with her family. After getting married, she and her husband started to go to his family in a nearby village every year to celebrate the Lunar New Year. Zhangjie explained that when at home, it is always her mother, mother-in-law, and herself who do most of the housework: "No matter if women are working outside, like their husbands, or not, women are just doing all the housework at home. In the village, every family is like that." While middle-class women can offload the burden of housework onto domestic workers, female rural migrants do not enjoy such a privilege. Patriarchal norms persist and influence female migrants' lives across generations. Huamei is a twenty-five-year-old young female migrant working at a beauty salon in Beijing. After breaking up with her boyfriend, she had several dates with young men introduced by her family and friends. Huamei complained that her parents often warned her that if she did not get married soon, she would become too old to attract a husband. She observed, "I am not against marriage. But I am working ten hours every day at the salon, then if I am married, who would do the housework and take care of the baby? I don't think men will do it."

Neoliberalism promises that further marketization and privatization can bring economic prosperity and improve people's lives, but the reality of neoliberal globalization is that it has detrimentally affected the well-being of workers across the globe. Backed by state policies, capital continues to make profit through disenfranchisement of workers. Yet a global working class continues to form. Rural migrant workers, subject to discriminatory state policies and market power, have become a new working class in reformist China. Among the structural and institutional forces, mainstream media and culture play a primary role in distributing symbolic capital. The next section interrogates how media representations of migrant workers perpetuate and justify their social marginalization in global contexts and in China.

MARGINALIZING AND DEGRADING MIGRANT WORKERS THROUGH MAINSTREAM MEDIA AND CULTURE

Mainstream media and culture reinforce the inequalities of migrant workers and intensify the division between local people and migrant workers. Dominant discourses about transnational migrant workers and undocumented immigrants are often racist, xenophobic, and classist. For instance, news media in Canada represent migrant workers as outsiders and threats to local communities.[23] Former US president Donald Trump calls undocumented immigrants "rapists," "drug dealers," and "criminals."[24] In the United Kingdom, migrant workers are depicted as disposable labor and alienated others in television documentaries.[25] In Taiwan, news media portray migrants from Southeast Asian countries, who work in construction and in caregiving in private homes and nursing facilities, as perpetrators of crime and unwanted others invading Taiwanese society.[26] Such degrading discourses implicitly justify the suffering of migrant workers and become a constitutive force of the unequal social structures of neoliberalism.

Stereotypical representations of transnational migrant workers and undocumented immigrants perpetuate nationalist ideology and sentiment. Nationalism constructs a binary division of "us" and "them" between local workers and migrant people, which prevents the formation of worker solidarity. For instance, amid the COVID-19 pandemic, mainstream news media and politicians in Western countries started to acknowledge the significant contribution of essential workers, many of whom work in low-paid sectors, such as agriculture, transportation, caregiving, and retail.[27] Although media and government discourse highlights the need to protect the well-being of low-income essential workers, it downplays the reality that a large number of people who work in low-paid essential services are temporary migrant workers, undocumented immigrants, and refugees. Their precarious immigration status makes them more susceptible to violations of their rights.

In China, mainstream media and culture act as primary sites to represent and construct rural migrant workers as alienated and deviant others. These representations objectify rural migrants as despicable and undesirable in urban social and cultural life. The popular television drama *Professor Tian and His Twenty-Eight Maids* provides a good example. The drama tells the story of an urban middle-class family who seeks a "proper" maid. Urban viewers' media consumption of the maids' images and their disidentification with those maids become a way to affirm and perpetuate consumers' urban and middle-class identities. The show thus gives urban consumers the fetishistic pleasure of watching female migrant maids as exotic others entering their lives.[28] Another drama, *Mingong*, which narrates rural migrants' lives in cities and is broadcasted on China Central Television (CCTV), reinforces the rural-urban binary through stereotypical visual representations of rural migrants and urban residents.[29] In the realm of nonfiction, or documentarian, representations, compassionate journalism, while ostensibly paying sympathetic attention to the hardships of female migrants and framing them as individual victims, in reality commodifies the suffering of women migrants as a selling point to appeal to readers.[30] Under the gaze of an urban- and middle-class-oriented viewership, rural migrant workers are portrayed as undesirable others.

The Chinese media system has undergone a transformation in the market reform. The party-state, market, domestic private capital, and transnational capital negotiate and cooperate to allocate and exploit media and communication resources. When the People's Republic of China (PRC) was founded in 1949, the central government was in control of all media production and distribution, and the media system primarily served to reproduce party ideology.[31] In Mao's era, Chinese media, particularly news media, heavily controlled by the party-state, were basically "state ideological apparatuses," to use Althusser's term.[32] In the late 1970s, media reform was initiated alongside economic reform as part of the Chinese government's drive to boost economic development. The production of media gradually incorporated market forces. It became insufficient to rely completely on state economic support for the survival of media organizations. The government also launched policies to cut subsidies and commercialize the media system. The pattern of coproduction between the state and market became increasingly noticeable in the twenty-first century, especially in the film industry. With the rise of the Chinese media market, investment in film production became a popular way for domestic and transnational corporations to make profits. The state takes a regulatory and gatekeeping role to preserve ideological control while making profits through rent seeking and outsourcing production work to private capital.[33] Since the 1990s, mainstream-media outlets have mostly relied on advertising for revenue and profit. The structural changes in Chinese media and communication systems have exacerbated existing unequal power structures by benefiting certain groups, such as urban elites, while further marginalizing the underprivileged.

Cultural inequality in reformist China manifests itself in the unequal distribution of media and cultural products as well as communication technologies, particularly between urban and rural populations. With little political and economic capital at their disposal, rural migrant workers also lack cultural capital. Despite the large size of China's rural population, newspapers aimed at rural readers sharply declined as the newspaper industry commercialized.[34] Depending on advertising for survival and profits, commercialized newspapers are not interested in the rural population, which is not considered profitable. When new information technologies like mobile phones, personal computers and the internet first appeared in the 1990s, only a small group of the elite could afford them.[35] As information-communication technologies (ICTs) get less expensive and more prevalent, less privileged groups are able to possess them and integrate them into their everyday lives. Unlike middle-class consumers, who are devoted to fancy foreign brands, like mobile phones from Apple and Samsung, less privileged groups tend to buy secondhand phones or cheaper knockoff products.[36] In recent years, as domestic brands have become more popular, middle-class consumers prefer expensive brands, such as Huawei, while cheaper brands are more commonly used among the working class. All my interviewees are now using domestic brand phones, including Oppo, Xiaomi, and Vivo, which are much cheaper than iPhones.

Cultural inequality not only manifests through consumption at a material level but also is sustained discursively. The domination of urban middle-class values and lifestyles is consolidated by degrading rural migrants. *Suzhi* (素质; quality or character) is the term proposed by the Chinese government in the early years of its economic reforms as the desired characteristic of the "high-quality" citizens the government aimed to cultivate to meet the demands of modernization. Initially promoted by the party-state in the early 1990s, *suzhi* has been quickly adopted by media and popular discourse to refer to an ideal and desirable type of subjectivity that modern Chinese citizens should embrace, and it has been used effectively to justify the established social hierarchy and status quo.[37] *Suzhi* means having civility, the ability to discipline oneself, and the capability to achieve modernity. Rural people and migrant workers are primary targets for the disciplinary power of *suzhi* discourse. For example, an article from a state-run magazine contends that "we must admit that the *suzhi* of Chinese peasants is not high. The grave concern is to educate the peasantry."[38] Tamara Jacka notes that the discourse of *suzhi*, which in turn fundamentally shapes the subjective position of rural migrants, is "bound up with a form of 'internal orientalism' on the part of Chinese intellectuals searching for ways to respond to western projects and colonialism in the late nineteenth and early twentieth centuries."[39] In this sense, the subordination and displacement of rural populations have arisen from China's search for modernization over the past century. In reformist China, the discourse of *suzhi* underpins the superiority of urban status, which is also a legacy of Mao's era, while it disdains and stigmatizes rural identity.

Along with *suzhi* discourse that degrades rural migrants as "low quality" people, *tu* (土; earthy) is another common term to address rural people with "low taste." In urban middle-class consumer culture, rural people are reprobated as symbols of being *tu*, with little aesthetic taste and fashion sense. Pierre Bourdieu conceptualizes "taste" as an arbitrary distinction created by the dominant class to produce hierarchal differences between the habitus of the dominant and those of the dominated.[40] Correspondingly, the disparaging discourses of "low" *suzhi* and of *tu* position the cultural habitus of rural migrants, including their manners, media consumption practices, and lifestyles, as negative references to sustain the supremacy of an urban middle-class way of life. The domination of middle-class consumer culture in China conveys an implicit message: rural migrants should be shameful of their lack of *suzhi* and aesthetic taste and need to be educated to become modern and capable citizens. The hierarchal distinction between rural and urban populations conceals the structural inequality in the distribution of cultural capital.

Media construction of the backwardness and deviance of migrant workers creates an obscuration of political, economic, and cultural inequalities in contemporary China. Such displacement becomes a way to gain popular consensus for neoliberal ideology among ordinary Chinese citizens so that people gradually accept and normalize privatization and marketization of public resources. Official media legitimize the political leadership of the party-state by sidestepping any discussions of structural inequality and disparity. A show from CCTV includes a "song for rural migrant workers" in the Spring Festival Gala. The song celebrates how rural migrants' experiences in cities were satisfying and empowering while failing to acknowledge any suffering or difficulties they might face. The official discourse propagates the national agenda of economic development and underscores the necessity of market competition and individuals' entrepreneurial spirit. Party media endorse rural women's migration as a significant step for self-improvement and celebrate stories of migrant women who return to help with their villages' entrepreneurial setups and promote a model of female rural migrants as independent and strong.[41] The state championing of individual achievement cultivates a neoliberal ethos and subjectivity among the population in order to facilitate China's market reform.

In the winter of 2017 after a fire in suburban Beijing caused nineteen deaths, the Beijing government launched a campaign in the name of public security to demolish "unsafe" residential and commercial buildings in suburban villages, where thousands of millions of rural migrant workers reside. Rural migrants work in low-income sectors and live in suburban villages where many buildings do not meet fire-safety standards. But instead of improving living conditions and providing temporary accommodations, the government simply expelled the migrants. Many had no place to stay during that especially cold winter and were forced to leave the city. In the campaign, rural migrant workers were labeled as a "low-quality population" (*di duan renkou*; 低端人口) in official and media discourse. The insulting term belongs to the continuum of state- and media-perpetuated *suzhi* discourse to justify the mistreatment of rural migrants. In Western countries, the stereotyped negative image of migrant workers and undocumented immigrants leads to their becoming scapegoats during economic crises. In China, rural migrants are excluded from urban communities and scapegoated by the government and media as problems to be solved. Encountering structural inequalities, workers resist in various ways.

WORKERS' STRUGGLES, RESISTANCE, AND RESILIENCE

While capital has become ever more dominant globally, workers have resorted to varied strategies to organize, protest, and demand rights and equality in different contexts. Informal workers have become a leading force in organizing labor strikes at different sites, workplaces, and communities and at different scales—local and national. Along with the informalization of employment amid neoliberal globalization, there has been an increasing trend of labor protests and strikes among informal workers worldwide. In South Korea, since the 1990s, burgeoning labor movements have been organized by contract workers from public and private companies and those working in low-income service and retail sectors.[42] In North America and Europe in the past decade, young gig workers in service sectors have launched strikes and formed their own unions to demand higher salaries, job security, and benefits. In Canada, young baristas have organized strikes and formed their own unions.[43] In the United States, Starbucks baristas from hundreds of stores have protested and some have successfully unionized. Uber drivers have organized a series of labor protests and demonstrations in California. In the United Kingdom, food-delivery workers have organized collective actions to protest labor exploitation of digital-service platforms.[44] Historically, women and minorities have constituted the main workforce of the informal gig economy and have often been excluded from mainstream unions. But in today's advanced economies, a notable characteristic of the new trend of worker resistance is that women, along with racial and sexual minorities, often become leaders in organizing labor protests and movements. For instance, it is young women and queer people who led the barista protests in Canada.

In developing countries, engaging informal workers becomes an important strategy for trade unions and labor movements. Broader alliances among workers and with the general public are formed—a trend which is particularly evident in Latin America and Africa. In Argentina, formal and informal workers, the employed and unemployed, have formed a working-class alliance, and they also unite with other political and social actors to form broader political movements to challenge the power of global capital and seek alternatives to neoliberalism.[45] In Brazil, workers are organizing strikes along with other social movements, such as peasants' landless movements in rural areas and women's rights movements in cities, to protest neoliberal policies and advocate for a new model of development.[46] In Mozambique, labor movements have witnessed the alliance between trade unions and community organizations representing the interests of informal workers.[47] In India, permanent workers and contract workers were united in the labor protests in automobile manufacturing.[48] Promising signs of solidarity emerge from a wide range of worker struggles and efforts of alliance building.

In reformist China, rural migrant workers are the main force of working-class resistance. They have engaged in a range of forms of resistance. An extreme form is suicide. In the late 1990s and early 2000s, news media reported many cases of migrant workers threatening to commit suicide in circumstances where they were demanding wages in arrears from their employers. Public attention to migrant workers' wage arrears reached a peak when former premier Wen Jiaobao addressed the issue and numerous media outlets reported the supreme leader's demands of payback of workers' arrear wages. In the last few years, the most notable case has been the so-called Foxconn suicide express. Foxconn is a manufacturing company that employs a great number of rural migrant workers and is notorious for sweatshop working conditions and military-style management. Jenny Chan and Mark Selden interpret

Foxconn workers' acts of suicide as "one extreme form of labor protest chosen by some to expose an oppressive production regime in which migrant workers are deprived of dignified work and lives."[49] While the Foxconn suicides might seem like a series of individual actions, their multiplicity embraces the collectivist spirit of labor protest. In a detailed account of Foxconn suicide survivors' testimonies, Qiu (Jack) Linchuan makes a compelling argument: "This unprecedented string of suicides at Foxconn was so much more than individual attempts to relieve pain. . . . The suicides can also be interpreted as a subliminal collective endeavor to expose the unbearable conditions that manufacturing iSlaves have to endure. They constitute a defiant act of resistance, too." [50] The tragedy of the Foxconn suicides gained widespread public attention through national and international media. Some concrete changes did occur when public pressure compelled the company to improve working conditions and the intervention of national political leaders prodded municipal governments to take some action to protect workers' rights.[51] Still, the impact was limited to only a few companies, and official state and media discourse avoided mention of structural inequalities. In reporting workers' suicide cases, Chinese mainstream news media avoid framing the actions as resistance and only represent them as tragic individual occurrences.

Commenting on the Foxconn tragedy, Jianlin, a young migrant worker, said to me, "I had worked in a factory in Zhengzhou for two years, and I know how suffocating the working environment is. I didn't feel like a human anymore, and we workers live like machines every day. I totally understand why these workers committed suicide—because life is too intolerable, and this is just the way they resist fate. They are certainly not cowards. They are brave. I am so furious. Why are we facing all these issues?" Jianlin also interprets workers' suicides as a form of resistance and is quite aware of the inequalities as the root cause. In contrast to the way mainstream media frame the Foxconn case, workers understand it as evidence of ongoing social problems rather than mere individual incidents. Jianlin was very critical of media reports on the Foxconn case: "Well, I am not surprised at all. Of course, media will trivialize the event and not condemn the government. Isn't it government policies that allow the company to treat workers like this?" Jianlin now works at a hostel, and he is very determined to not work in factories anymore. Compared with the previous generation of migrant workers, more and more young migrant workers regard factory labor conditions and military-style management as unbearable and, more importantly, unacceptable. Huamei said of assembly-line jobs, "Although I often need to work very long hours at the beauty salon, the working environment is much better than at factories. And I can talk to my customers, which is kind of fun." In the past five years, factories in China have reported an increasing shortage of labor.[52] Young workers' refusal to work in factories is at once the cause of the recent labor shortage and the result of longer-term structural inequalities in reformist China.

Migrant workers' collective actions, including bargaining, protests, marches, and demonstrations, are common among factory workers. The collective resistance at industrial production sites aims to secure substantial gains in higher wages, better working and living conditions, and more benefits.[53] Since the early 2000s, there has been an ever-growing use of social media by migrant workers during instances of industrial strikes in China; QQ (Tengxun; 腾讯), blogs, and online forums were common tools in the early years of the internet, and Weibo (微博; Microblogs) and WeChat have recently become popular among migrant workers.[54] ICTs help facilitate the process of mobilizing and organizing. For instance, in the factory strikes in Shaanxi, Shenzhen, and Shandong, among other provinces, workers relied on social media to spread the word, document and share photos and videos of their strikes, narrate stories, and express opinions and commentary to inform and, more importantly, mobilize action.[55]

It is not surprising that workers' protests often face brutal crackdown from local governments. Compared with individual grievances, collective actions, such as labor strikes and demonstrations, seldom get coverage in mainstream media. In China's political context, the relations between the party-state and workers' collective actions are repressive and regulatory. During Hu Jintao's administration from 2002 to 2012, the state resorted to a wide range of repressive strategies to suppress workers' protests, including sending paramilitary police to crack down on the rebellions, harass the relatives of activists, and arrest leaders of the protests.[56] Due to state violence and suppression, labor strikes may succeed in one factory while facing "formidable difficulties in extending success throughout an industry."[57] Since 2013, under Xi Jinping's regime, harassment and brutal oppression against labor unrest and activism have become even more frequent and have further restricted the political opportunities for labor movements to burgeon.[58] Instead of protecting workers' rights and well-being, labor law in contemporary China has become a regulatory regime for the party-state to discipline labor power: when workers seek legal protection of their violated rights, the response strategy that the government deploys often relies on channeling workers' grievances through the mediation process or legal process, which turns collective labor unrest into individualized and isolated labor-dispute cases.[59] Local governments strategically mediate conflicts and cautiously prevent any autonomous organizing power among the workers.[60] Cases of labor disputes have shown that workers' attempts to seek legal protection are costly, time-consuming, and often rejected, and the requests are hard to pursue outside the domain of law.[61]

Guo shared his experiences of dealing with wage arrears. He and the other five construction workers first requested the back wages from the contractor who was subcontracting the job to them. This initial attempt was not successful. He then turned to a volunteer lawyer whom he got to know at an NGO. With the lawyer's help, the workers reported the case to the labor and social security department of the local government. After almost a year, they finally received their wages. I asked Guo about his thoughts on labor protests and strikes. He said, "I am more concerned about getting my wages. When we went to the boss and the government, we were cautious and did not want to cause troubles. We didn't want to get arrested." Workers recognize the intimidation tactics that the state uses to deny them their political rights to protest and strike. Jianlin's view reflects the impact of state suppression: "I respect those workers on strike very much, but I will not join them. I don't want to get arrested. I know people who were arrested." Arresting workers who have engaged in direct actions persists as a means of exercising a state's coercive power to suppress resistance in historical and contemporary contexts across different countries, including China. But the decision not to join a strike does not necessarily prevent workers from feeling solidarity with their fellows.

Beyond labor protests and strikes, migrant workers also contest the dominant discourse. For instance, being exposed to the disciplinary power and condescending gaze of *suzhi* discourse, migrant workers become very aware of stereotypes and judgements. In Sun Wanning's ethnographic study on domestic workers in China, one worker remarked, "I'm tired of being told that we domestic workers have low *suzhi*. Our level of education may be low, but that has nothing to do with low *suzhi*."[62] In our chats, Jianlin questioned the classism embedded in the *suzhi* discourse: "They just think rural people have low *suzhi*. That is ridiculous. Do they think the rich and corrupted officials have high *suzhi*? One's characters (and behaviors) have nothing to do with money or social status." In our conversation about the Beijing government and its eviction of the "low-quality population," Hua, a middle-aged migrant worker, criticized the term strongly: "They consider us poor people to be low-quality. But we work so hard every day, and we don't steal or commit crimes. How can they say we are a low-quality population?" Hua is a self-employed painter, and he has worked in several cities for almost two decades. Reflecting on his experiences, Hua said, "In early years, contractors often didn't pay us on time. Employer families accused us of cheating on labor and materials, which I never did. So does the government think these people are high quality?"

Migrant workers also take active roles as cultural producers to write migrant stories. The emergence of *dagong shiren* (打工诗人; worker poets) and *dagong zuojia* (打工作家; worker writers) forms an important part of rural migrants' engagement with cultural production. *Dagong shige* (打工诗歌; worker poems), which is characterized by a small number of migrant workers who write poetry to document their lives and express emotions, has become a specific genre of subaltern literature.[63] Some female migrants self-publish their stories about migration in popular online forums; if these stories attract a sufficient number of readers, publishers approach these writers to sign book contracts. Online publishing enables migrant women writers to "reach out without having to go through the conventional institutions of publishing," which is often dominated by male elites.[64] In recent years, with the rapid development and increasing popularity of short-video platforms, such as Kuaishou (快手; Quick Hand) and Douyin (抖音; TikTok [China edition]), the younger generation of rural migrants has become content creators on these platforms. Xiaoli has both Kuaishou and Douyin accounts. He has produced dozens of videos but does not have many followers. We talked about the influencer culture, and Xiaoli showed strong interest: "If I can become an influencer, I would be able to make more money. But I'm not that dedicated to becoming an influencer. I just use my accounts to document my life."

Xiaoli's thoughts are common among migrant workers engaged in writing and making videos. They may have some aspirations to earn money through their cultural practices, but their main goal is to find fulfillment through self-expression. Although these forms of self-expression are not necessarily driven by political goals, their practices do confront the urban elites' cultural domination and increase the group's visibility in the public sphere. Female migrant writers explore their sexual lives in novels. Feelings of sexual repression are common among rural migrant workers, especially women, as young female migrants "face the added difficulty of having far fewer outlets than other social groups, including male migrants, for pursuing their desires, and they often live in much more circumscribed, deprived and scrutinized spatial arrangements."[65] The body of migrants' self-published literature describes diverse accounts of migrant women's sexual desires, activities, frustrations, and struggles.[66] These narratives depict the details of migrant women's lives, which are seldom represented in mainstream media and cultural accounts. Coping with the precariousness of digital platforms and the attention economy, migrant youth resort to collaborative production to create various content in the hope of generating income and gaining social mobility.[67] Similar to *dagong* poetry and literature, creating and posting videos of their lives by young rural migrants is also a form of self-expression and a way of seeking social, cultural, and economic capital.

Workers' various forms of resilience suggest a promising possibility of social change at the present historical juncture when the repressive powers of capital and the state often seem insurmountable. In worker struggles at local, national, and transnational levels, unions remain an enduring and important force, and NGOs have gradually emerged as an additional significant organizational force. The next section discusses the historical and contemporary roles and strategies of unions and the rising influence of NGOs in labor movements and worker struggles in world history and in China.

LABOR UNIONS AND NGOS AS ORGANIZATIONAL FORCES

With the rapid development of industrial capitalism and the colonial and imperialist expansion of global capital in the nineteenth and twentieth centuries, labor unions have become an important institutional force to represent workers' interests and defend their rights. In Western countries, mainstream labor unions have successfully built partnerships with the state and industries to negotiate for employment standards and workers' benefits.[68] The immense power of unions in the post–World War II moment represents something of a peak in this history—a moment when unions guaranteed high salaries and job security for industrial workers in North America and Europe. In non-Western countries, labor unions have not only represented workers' rights but became an integral part of the nation building in the postcolonial period. For instance, in late-colonial India, workers sought collective bargaining power through unionization. After India's independence, major unions were affiliated with major political parties and embraced a state-led centralized bargaining structure.[69] From 1860 onward, labor unions in South Africa have been an essential by which workers have fought for their rights and for racial justice.[70] Prior to neoliberal globalization, a common characteristic of labor unions in Western and non-Western countries, albeit with variations, is that their members are workers/employees in formal economies that are well regulated by the government.

In the neoliberal era, the concentration of union membership among organized industrial workers has ironically become an impediment as the world's workforce has grown increasingly informalized. The declining power of labor unions is the result of an overall restructuring of national and international labor markets, where the numbers of formal employees have dropped greatly, while subcontracted and informal workers have become the main labor force in the manufacturing and service sectors. The state also plays a critical role in constraining the power of labor unions. For instance, in the postwar United States, the welfare state focused on ensuring mass employment and workers' rights in the Fordist economy. In the era of post-Fordism, the neoliberal state has set policy obstacles to prevent workers from unionizing and collective bargaining, while employers have rapidly expanded their antiunion campaigns.[71] Both trends have enabled a new wave of capital accumulation. Additionally, states have used coercive means to quell instances of labor organization. The South Korean state responded to manufacturing union strikes with violent interventions, using riot police and tear gas.[72] In India, the state represses workers' movements and unions' strikes in manufacturing sectors through police violence and mass arrest.[73]

Responding to the challenges that the entwined powers of market and state pose, community and social-movement unionism emerged as new types of unions at the end of the twentieth century.[74] Unions have reached out to formal and informal workers and both members and nonmembers beyond the workplace to organize collective actions in collaboration with local communities. In the late 1990s, labor unions in the United Kingdom faced the continuing decline of manufacturing employment and union membership; in response, these unions have built relationships with local communities as an effective way to address the well-being of community members and bolster union power.[75] In Canada, building coalitions with community members has become a vital strategy for unions to organize nonunion workers in the ever-expanding informal sectors of the economy.[76] Unions also seek alliances with social-movement actors with broader political goals to contest structural inequalities, as can be seen in many developing countries where unions have become a leading force in wider social and political struggles. Since the 1980s, workers in Brazil, Argentina, the Philippines, South Africa, and South Korea have created new labor movements that go beyond the conventional mode of union activities and ally with varied social movements, with the goal of effecting radical changes in society.[77] These changes in labor organization indicate new conceptions of the constitution of the working class and of social-justice struggles.

Unions are not the only prominent organizational force in worker struggles. Since the late 1980s, NGOs have played an increasingly important role in advocating for the rights of underprivileged migrants, including migrant workers, undocumented immigrants, and refugees, who serve as an essential labor force in the global economy. Due to legal obstacles and precarious immigration status, these migrant people are often not permitted to unionize in many countries and areas. For instance, in Singapore, Canada, and the Middle East, it is illegal for foreign migrant workers, not to mention undocumented immigrants, to form unions. NGOs thus become a main organizational force to provide service and organize and mobilize collective actions. Community-based organizing and the formation of national and transnational alliances are the main strategies of migrant-worker NGOs. In Singapore, two NGOs, Transient Workers Count Too (TWC2) and the Humanitarian Organisation for Migrant Employees (HOME), in alliance with international NGOs and advocacy groups, act as the leading forces in domestic workers' efforts to demand their labor rights.[78] In Canada, since the early 1990s, national and local NGOs, such as Migrant Workers Alliance for Change (MWAC) and Committee for Domestic Workers' and Caregivers' Rights (CDWCR), have advocated political and labor rights for precarious migrants, including care workers, agricultural workers, and undocumented immigrants. In the Middle East, a group of local NGOs were established in the late 1990s and have provided various types of service to migrant domestic workers and refugees and advocated for their rights.[79]

Unions in China are part of the state apparatus and subject to corporate management; they are not an autonomous force to represent workers' interests. Founded by Chinese Communist Party in 1925, the All-China Federation of Trade Unions (ACFTU; Zhonghua quanguo zonggonghui; 中华全国总工会) has the largest membership and number of branches in the world. To this day, it remains a top-down, centralized affiliate of the party-state.[80] In Mao's planned economy, members of ACFTU were mostly workers from state-owned enterprises (SOEs). In the era of economic reform, the dissolution of SOEs has resulted in the decline of ACFTU's membership. ACFTU strategically broadens its membership by establishing local union branches at private and foreign-owned companies and by actively recruiting rural migrant workers.[81] Leaders of local unions are appointed by corporations or upper levels of unions, and very few are directly elected by workers. The primary function of unions in China is to appease workers' unrest and direct labor disputes to state-sanctioned channels so that confrontation with state power is avoided.[82] Since the founding of the PRC in 1949, independent labor unions have officially become illegal and politically taboo.[83] Workers' attempts to form independent labor unions and organize collective actions are frequently suppressed by local government in the name of maintaining social stability and creating a favorable environment for capital investment. A recent case is the crackdown on Jasic factory workers' protests and arrests of labor activists in 2018 in Shenzhen, Guangdong Province.[84]

In contrast to the state affiliations of unions, labor NGOs have gradually emerged as a vital grassroots source of labor activism for more than three decades. Since the mid-1990s, labor NGOs began to emerge in the south coast area of China.[85] Activists and nonprofit organizations from Hong Kong, including China Labor Bulletin (Zhongguo laogong tongxun; 中国劳工通讯) and Chinese Working Women Network (Nügong Guanhuai; 女工关怀),[86] along with international civil groups and foundations, helped to establish labor NGOs in the Pearl River Delta region, where the economic reforms were pioneered, labor-intensive and export-oriented factories were built, and millions of rural migrants first worked and settled. In the ensuing years, labor NGOs have spread from the south to other regions in China, including the east coast, the central area, and the capital city, Beijing. Numerous labor NGOs have been established in major cities, like Beijing, Shenzhen, and Guangzhou, and secondary cities, like Wuhan, Qingdao, and Chongqing. The primary functions of most of these NGOs are to provide legal services, education about labor policies and rights, and cultural activities.[87] Labor NGOs respond to the concerns of rural migrant workers that the state and market often fail or are unwilling to address.

On the other hand, scholarly critiques have pointed out labor NGOs' limited ability to effect radical structural change. Challenging the idea that labor NGOs in China can promote progressive political change, Ivan Franceschini lists some critical facts: as a highly mobile population, rural migrant workers rarely maintain long-term connections with local NGOs; Chinese migrant workers often do not trust them and their "free services"; and in politically sensitive situations, such as demonstrations and strikes, labor NGOs often fail to represent migrant workers.[88] Some scholars have argued that NGOs' advocacy is really just a form of lip service as they primarily attend to individual cases without addressing structural inequalities.[89] For instance, some NGO training programs, such as those providing computing skills, often serve government policy by nurturing a spirit of entrepreneurialism in migrant workers, thus reaffirming the state agenda of self-development and discipline.[90] Labor

NGOs can be politically cautious and tend to avoid cultivating solidarity and collective power among migrant workers, instead maintaining a cordial relationship with the state.[91]

But the potential for NGOs to act as a grassroots organizational force in enabling collective actions should not be dismissed out of hand. Through an extensive exploration of labor NGOs under Hu's regime, Diana Fu demonstrates that although not directly involved in worker strikes, labor NGOs are a vital force in providing strategies and support to workers in individual conflicts and small-scale collective actions, such as flash demonstrations.[92] Fu's work has significant implications in making legible the mobilizing and organizing capacity of labor NGOs in China. Few of the migrant workers I met during my fieldwork had joined any unions. As most of them work in informal economies, such as low-income service sectors, unions are not even present in their workplace. Some factory workers were highly suspicious of the capability of unions to defend workers' rights. As one worker said, "We had a union in the factory I worked in in Shanghai, but it is useless. The union is just like part of the factory. It is standing with the boss, not us workers." Workers' attitudes toward NGOs contrast with their criticism of unions. Workers who have participated in NGOs' activities or received services, such as free legal consultation, hold very positive views of labor NGOs. Guo, for instance, said that the main reason for him to live in his suburban village rather than others is that the NGO he participates in is in the community. Though workers have different expectations for their involvement in NGOs, their general perception of NGOs is positive.

The differences in practice and strategy between labor unions and NGOs arise from the emergence of each type of organization in a different historical and politico-economic context. Both labor unions and NGOs apply themselves to the urgent, ongoing tasks of combating the repressive power of the state and growing domination of global capital and of finding political opportunities to serve as a genuine organizational force for working people.

CONCLUSION

Rural migrant workers' inequalities are the outcomes of China's transition to a market economy while maintaining its authoritarian political system, the legacy of urban-rural division, and patriarchal culture. These workers have made enormous contribution to China's economic miracle, yet they continue to be socially marginalized and are deprived of labor and civil rights. A rural migrant worker like Guo may not find that his practices of resilience and self-expression and his participation at labor NGOs gain him social mobility or substantially improve his life in the short term. Yet his continuing efforts, along with those of similar workers, could coalesce to form a collective, bottom-up, resistant force to challenge power asymmetries in China.

In neoliberal capitalism, the state, transnational and domestic capital, and mainstream media intertwine to become a hegemonic power and give rise to the formation of a contemporary global working class. Confronting increasing precarity and exploitation, informal workers and migrant workers become key actors leading workers' struggles across the global North and South. New alliances are formed between labor movements and social movements in varied national contexts. Trade unions endure as a major organizational force with revitalization, while labor NGOs emerge in the contexts where unions are not accessible to workers. As the new working class in post-Mao, reformist China, rural migrant workers are an important segment of the global working class. Despite the state suppression in China, rural migrant workers have persisted in strikes and protests over the last two decades.

Informal workers and migrant workers should be recognized as a new historical subject who have demonstrated their determination, capability, and potential to fight for more equal and just societies. Durable systems of power, such as capitalism, patriarchy, colonialism, and authoritarianism, have had a global reach, and there are both global commonalities and regional specificities running through the structural conditions that shape the formation of new historical subjects. Meanwhile, the entrenched inequalities manifest in different ways and with different consequences depending upon the specific politico-economic and sociocultural landscapes. To attend to structural forces is not to fall into the methodological trap of structural determinism. There is no guarantee that this new historical subject will be formed in any given context. The formation process is embedded in everyday life and struggles, and those are shaped by and respond to structural forces.

In contemporary China, rural migrant workers take on the role of the new historical subject as they encounter inequalities and oppression while showing the potential for creating new forms of resistance. To explore to what extent rural migrant workers' resistance can subvert the established systems of power, one of our first steps must be to consider how a rebellious subject can be formed. A look into subject formation moves us beyond structural determinacy toward a path that seeks possibilities for change. In the next chapter, I explore how rural migrant workers develop a subjectivity of resistance through analysis of a particular case of migrant domestic workers' group advocacy.

TWO

TRANSFORMING SUBJECTIVITIES

*Female Migrant Domestic Workers and Advocacy
through Theater Performance*

In an interview with me, Yan Chengmei, a staff member of Migrant Women's Club (MWC), talked about the circumstances of domestic workers: "Domestic workers nowadays earn ¥5000–6000 [about $1000] a month, even more than some recent college graduates. Though the salary may seem good enough for these workers, people should be aware of the extremely heavy workload, long working hours, and difficult situations they have. There is still much prejudice toward domestic work as a degraded and undesirable profession."[1] In the past decade in China, the number of domestic workers has reached twenty million and most of them are rural-to-urban female migrants.[2] Like domestic workers in other countries, Chinese domestic workers often experience poor working conditions and low wages, mistreatment by employers, and social exclusion.

In 2011, the International Labor Organization passed a resolution calling upon countries to protect domestic workers' labor rights, improve their working conditions, and guarantee social security.[3] During this process, MWC served as an active local representative. Yet China is still not among the thirty-five countries that have ratified the convention to date. In the same year, MWC founded Didinghua Theater, a performance program, as part of its advocacy efforts to secure labor legislation to cover domestic work as formal employment in China. Didinghua is named after a small hardy wildflower that grows at roadsides and in the wild. The name symbolizes the determination and resilience of female migrant workers who make their livings in difficult situations. Most of the domestic workers participating in Didinghua are middle-aged female rural migrants; a few are laid-off workers among the urban poor. At Didinghua Theater, domestic workers tell their stories and adapt those stories into performance with the goal of raising public awareness of domestic workers' situations and earning respect for this marginalized community.

Focusing on female migrant workers' participation in Didinghua Theater, this chapter aims to demonstrate how workers begin to see themselves as part of a potential counterhegemon. Drawing upon feminist scholarship on reproductive labor, poststructuralist theories of subject and subjectivity, and critical performance studies, I address the following questions: What are the typical material conditions of domestic workers in China? How are domestic workers mobilized to participate in the performance program for advocacy? What change has performance brought to their lives? To what extent does female migrant workers' performance function as a form of collective resistance? Attending to the politics of grassroots mobilizing and organizing among domestic workers who have long resided in the informal sector of the economy, this chapter shows how subjective transformation among underprivileged and subordinate groups is possible through performance as a specific form of mediated labor activism.

From March to September 2016 and in the winter of 2017, I frequently visited the site and attended their activities, including the practices, rehearsals, and stage performances, and gradually became close with a few dozen female migrant workers.[4] They were very friendly to me and treated me like a little sister. I helped document their rehearsals by taking photos for them. When they had breaks, we chatted and shared snacks; sometimes we went out for lunch, talking about our families and lives. All these middle-aged women workers were mothers, and some had long-distance relationships with their husbands. A few were divorced. Most of them came from rural villages and had dropped out of school at an early age. Their work experience varied: some of them had run small businesses in towns close to their home villages, and some had worked in factories, shops, and restaurants at a young age in various cities and towns. To make money for various reasons, including to pay off debts, support families, or pay for children's education, they later migrated to Beijing. Given the constraints of age, low education levels, and lack of professional skills, many of them decided to work as live-in domestic workers in Beijing as these positions are among the few available jobs in low-income service sectors.

COMMODIFIED AND DEGRADED DOMESTIC WORK: FEMALE MIGRANT WORKERS

Exploitation and commodification of women's reproductive labor, including birthing, childcare, and all sorts of domestic work, are fundamental to sustain patriarchal and capitalist systems. Capitalism merges with patriarchy to create a wage differential between men and women, compel women to fulfill domestic duties, and justify the disregard for women's reproductive labor.[5] Patriarchal norms limit women to lower-status work and make women's domestic work unpaid or lower paid, and capitalism correspondingly exploits women's free or cheap labor to facilitate capital accumulation. In the global care industries, domestic workers are mostly women who are working class, migrants/immigrants, and racial minorities. For instance, in the United States, white middle-class women displace the burden of housework onto working-class, immigrant, and racial minority women, who take on heavy workloads for low pay.[6] In Singapore, nationalist and gender ideologies lower the labor value of transnational maids from the Philippines, Indonesia, and Sri Lanka.[7] In Hong Kong, migrant women from the Philippines, Malaysia, and other Southeast and South Asian countries are recruited as cheap labor to fill the area's shortage of domestic service.[8] Globally, domestic workers face long-standing problems stemming from the lack of regulation over domestic work, including inadequate protection of workers' rights and various forms of mistreatment and discrimination.

Household servants were among the most deprived social groups in feudal China for centuries. It was the poor and disenfranchised people who served as household servants to the privileged. The feudal political system regulated and categorized servants as inferior people with no entitlement to land or civic rights.[9] Given its low social status, the position of household servant became a contemptible social identity. In Mao's China, to dissolve feudal and capitalist labor relations, the old form of domestic servants was abolished; only a few political and intellectual elites were allowed to hire household maids.[10] Economic reform in the late 1970s facilitated a resurgence in the hiring of domestic helpers. Demand for domestic service among urban families has been increasing ever since. Similar to other countries and areas in the world, most families that employ domestic workers in contemporary China are middle- and upper-middle-class urban ones. Middle-class working couples are often in crucial need of domestic service for housework, childcare, and elder care. From the late 1980s to early 2000s, young female rural migrants and laid-off urban workers formed the main labor pool for domestic work.[11] Critiquing the maltreatment of domestic workers, anthropologist Yan Hairong characterizes the relationship between urban employer families and domestic workers as a new type of master-servant relationship in reformist China.[12]

The experience of Fangfang, a middle-aged rural-to-urban female migrant, is typical of similar workers in the 1990s. In 1993, when she was only sixteen, Fangfang was introduced by a relative to work at an urban household in Beijing. The employing family promised to pay her fifty dollars (¥300) per month for taking care of their new-born baby. But once she began the work, they only paid her forty (¥250) and also demanded that she do all the housework. Fangfang recalled her unpleasant experiences: "The workload was very intense, and what was worse is that I felt so depressed living with them. They were not bad people, but they made a very clear boundary with me and treated me in a way that made me very uncomfortable. For example, they would rather have the fruit go rotten than have me eat it." Back then, the two main methods for recruiting female migrants as domestic workers were through personal referral and through local women's federations in cooperation with local labor departments. Many domestic workers, like Fangfang, did not even have contracts with their employer families. Similar to rural migrant workers in construction and other service sectors, wage arrears were common among domestic workers in the 1990s and early 2000s. The lack of protection provided by labor laws and the unequal relations between employer families and domestic workers left female migrants in a rather vulnerable situation. Wage arrears, verbal and physical abuse, and workplace injuries without compensation were widely documented by scholars and NGOs.[13]

A former volunteer lawyer of MWC commented that in the early years, when workers encountered mistreatment, the government departments were not helpful and domestic workers were reluctant to resort to legal actions. "Many of them chose to either tolerate [the conditions] or just left the family," the lawyer said in the interview. Fangfang is among those who left. She left the family after two years and never worked as a domestic worker again. She told me about her determination to have an office job: "I was so desperate to find a secretarial job back then, and I did not even know why. I knew I have no degrees and few skills. But my handwriting is very pretty, and my writing skills are good. I believe they can be my advantages."

As a young rural girl who dropped out of school at sixteen, Fangfang took every chance to acquire knowledge and professional skills after she came to Beijing. She read from books about speech skills, learned Microsoft software at a neighborhood printing shop, and even acquired a college diploma through self-study. Her hard work paid off: all her later jobs have been as a secretary in small or medium-sized companies, just as she had hoped.

But not all female migrants are able to land white-collar jobs. Domestic work remains one of the few reliable job opportunities for most rural female migrants. Since the beginning of 2000, middle-aged female migrants—from thirty-five to fifty-five years old—have gradually become the main labor force for paid domestic work in major Chinese cities.[14] As factories, restaurants, retail shops, and salons usually prefer to hire young migrant workers,[15] middle-aged female migrants face limited employment opportunities and often have few other choices than to serve as domestic workers. Despite the increased salary today compared to wages in the 1990s, domestic workers still lack labor-law protection, employment security, pensions, and other social welfare.[16] The group also faces substantial bias and discrimination. The feudal heritage of household servants' low social status has left an inferior and stereotyped image of domestic workers. Patriarchal norms define domestic work as primarily women's tasks and lower the value of reproductive labor. The market economy commodifies female migrants as a desirable labor force to fulfill the rising demands of domestic service. Urban supremacy creates a distinct hierarchy between urban residents and rural migrants. All these forces intertwine to produce female migrant domestic workers as subordinate, feminized, cheap, and flexible labor.

Malan is a forty-six-year-old domestic worker. Coming from a rural village, Malan dropped out of school at the age of seventeen and moved to a city to sell clothes with her older sister. She returned to her home village in her early twenties and, with mounting pressure from her parents to marry, later got married to a man from a neighboring village. After their wedding, she and her then husband moved to a nearby town to start a small furniture business there. They ran the business for almost twenty years until she decided to get divorced after finding out about her husband's infidelity. Initially, her husband did not agree to the divorce. Malan, disillusioned by her husband and determined to move on, decided to forfeit property to help accelerate the divorce proceedings. Malan left the town in 2009. She first went to Shanghai, where she found work as a domestic worker and restaurant waitress. As she was not used to the humid climate of Shanghai, she relocated to Beijing in 2011, where she has stayed and worked as a domestic worker. Malan recalled in our interview that she encountered many employers who looked down upon domestic workers. She did not like to be referred as *baomu*—a Chinese term used to refer to domestic workers, often carrying demeaning connotations—by her employers and found the term discriminatory.

Malan's experiences are not uncommon among the middle-aged female migrants I met during fieldwork. To earn a living, these women have migrated and remigrated around the country. But years of work have brought them little social mobility. They are enticed by the comparatively high wages of domestic work but constantly face discrimination in their daily lives. Before coming to Beijing, Xiaohong had worked at a wedding photography shop in a town close to her home village for almost ten years. She was initially responsible for doing make-up for customers and was later promoted to a sales position. She did not like sales work and always felt pressured and stressed, so she quit the job. After getting married, she and her husband moved to a southern coastal city, where they both worked at a supermarket. Through a friend's recommendation, she took some training classes offered by a domestic-service company and obtained a certificate. Attracted by the relatively well-paid domestic jobs in Beijing, she moved to Beijing alone at the age of thirty-six. Most of her work involved taking care of small children. She had two main criteria when she chose employing families: good wages and being happy at work. She told me, "I don't mind a heavy workload if they can pay me well. But if I feel unhappy and uncomfortable, I will leave and quit immediately." To explain what her standards for being "happy and comfortable" entailed, she described an instance when a grandmother of her employers' child often challenged her on her childcare methods. One day, during a disagreement, the elder woman used curse words to scold and threaten her. She quit the job following that incident, commenting to me, "They were so rude and disrespectful because they think I am just a *baomu* and my education level is low."

In my conversations with them, domestic workers consistently brought up respect as one of their key concerns. Jiajie was born in 1960 in a town in northern China, graduated from high school in 1977, and did not go to college due to the Cultural Revolution. She worked in a state-owned enterprise in the 1980s and got to know her husband at work. They started their own small business in the early 1990s when the state started to boost the market economy. The business did not do well and led them into debt. In 2007, Jiajie decided to go to Beijing after seeing a job ad posted by the municipal labor ministry to recruit domestic workers. She recalled why she made this decision: "The minimum wage posted for domestic workers in Beijing was higher than the maximum wage I can get from my town." To pay back the debt, Jiajie moved to Beijing alone at age forty-seven. Jiajie was very proud of her skills as a domestic worker because she was "different from those who came from rural villages given her background and experiences." Yet despite her better background than most female rural migrants, Jiajie's early years of domestic work were not pleasant. She worked with many employers who were unfriendly and excessively demanding, and once she was even wrongly accused of stealing her employer's possessions.

Jiajie was lucky to finally work for a nice family, and she stayed with them for seven years. The wife and husband both worked as executives of state-owned companies. Jiajie's daily routine was to cook for the family and do housework. The primary reason that she worked for the family for such a long time was because, as Jiajie said, "they do respect me." She related several instances: the employer's family always waited for her to have meals together; when she had just started working for the family, the employers told her that "we are all equal, you *dagong* [work] for us and, we *dagong* for the party; there are no differences between us." Jiajie said to me, "My employers are not like many other [employer] families, which only give their domestic workers the leftovers to eat. Regardless of whether they really think so [that we are equal] or not, at least their words made me very comfortable and feel respected. Once when I was ill in the hospital, the employer family did not cut my salary for the leave and instead paid me extra to show their concern. They also visited me in the hospital and brought fruits and healthcare products." Although some domestic workers may be fortunate enough to work for respectful employer families, discrimination against domestic workers has been a common phenomenon in China and worldwide, as evidenced by one of the principles in the International Labor Organization's Domestic Workers Convention: "the elimination of discrimination in respect of employment and occupation."[17] Respect toward domestic workers should not rely on the morality of individual employer families but rather on the societal recognition of the value of their work and labor and protection of their labor and human rights.

Many domestic workers have internalized the pervasive discourses that demean the profession. Middle-aged female migrant informants often confessed to me that they considered domestic work a shameful and inferior job. These women workers recalled that they had to try incredibly hard to get themselves prepared to "serve people" (*cihou ren*; 伺候人) before they decided to take the job. One worker shared that in her first couple of years as a domestic worker, she saw herself as "losing face" (*diuren*; 丢人). When she was working at employers' families, she avoided eye contact with others and often spoke with her head down. Other domestic workers related similar experiences. They felt ashamed to tell relatives and friends back home that they were taking jobs as domestic workers. Domestic workers prepared themselves to assume the submissive role of servant, supposing that it was what the occupation demanded. But at the same time, these women felt a constant conflict between their perception of domestic work as a degraded profession and their strong feelings as dignified subjects who desire respect and recognition. Bias and prejudice toward their jobs stands as one of the issues of most concern for many middle-aged female migrant workers. A wish to combat that stigma has become a primary motivation for female migrant domestic workers to participate in the performance program of Didinghua Theater.

MOBILIZING FEMALE MIGRANTS AND BECOMING ANTAGONIST SUBJECTS

Didinghua's mission grows out of MWC's long-term advocacy efforts for domestic workers' rights. Before the founding of Didinghua, MWC assisted many domestic workers in negotiating with employing families to obtain wages in arrears or compensation for work-related injuries. Interaction with domestic workers made Yan Chengmei and other MWC staff realize that the organization's work should move beyond the mere provision of such services to a call for wider awareness and recognition of domestic workers' situations. As many domestic workers were interested in singing and dancing as leisure activities, performance seemed an ideal means by which to mobilize these workers—and it offered an appealing, reflexive, and participatory way to tell domestic workers' stories. Didinghua's performances are not staged in highbrow or commercial theaters; rather, Didinghua's approach to performance, to use Dwight Conquergood's definition, embodies political and cultural articulation by subordinate groups, researchers, and activists to question and challenge oppression and domination.[18]

With the help of two other MWC staff members, Yan Chengmei founded the Didinghua Theater in July 2011. Chengmei told me, "When I first met these women at Didinghua, many of them felt they were 'losing face' for doing this job. In the society, there is still a lot of discrimination against domestic workers and bias in terms of viewing domestic work as a degrading profession. We want to change the situation." In the first few years after its establishment, Zhao Zhiyong, a professor from the Central Academy of Drama, together with two of his graduate students kindly served as voluntary instructors to offer performance training and guidance for women participating in Didinghua. In an article reflecting on his experiences with underprivileged groups on performance, Zhao refers to Augusto Boal's "the theatre of the oppressed" to interpret the political implications of domestic workers' performance: "Although one or two performances cannot change the disadvantaged situations of these people, their performance contributes to a 'new cultural' movement for social equity and justice."[19] This statement aligns with the organizers and activists' clear advocacy goals for the performance program of Didinghua. To cater to the working schedules of domestic workers, most of whom only have one day off per week, Didinghua initially held its activities on Saturdays, and it gradually became a routine. Chengmei and Professor Zhao organized workshops for the female migrants to share their experiences. They helped workers to recognize the unfair bias against domestic work and to confirm the value of their labor and jobs. Chengmei and Professor Zhao's advocacy goal for Didinghua Theater resonated well with domestic workers' longing for respect and recognition.

More than forty domestic workers attended the early years' activities at Didinghua. Instructors offered them classes on basic performance skills, such as body language, voice, and acting. None of the workers had prior experience in performance or acting. Many of them were attracted because of their interests in singing and dancing and by the offer of free acting classes from a college professor. Yet many of the women got bored with the training after several classes. Professor Zhao adjusted the strategy and encouraged them to share stories about their lives and work experiences and to practice improvised performances. The three instructors then used material from the collected stories to construct plays. Over dinner, one domestic-worker participant recalled the storytelling experiences: "Many of us cried when we were sharing the hardship and difficulty of working as maids. We are treated badly and feel so lonely and depressed living in employers' households. When we were talking about it together, we all got so sad and angry." The off-stage storytelling and experience-sharing activities transform domestic workers' individual suffering into collective experiences. By telling personal stories, subordinate groups can nurture self-awareness of their personal history and interrogate the systematic inequalities that limit their lives.[20]

Performance becomes a powerful collective action that creates a space of contestation. In that space, subordinate people can seek alternative and/or oppositional subjectivities that resist oppression and domination. Female migrants are able to cultivate new subjectivities[21]— that is, they gradually change the degrading perceptions of their job through performance and embrace being domestic workers as dignified and valued. Self-confirmation and awareness are both the means and the end of domestic workers' collective resistance. As one worker told me, "After participating in many discussions and performance activities, I started to realize that the purpose of performance is not only to tell stories of our suffering but to demand respect for us domestic workers. It [performance] makes me believe that domestic work is an important job and that there should be mutual respect and understanding between employers and us. They should not disdain us." These female workers become what Kathi Weeks calls "antagonistic subjects." Weeks views women's labor practices not just as "instances of oppression and exploitation" but as bearing the potential to "inspire disloyalty and disobedience to the values of the larger social formation."[22] In the context of female migrant domestic workers, performance is the intervening force to realize the enabling potential of these women's everyday laboring practices.

The process of resubjectification opens possibilities for further change. The self-cultivation of subjects can also transform the places where people are situated.[23] These places include the household, workplace, communities, and urban spaces. This self-cultivation acts as an intervention to bring practices into contexts that could not generate them but in which they are helpful to undermine dominant power. Female migrant interviewees reflected that in their workplace households, they abandoned the belief that domestic workers were subordinate or even submissive to employers and became more confident in communicating, negotiating, and even disagreeing with their employers regarding work, particularly when they encountered conflicts. Such self-confirmation, generated through their activities with Didinghua, brings confidence and power to female migrant participants to help them deal with difficulties in other spheres of life. When I interviewed her, Fangfang had only been participating in Didinghua for several months. She was excited about the change performance brought to her life: "I was very stiff when I first started rehearsing, but I gradually improved my performing skills, and I do gain a lot from the practices. I always remind myself to behave more naturally when we rehearse, and then I apply this strategy to real life and become more confident when I interact with people."

These feelings of confidence and accomplishment were frequent themes in female workers' reflections on their participation in Didinghua. Thinking back to early performances with Didinghua, Jiajie still remembered the excitement that she and other domestic workers felt when they did their first onstage performance in a local community theater: "I never expected I could perform on stage one day, and these were stages in Beijing! We were all super excited and proud at the time." Ying is also a new member of Didinghua. She was an early member of MWC back in the 1990s but later went to other cities to work. Ying returned to Beijing with her husband and son in 2012, and they now rent a small apartment in a suburban village. In her twenty-five years of *dagong*, Ying had worked as a waitress, a domestic worker, and a street food seller. Though she has no prior performance-related training or experiences, Ying appears to be a talented performer. She once played a role as a cruel employer in a staged performance at MWC's Twentieth Anniversary Gala in April 2016, and her vivid performance received high praise from the gala attendants. When I complimented her on the performance, Ying talked about why Didinghua appealed to her: "I am very willing to come [to Didinghua] because I feel refreshed here, especially when I have to deal with endless housework. It's already so tiring at work, and then there is more housework waiting for me at home. I don't have any experience in performance. Everything just feels natural to me. I am very pleased to see that my sisters here like my performance. I feel accomplished."

Experiences at Didinghua become an enabling space where female migrant workers embrace new subjectivities. Xiu is a fifty-year-old domestic worker whose early years of working experience in urban households left her feeling depressed. She was rather introverted and barely talked to anyone when she first participated in the activities at Didinghua. But after two years' participation, she has gradually become an active member. It takes Xiu two hours by bus to get to Didinghua, but she is always the earliest one to arrive. Although she is still not a talkative person, she looks very relaxed and delighted when she is with other domestic workers. Xiu has made some good friends at Didinghua.

Becoming a core member of the team brings her a great sense of emotional support and recognition.

Another participant, Hua, had suffered from domestic violence for years. She got divorced from her husband and left their rural village after her children had grown up. She went to Beijing at the age of forty-two and became a domestic worker. At first, she felt ashamed to tell others about her husband's abuse. She gained trust and courage from participating in the performances and finally told the other participants her story. Hua's experiences were later written into the Didinghua play *Huangwu de jia* (荒芜的家; Desert home), which advocates against domestic violence. Being marginalized and excluded from urban social life, participants like Xiu and Hua regard Didinghua as an intimate and secure place where they have friends and social support. Through performance, female migrants transform themselves from disadvantaged individuals into a collective group actively fighting against their real-life suffering in various ways.

NGOs have been an important organizational force in providing

FIGURE 2.1 *Female migrants rehearsing a performance*
at MWC's office, March 2016. Photo by author.

community spaces for marginalized groups in China and many other countries.[24] MWC also serves as a social and alternative space where domestic workers can meet friends, chat, and relax after tedious and heavy workdays. Every Saturday since the founding of Didinghua in 2011, a group of domestic workers arrives at the MWC activity room around 9:00 a.m. The room is big, about forty square meters, with wood floors. Before the activities start, usually at 10:00 a.m., these women sit together and chat about their work and personal lives. They share practical information, such as how their employers treat them, which domestic-work companies have more benefits for workers, and strategies and tactics to deal with employers.

As domestic workers are normally confined within households and urban apartment complexes, their gatherings at MWC transgress those spatial constraints. Feelings of sisterhood and mutual trust and support have emerged among these female migrant workers through their many shared days of practice and exercises. In rehearsals and practices, only a few women have a talent for acting, while many others recite their lines

FIGURE 2.2 *Female migrants preparing for a performance rehearsal at MWC's office, March 2016. Photo by author.*

with stiff facial expressions and body language. Some women admitted in our interviews that performance was difficult for them as they had no prior performance training or simply lacked such talent. One female worker shared, "I have devoted so much spare time to memorizing the lines of my roles [assigned in the plays]. Memorizing lines is not a problem, as I just repeat and repeat them many times. But to perform with vibrant expressions and emotions is very challenging for me. I don't have a talent for performing! I can't perform well, but I do enjoy the activity very much."

Although they often had to rehearse many times, which can easily become tiring and draining, these female workers found the activities joyful and reassuring. They joked with each other, reminded others of forgotten lines, and shared suggestions and ideas about acting.

In the years since its founding, Didinghua Theater has apparently attracted many domestic workers to participate in activities centered on performance. What kinds of performances have these women created? How do such performances become a form of collective resistance? And what dominant values do these performance challenge?

PERFORMANCE AS COLLECTIVE CRITIQUE AND RESISTANCE

Resistance efforts by domestic workers have attracted scholarly attention, yet extant studies either look at individualized tactics or fail to recognize the possibilities of forming collective resistance in China.[25] Different subaltern groups have used performance as a form of collective political action in the past and present.[26] At Didinghua, domestic workers' stories were incorporated into a play titled *Wo de laodong, zunyan yu mengxiang* (我的劳动,尊严与梦想; My labor, dignity, and dream) by three volunteer instructors.[27] This play was the first production of Didinghua and the most formative event in the theater's history. The performance consists of eight stories based on these women workers' experiences. The performance highlights the unpleasant experiences domestic workers encounter in their daily lives, including mistreatment by employers, discrimination and bias they suffer more broadly, their tedious and demanding workloads, the loneliness and isolation of their emotional lives, and their feelings of helplessness and powerlessness. Domestic workers' performance stories are critical personal narratives and counternarratives that expose inequality and oppression, offer hope, and mobilize action.[28] By revisiting their experiences in a performance context, domestic workers voice their critique of the unequal power relations they are constantly subject to. Performance transforms the individual, private, and invisible cases into collective, public, and visible issues.

Three of these stories expose the bias, prejudice, and discrimination domestic workers regularly face. The first story presents the biased attitude that security guards of a residential complex hold toward domestic workers. The story starts with the worker's monologue describing how security guards often did not allow her to enter the apartment complex. She then shifts to a prouder tone of voice while dressing herself up in an expensive-looking coat and scarf and says, "The security guard used to not let me in, but when I started to wear good clothes, they thought I was a resident here."[29] The security guards' prejudice affirms the view that the rich residents are inherently superior to those who are poor or less privileged. Dressing like a rich resident mocks the hegemonic performativity of the urban middle class. Most urban residential complexes in China have security guards at their front gates. The more "luxurious" the complex, the stricter the security guard. As people who live and work in the households of the complex, domestic workers should be granted access easily. Yet they can be prevented from entering just because they do not dress well, like residents. The security guards judge domestic workers based on their appearances, including the way they dress.

The second story displays a scene where a female employer demands that domestic workers call her and her husband *taitai* and *laoye*, respectively. *Laoye* means "master" or "sir," and *taitai* means "madam" or "lady"; these were forms of address used by domestic servants in pre-1949 China. Although such demands are uncommon in post-1949 China, when they do occur, they unmistakably evoke the master-servant relationship that domestic workers operated within in pre-Communist China. In story number three, a middle-aged woman employer expresses a widely held contempt for domestic work as an undesirable and even despicable profession when she says to her domestic worker in an exaggeratedly sarcastic and loud voice, "Even if someone paid me 1 million [Chinese yuan], I would never work as a domestic worker."[30] Domestic workers worldwide experience this type of obvious discrimination and degradation regularly.[31] By exposing these encounters through performance, it brings to light what is usually unseen.

In the fourth story, a domestic worker is forced to leave her employers' house at midnight. A wife suffering from postpartum depression takes it out on her domestic worker through verbal abuse. The husband, while apologetic to the worker, does not take any meaningful action to curb his wife's abusive behavior. In the climactic scene of this story, the wife loses her temper late one night and orders the worker to leave the house immediately. The husband simply apologizes to the worker and suggests that she leave. The worker packs her things and helplessly leaves the house at midnight. Story five shows a typical case of an employer taking advantage of domestic workers. An employer asks a domestic worker to do housework at the home of the employer's mother—a task beyond what the worker was hired and paid for. The employer promises the worker extra pay for the work but ends up paying nothing. The absence of proper regulation results in a lack of protection for the labor rights of domestic workers. Employers who violate labor rights encounter minimal consequences.

Story number six presents a case of an employer deliberately making trouble for a domestic worker. The employer, an elderly woman, asks the worker to take her in a wheelchair to a park. In Chinese cities, parks are social spaces where elders, housewives, and children from nearby neighborhoods socialize as part of their daily routines. In the next scene, the employer requests that the domestic worker collect her urine in a container in the corner of the park. The worker is embarrassed to perform this task in a public space, so she suggests to the employer that she can accompany her to the restroom to collect the urine. But the employer refuses, insisting that the worker do what she asks. The worker reluctantly collects the urine and heads to the park restroom to dispose of it. Meanwhile, a neighbor, another elderly woman, shows up and greets the woman employer. After bragging to the neighbor about her son's well-paid job as a company manager, the employer suddenly stands up from her wheelchair. Surprised, the neighbor says, "You can walk! Then why did you sit in the wheelchair?" The employer replies, "I hire her so she will do whatever I demand." The two elderly women then walk home together. The domestic worker returns from the restroom to find only an empty wheelchair. She sighs and wipes away tears, saying, "Why is it so difficult to do this job? I really want to quit, but I need money to pay for my daughter's tuition fees."[32]

The employers' mistreatment of the domestic worker seems not to be deliberate. Yet regardless of whether these actions are done on purpose or not, the situations represented in the play expose the unequal power relations between domestic workers and their employers. The performances of these situations do not merely depict domestic workers as helpless and powerless in order to provoke sympathy; rather, they help reveal domestic workers' disadvantaged conditions to raise empathy and awareness. The way the scenes are performed, such as the worker's sighing in story three, appeals to the audience's affects. The worker's hopeless confession that "I really want to quit, but I need money" reflects the struggles that the majority of middle-aged female migrants experience. They have few job choices, yet they bear heavy economic burdens. While quitting could serve as a way to resist the mistreatment and unpleasant working conditions, it could, at the same time, represent an unaffordable price for these female migrants to pay.

The last two stories highlight how a gender-based division of labor and class hierarchy intersect to produce female migrants as "ideal and suitable" labor subjects for domestic work. In story seven, a domestic worker is hired to take care of an employer's child. The episode depicts an occasion when the child falls while playing in the living room while the worker is busy cooking for the family. The mother blames the worker for paying insufficient attention to the child, and the worker does not defend herself. Head down, she mutters to herself, "I was cooking in the kitchen, and I thought the mother was in the living room with the kid, so she can at least take care of the kid for a moment."[33] Story eight presents a genuine emotional bond that develops between a domestic worker and a child and elder from the family who employs her. In one scene, the elder says to the worker, "Xiaoju [the name of the worker], my children are too busy with their jobs to take care of me, and you have taken care of me so well that I regard you as my half-daughter."[34] The old woman had been sick for years and relied heavily on Xiaoju in her daily life. In a later scene, Xiaoju must leave her employer family to return home because of family obligations. She is sad to leave the child she has been taking care of for several years.

Just as white middle-class women have displaced the burden of domestic work onto working-class racial-minority women in Western capitalist countries, Chinese urban middle-class women have passed on domestic duties to impoverished female migrants. Paid domestic work, as one of the few available employment options for these women, bolsters the privilege of the urban middle class. The consumption of female migrants as domestic workers underpins the long-established gender-based division of labor that regards domestic work as primarily the work of women. Xiaoju's story provides a vivid example of the kind of emotional labor and devotion that can become a crucial part of a domestic worker's duties. In the commodification of female migrants as ideal cheap laborers for paid domestic work, the exploitation of their emotional labor is often concealed. The stories contained in *Wo de laodong* also reveal the ironic predicament of domestic workers who are unable to be with their own children and aging parents because of their responsibilities to care for employers' children and elders. Such displacement also occurs in the lives of millions of transnational domestic workers. To earn more money for their families, they migrate to work for middle-class families in developed countries, leaving their children and parents far away in their home countries.

Although these stories emphasize the suffering and maltreatment of domestic workers, they are more than just victimhood narratives to provoke sympathy. Rather, the stories expose the group's disadvantaged conditions and criticize the unequal power relations the workers must face: the urban superiority that creates a distinctive hierarchy between urban residents and rural migrants; the low social status of servants in feudal times, reproduced in only slightly modified form in the inferior position and stereotypes of contemporary domestic workers; patriarchal values that designate domestic work as primarily women's work and minimize the social value of domestic labor; and a market economy that exploits domestic workers' physical and emotional labor. While domestic workers appear to make their employment choices individually, it is the interlocking system of feudal heritage, patriarchal norms, market economy, and urban supremacy that produces middle-aged female migrants as subordinate, feminized, cheap, and flexible laborers. Despite the significant increases in domestic workers' salaries, the narratives that Didinghua presents emphasize that the heavy workload and longstanding prejudices against domestic work should not be overlooked.

Discourses of labor are central to Didinghua's resistance framework. In calling for recognition of domestic workers' labor value, Didinghua's performances directly critique the intersection of the capitalist market, feudal stereotypes, and patriarchal values that degrade the value of women's labor. That value has both material and symbolic dimensions, and Didinghua's approach to resistance emphasizes the symbolic dimension through its invocation of terms such as "respect" and "dignity." Labor value was once a state-promoted ideology and one of the most essential components of socialism in Mao's China. Although such discourse has greatly diminished as China accelerates its economic reform, the concept of the "value of labor" is still tolerable in the present political environment, while feminist and human rights concerns are often dismissed by state propaganda as too Western. Since it is a legacy of state socialism, the value of labor is better received among the general public than other ideologies, especially among working-class people. Therefore, the concept of "labor value" can effectively mobilize female migrant domestic workers to use theatrical performance as a collective form of resistance against the inequalities they experience. At the end of story three, a domestic worker says in her closing monologue, "You look down upon me, but I make a living by my own hands. What should I be ashamed of?"[35] This moment directly challenges the audience to question its own biases against domestic work and discrimination of domestic workers.

Because of their attention to moral responsibility, Didinghua performances have also become a form of public pedagogy to imagine hopes and create radically democratic spaces.[36] Over the years, Didinghua's performances have been staged at various public spaces and on different occasions, such as the Feifei Festival (Feifei xijujie; 非非戏剧节). The Feifei Festival is an annual performance event organized by the municipal government of Chaoyang District in Beijing.[37] Didinghua has also performed at community spaces and universities in Beijing, Jinan, and Xi'an. Audiences who attend Didinghua's performances are often domestic workers, migrant workers, NGO staff, activists, scholars, students, and other concerned members of the public. After a show, performers sometimes hold interactive sessions with the audience to further share their experiences as domestic workers. Some audiences wrote on the

Feifei Festival's message board that, while the performance was not of professional caliber, they found it touching to see domestic workers sharing and performing their experiences. Some audiences welcomed the performance's capacity to raise public awareness of the conditions of domestic workers. One audience member incisively remarked that domestic-worker issues are not individual but social and structural problems and that these workers are victims of the country's approach to economic development. But not all audience responses were favorable. Some who had employed domestic workers found the performance offensive and uncomfortable. They complained that Didinghua's representation of employers is inaccurate, as they are nice to their employees. Despite these complaints, the majority of the audience appreciated Didinghua's goal of advocacy.

Domestic workers' performances enact a form of public pedagogy by making the invisible visible and generating public reflection around inequalities. The pedagogy inherent in performance can generate sympathy and reflection and mobilize change toward a more just and

FIGURE 2.3   *Didinghua group performing at a prestigious university in Beijing, May 2016. Photo by author.*

egalitarian world. As D. Soyini Madison promisingly argues in the "per-formance of possibilities," "when the audience member begins to wit-ness degrees of tension and incongruity between the subject's life-world and those processes and systems that challenge and undermine that world, something more and new is learned about how power works."[38] By reaching out to wider publics, Didinghua's performances create the conditions of possibility for broader interventions.

CHANNELING RESISTANCE VIA NGO-INTERMEDIATE ACTIONS

As an NGO-based program, Didinghua organizes its advocacy activi-ties within the institutional boundaries of MWC. It benefits from the support and resources of MWC, but its programming is shaped by and channeled through the political agenda of MWC. A main obstacle Did-inghua faces is the high mobility of its domestic-worker participants. Except for several members who have remained active participants since Didinghua's founding, most participants can only partake for limited periods due to job switching or relocation to other cities. It is common for domestic workers to change employers for better working conditions or higher salaries. If the new employer household is too far away from MWC's office, this may prevent some workers from attend-ing Didinghua activities. Participant mobility also poses challenges for the production of stage performances, and cast substitutions happen frequently. Even with these ongoing difficulties, Didinghua's perfor-mance program remains one of the most popular activities at MWC.

The high mobility of rural migrant workers poses a challenge for labor NGOs in maintaining long-term relationships with their worker participants.[39] Yet MWC and its participants find ways to overcome these obstacles and form long-term alliances. Even after leaving Bei-jing, many workers remain connected with other participants and staff members of MWC. Some workers have rejoined Didinghua upon returning to Beijing. The support and empowerment workers experi-ence when performing with Didinghua strengthen the sense of commu-nity at MWC, enabling the NGO to go beyond a service-provider role to building stronger connections with female migrant workers.

Since the success of *Wo de laodong*, performance has remained an effective means of collective expression for female migrant workers' activism at MWC. Professor Zhao served as instructor at Didinghua until 2014. Since then, many college professors, students, and activists have volunteered and worked with domestic workers to craft new stories and rehearse performances. In 2016, when MWC celebrated its twentieth anniversary, many new participants joined Didinghua, and together, they created a new play titled *Dagong wu ze* (打工五则; Five stories of work). Most of these new participants had been members of MWC in the mid-1990s and early 2000s. *Dagong wu ze* presents life experiences of migrant workers since the early 1990s: their departure from their home villages, working in factories and low-income service sectors in cities, an entrepreneurial story of a middle-aged female migrant who runs a domestic-service agency, and the difficulties and struggles migrant workers' children face when attending school in cities. The play ends with a group of female workers telling of their dreams and expectations. Through performance, female migrant workers reflect on the commonalities of their life trajectories. With few exceptions, social mo-

FIGURE 2.4 *Female migrants performing at the MWC's Twentieth Anniversary Gala, April 2016. Photo by author.*

bility and fair education opportunities for their children are unattainable goals for these women workers.

Domestic-worker performance has gained visibility in mainstream media, albeit in a limited way. The mainstream media's representations of Didinghua fall into three basic types. The first frames domestic workers doing performances on stage as a spectacular event. This type of news report interprets Didinghua as an aesthetic activity that provides opportunities for domestic workers to fulfill their cultural needs and to improve themselves through performance. For instance, *Jiaodian fangtan* (Focus report), one of the most influential news programs on China Central Television, broadcast a report on Didinghua in its ten-minute-long program in 2016. The *Jiaodian fangtan* represents domestic workers' performance as a "pursuit of artistic dreams." The news program highlights the contrast between the highbrow of the drama and domestic workers as an eye-catching point. It did not mention the advocacy mission of the domestic workers' performance and framed it as merely "art for art's sake."[40]

The second type of media report presents individualized narratives of domestic workers who participate at Didinghua. While these reports do discuss the women's hardships as migrant workers, they strategically omit mention of structural inequalities and possible solutions.[41] These sensational stories belong to what Sun Wanning characterizes as "compassionate journalism," which sensationalizes the predicament of migrant workers in order to draw larger audiences to the news venue.[42]

The third type of media representation explicitly discusses Didinghua's advocacy activities for domestic workers. For instance, a report by a mainstream-news website on nonprofit and charitable organizations providing service to rural migrant workers highlights Didinghua and MWC as an exemplary case.[43] But this type of report cautiously avoids representing domestic-worker performance as collective resistance. One journalist, who has reported on Didinghua, reveals the following about the institutional constraints of mainstream media in China: "I do agree with what Didinghua advocates, and I believe people's discrimination against domestic workers is wrong. We should change that. But in my reports, I cannot use sensitive words or say things that imply a criticism of inequalities or an acknowledgment of these workers' performance as a form of resistance. I actually had my first version of the report rejected by the editor, who thought it was too critical to publish in our newspaper." Didinghua cofounder Yan Chengmei was quite aware of the mainstream media's selective coverage of Didinghua, but she believed that at least media reports had the potential to draw wider public attention to Didinghua and domestic workers' difficulties. Considering the dearth of coverage of workers' strikes in Chinese mainstream media, Didinghua's penetration into the mediascape is indeed an achievement.

While Didinghua's attention to domestic workers' labor value has successfully mobilized these workers to participate in collective resisting actions, the group's advocacy has insufficiently addressed other types of discrimination, such as geographical discrimination. In China, one's province of origin can be the cause for biases and stereotyped perceptions. In the domestic-service industry, commonly held geographical discrimination is toward people from Henan and the three Dongbei provinces in northeast China.[44] Many employers are reluctant or even refuse to hire domestic workers from Henan and Dongbei. Stereotypes persist that construct people from Henan Province as cunning and dishonest and those from Dongbei as bad-tempered and irritable. To mitigate geographical discrimination, many domestic workers intentionally conceal their true province of origin and claim they come from those provinces more favored by employers. But faking one's origins poses challenges as people have different characteristic accents or even dialects in different provinces. Only workers who can speak Mandarin with little to no regional accent are able to conceal their provincial origins.

Malan is one such worker. A native of Henan, she often encounters employers who explicitly state they do not hire domestic workers from her province. So she pretends she is from another province. Sometimes it works; sometimes it does not. Malan suggested to Chengmei that Didinghua should produce a performance to advocate against these geographical biases, but her suggestion was opposed by some other Didinghua members. They were worried that such perceptions were widely accepted in the domestic-work industry and believed they should not jeopardize their job opportunities by challenging the industry. The opposition and lack of support disappointed Malan: "I don't understand why they did not adopt my suggestion. There are lots of biases in the job market [of domestic work] toward people from Henan and Dongbei.

It's so unfair to those of us from these regions. Why shouldn't we create performances to change people's perceptions?" Malan's question has powerful implications as it shows that domestic workers have started to accept performance as an advocacy action. On the other hand, her comments expose the lack of an inclusive agenda within Didinghua to address certain forms of discrimination and inequalities.

Among some domestic workers, there often exists an us-versus-them mentality based upon a binary of rural and urban origins. Recalling her first training classes with domestic-service agencies, one worker looked disdainful and complained, "The training was too basic, and it was all about how to use washing machines, ovens, and refrigerators, which only those from rural areas needed to learn. But I am different from them." This person was a laid-off worker from a state-owned enterprise. Prior to the mass layoff of the late 1990s, urban residents had much better opportunities in education and work than rural people. Yet dominant discourses ascribe the inequalities of the rural-urban binary to the incompetence of rural people. Mei has been a domestic worker for almost ten years and believes she is a highly skilled and qualified worker. Mei blamed workers of rural origins for the persistence of employers' disrespect of their domestic-work employees: "There are some [people] who are from very poor rural areas, and they regard the relationship with employers as that of old times and think employers can scold and even curse maids. Why do some employers look down upon us? It is just because of those maids who only want to make money no matter how employers treat them. If everyone had self-esteem and didn't allow employers to hurt our hearts, do you think employers would still treat you like that?" The neoliberal discourse of self-governance is deployed to judge individual workers. And it appears that Didinghua's labor-advocacy agenda has not effectively worked against that form of judgement.

An explicit advocacy agenda to help form solidarity among female migrant workers across geographical divides and different industries remains lacking in MWC's labor activism. Not until 2016, when MWC celebrated its twentieth anniversary, did Didinghua begin to attract female migrant participants beyond the field of domestic work. Many of the new participants at Didinghua were previously members of MWC in the mid-1990s who had turned away from the organization after it shifted its focus to domestic workers. Some of these female migrants explained to me that they found it hard to socialize with domestic workers. One said, "Those domestic workers complain about bad working experiences, but we don't have such experiences. We found few things in common with them."

CONCLUSION

Recognition of the value of domestic work is a crucial step in combating systemic discrimination against domestic workers. The kind of advocacy work done by MWC challenges low social status of domestic workers and the degraded value of domestic work. Labor discourse resonates with a Marxist and socialist ideology, which was legitimized in Mao's China and remains part of the state's official discourse in contemporary China. This resonance makes the government more tolerant of advocacy efforts and collective resistance; it also engages domestic-worker participants who long for respect and recognition of their work. By participating in theater performance, women workers articulate their grievances from their perspectives and in their own words and make visible their everyday struggles.

Performance intervenes in the process of subjectification and disrupts domestic workers' internalization of inferiority as it contributes to the formation of a collective resisting subject. By telling stories, creating theatrical works, and performing on stages, individual workers form a collectivity of a subordinate group. It is through performance as an intervention that domestic workers' laboring practices are no longer just experiences of exploitation but are becoming an enabling ground for cultivating alternative subjectivities and actions.[45] Upon becoming self-assured antagonist subjects, workers liberate themselves from the cultural domination and social exclusion that demeans their profession and constructs them as depreciated others. The subjective transformation allows women workers to perceive themselves as part of a counterhegemonic force.

Domestic workers' advocacy through performance shows that informal workers, especially those in low-income service sectors and occupying separate workplaces, can be mobilized and organized in grassroots labor activism. As labor strikes are often thwarted by the Chinese government, performance serves as a sustainable form of mediated labor activism. Labor NGOs, such as the Migrant Women's Club, can provide essential organizational support and enact an institution-sponsored space to make labor activism possible. But the advocacy agenda of NGOs may selectively funnel resistance to align with certain themes and exclude others. Advocacy through theater performance at MWC is, therefore, simultaneously an enabling and a limiting process. Domestic-worker participants have formed a collective resistance against their marginalization, but they have not yet formed solidarity with other subordinate groups. To build broader forms of solidarity, a more radical and inclusive advocacy framework is required.

THREE

CHALLENGING CAPITALISM
AND NEOLIBERALISM

New Workers and Working-Class Cultural Production

Picun is a suburban village located in southeast Beijing, at the border between Chaoyang and Tongzhou Districts. As Picun is close to the airport, high-rise buildings are not allowed, and the village is full of old and dilapidated houses. About 1,500 local residents and ten thousand rural migrant workers live in the village. Roads are narrow, dirty, and messy. Picun exemplifies thousands of inner and suburban villages in large cities in China that are the product of the country's economic reform and urbanization. The rapid expansion of cities has brought the surrounding countryside into the urban territory. Inadequate regulation and infrastructure leave these previously rural communities with poor living conditions. Despite the crowded and shabby housing, the low rent attracts a great number of rural migrant workers. But the settlement is temporary and precarious. Along with accelerating urbanization and gentrification, many suburban and inner villages are demolished and rebuilt into residential and business districts.[1] Local residents can get large demolition compensations, which instantly raises their class status to that of the new rich. Migrant workers, on the other hand, are not able to afford the new gentrified housing and are forced to leave.

Rumors of demolition have spread in Picun Village for several years. In the summer of 2023, some of the existing older buildings started to be demolished.

Picun is unique among Chinese urban villages. It is not merely an affordable physical space inhabited by migrant workers but a migrant-worker community built by the efforts of a labor NGO, Migrant Workers' Home (MWH). In 2005, MWH relocated to Picun from another suburban village, where it rented several one-story houses in a corner of the village. Over a decade, MWH's series of cultural projects made it an influential NGO advocating for labor rights and socialist values. With an activist agenda critiquing labor exploitation of migrant workers and stressing class struggles, MWH's grassroots cultural advocacy has gained recognition among diverse groups of people who care about social equality and justice. Many migrant workers choose to live in Picun because of their interest in MWH's activities and events. Picun receives much more media coverage than other urban villages, with the news typically portraying it as a spiritual home of migrant workers. Domestic and international scholars have written articles about the significance of MWH's labor activism in Picun. Picun has become a symbolic site of the working-class community, a space in which workers may build collective resistance through cultural practices and activities.

The labor activism led by MWH, informed by an explicitly Marxist conception of "class struggle," adopts a more radical advocacy framework compared to that of the Migrant Women's Club (MWC) and Didinghua Theater. MWH's radical framework focuses on challenging capitalism and neoliberalism, seeking to bring about a fundamental transformation of the economic and social structures that perpetuate exploitation and inequality. MWH's labor activism aims to address the root causes of labor exploitation and advocates for systemic change. This chapter delves into how MWH engages in labor activism that challenges dominant ideologies and power structures. The facilitation of migrant workers' collective cultural production by MWH is a crucial strategy in their labor-activism efforts. This approach allows migrant workers to come together and engage in cultural and media practices and activities to assert a working-class standpoint and subjectivity. Migrant workers' collective cultural production becomes a prominent form of mediated labor activism by advocating change, cultivating class consciousness, and building solidarity.

In *The Long Revolution*, Raymond Williams critiques the problem of socialism in Britain in the twentieth century: "The main challenge to capitalism was socialism, but this has almost wholly lost any contemporary meaning, and it is not surprising that many people now see in the Labour Party merely an alternative power group, and in the trade-union movement merely a set of men playing the market in very much the terms of the employers they oppose. Any such development is generally damaging, for the society is unlikely to be able to grow significantly if it has no real alternative patterns as the ground of choice."[2] Williams's critique reminds us of the urgency of socialist projects to engage the great masses. One of the crucial steps in engaging people is to revitalize socialist ideas, values, and imaginations, which involves making them relevant to the specific social, economic, and political context. The revitalization requires envisioning and articulating alternative futures that go beyond the limitations of the capitalist system.

In reformist China, socialism faces a crisis of relevance and engagement in that it has little purchase on reality except for standing as empty words in the propaganda of the party-state. China has undergone significant economic reforms and embraced market-oriented policies while maintaining the party's authoritarian control. The rise of a state-led capitalist system has led to a divergence between socialist ideals and the reality of China's economic and political system. Meanwhile, market and consumerist ideologies are dominating public life and popular culture, interpellating neoliberal subjectivity and consumer subjects.[3] People are hailed by dominant ideologies of neoliberalism to view themselves as economic actors to prioritize their own self-interest and personal gain. In the formation of neoliberal subjectivity in China and elsewhere, "everyone speculates on the desires of others in the Darwinian struggle for position."[4] Individuals identify themselves through their consumption practices and material possessions and view consumerism as a normative and desirable way of life.

Chapter 3 explores how MWH's labor activism confronts dominant ideologies of neoliberalism and consumerism in China's present cultural and political context.[5] I analyze MWH's series of cultural activities and events and discuss the characteristics of its mediated labor activism and implications. What are the practices that have been incorporated

into the collective cultural production? How do these cultural practices serve as a form of resistance against the prevailing consumerist
and individualistic values promoted by neoliberalism? What alternative values, principles, and ways of life have been advocated by MWH's
labor activism toward a more just and equal society? By addressing
these questions, this chapter addresses how migrant workers' collective
cultural production contributes to the revitalization of genuine socialist ideas and imaginations in reformist China.

CONSTRUCTING A NEW-WORKER IDENTITY AND CULTURE

The main focus of MWH's labor activism has been constructing a "new-
worker" (xin gongren; 新工人) identity and culture that question the inequalities that migrant workers face, raise class consciousness among
the workers, and thereby promote social change. The construction of
a new-worker identity is intended to replace the identity category of
"peasant worker" (nongmin gong; 农民工)—a term carrying discriminatory connotations that is widely used in mainstream media and public
discourse to refer to rural migrant workers. Sun Heng, the founding
member of MWH, has advocated for this new identity in some of his
media interviews.[6] He contended that new worker is an identity that
places more emphasis on the subjectivity and dignity of workers.

Lü Tu, an independent scholar and a key staff member at MWH,
offers a thorough explanation of the implications of constructing the
new-worker identity in her book Zhongguo xin gongren (Chinese new
workers).[7] In Lü's account, the notion of the "new worker" represents
the new generation of migrant workers: "new" describes the new generation's position as urban workers who no longer identify as peasants
who happen to work in cities; they therefore differ from the older generation of migrant workers who have a strong attachment to peasant
identity and usually return to their rural villages after years of working
in cities. The new generation longs to settle in cities, but they generally
cannot afford to; and the term "new" differentiates migrant workers
from urban workers in state-owned factories who enjoy many privileges
that migrant workers never have.[8]

The new-worker identity is an essential component of MWH's construction of a class-conscious culture. The new-worker identity creates a

working-class-subject position that migrant workers occupy to respond to the economic exploitation, cultural domination, and social exclusion they face. MWH's recruitment literature states that members should identify with working-class perspectives and values. The construction of a new-worker identity and culture in MWH's labor activism has appealed to the young generation of migrant workers as well as the old ones. Migrant-worker participants at MWH are a mix of the two generations. After participating in MWH's activities, workers start to identify themselves as new workers. One worker said, "I was first attracted by the library of MWH, where I borrowed books. Later, I joined the organization because I agree with the values [equality and justice] they advocate." In contrast to dominant culture, which stigmatizes rural migrant workers as deviant others, new-worker culture emphasizes the subjectivity, voices, and power of rural migrant workers. MWH encourages workers to view culture as a lived totality, what Raymond Williams defines as a whole way of life that encompasses particular meanings and values.[9] The everyday life of migrant workers is made visible and acknowledged by the new-worker culture. New-worker culture incorporates socialist values and asks workers—and other members of Chinese society—to imagine a future in which workers are free from exploitation.

The integration of migrant workers' experiences into new-worker culture is different from the practice of "speaking bitterness" (*chi ku*; 吃苦) that was encouraged in Mao's China. "Speaking bitterness" was a state-led cultural project to persuade individuals to reflect on the "cruelty" of the presocialist past and to champion Mao's socialist state.[10] The construction of the new-worker culture is a grassroots, bottom-up project of labor activism. Migrant workers use their voices to reflect upon their conditions and nurture a collective consciousness and subjectivity among workers. The new-worker culture does not attempt to provoke public sympathy or pity in the way that mainstream compassionate journalism does; rather, it aims to raise public awareness of class inequalities.[11] MWH intends discussions about migrant workers' inequalities to revive the discourse on class equality, which has been marginalized in Chinese society since Mao's era. Culture and cultural practices serve as both sites and means for NGO-based labor activism.

Over the course of a decade, MWH built a series of cultural projects

with the explicit agenda of challenging both capitalism and urban supremacy, stressing the class struggles of migrant workers. For instance, Dagong
Art Museum (Dagong yishu bowuguan; 打工艺术博物馆), a grassroots
migrant-worker museum, documents the history of rural migrant workers in post-Mao China; MWH's musical band, New-Worker Troupe (Xingongren yuedu; 新工人乐队), writes original songs about migrant workers,
produces albums, and holds live performances; five Dagong Spring Festival galas (Dagong Chunwan; 打工春晚) and three New-Worker Cultural
Festivals (Xingongren yishujie; 新工人艺术节), organized by MWH in the
past ten years, have attracted many media reports and millions of audience members; *Picun shequ bao* (皮村社区报; Picun community newspaper) a community-based, alternative periodical, publishes stories written
by and for migrant workers; and a literature-writing group offers free
weekly lessons and workshops for migrant workers interested in literary
creation. These cultural activities, traversing different media, advocate
for class equality by presenting rural migrant workers' everyday lives
and subjectivities. Rather than continuing to see themselves portrayed as
objects of mainstream-media attention, migrant workers become active
participants in producing their own culture.

Compared to the scant coverage that labor strikes and protests receive
in Chinese mainstream media, MWH and its cultural activities and
events have been widely covered. Still, mainstream media are inclined
to highlight the "service" function of MWH. Rehearsing the official discourse, media reports on MWH tend to frame it as an organization that
provides cultural and social services to migrant workers.[12] Phrases such
as "Building a harmonious society"—an official phrase promoted during
Hu's administration—frequently appear in media articles to praise
MWH's contribution. With few exceptions, news media typically un-
derrepresent MWH's cultural production, and they therefore obscure
the organization's labor activism.[13] Around the globe, the relationship
between mainstream media and social movements/protests has been
contentious, with social movements often receiving distorted coverage
that either circumvents their actual political goals and messages or fosters public resentment and hostility.[14] Media coverage of MWH is thus a
mixed blessing: it helps increase MWH's public visibility and social influence, yet its representations—often misrepresentations—also curtail
the counterpower of the organization's labor activism.

Maintaining an independent space of cultural production and reception is therefore of vital importance for the creation of a new-worker culture. Dagong Art Museum is such a space. "Without our culture, there is no history; without our history, there is no future." This slogan, printed on the outer wall of the museum, highlights the importance of claiming rural migrant workers as a historical subject capable of making alternative futures. Established by MWH in 2007 and free to the public, it is the first and only museum dedicated to the history of rural-to-urban migration that has taken place in the four decades of China's economic reform. Until 2017, Dagong Art Museum had received financial support from a foreign foundation. The funding was later cut off, and the museum has since relied on crowdsource funding to maintain its operations. Located next to MWH's office in Picun, the museum only has two rooms, each about fifteen square meters. As a grassroots museum with rather constrained funding, its decoration is plain and simple. The exhibits present stories of rural migrant workers and their strength and hard work—stories that are often submerged in celebratory accounts of the country's enormous achievements of economic development.

Topics covered in the exhibits include major policies that profoundly affect migrant workers' well-being, high-profile events, workers' daily lives, and the history of labor NGOs in China. In particular, the museum documents how the *hukou* policy greatly limits rural migrant workers' access to social welfare and security and prevents their children from attending urban schools.[15] The high-profile events include the death of Sun Zhigang, cases of black lung disease among workers, and the worker suicides at Foxconn.[16] Since its establishment, the museum has received about fifty thousand visitors and various endorsements. For instance, Pan Jiaen, a domestic scholar, commented that "the museum reminds us of the secret of China's economic growth and development and makes us recognize the sacrifices of millions of workers."[17] Leung Man-tao (Liang Wendao), an influential writer and critic in Hong Kong, remarks, "Beijing is built by them [migrant workers], but they do not own any one of the buildings, except for this museum."[18]

Dagong Spring Festival gala is one of the most influential among MWH's activities and events that creates an alternative and independent cultural space for migrant workers. In 2012, MWH held the Dagong gala for the first time and invited a celebrity who had expressed

FIGURE 3.1 *Dagong Art Museum, 2021. Source: MWH's WeChat public account.*

concern for underprivileged groups to host the gala. The theme of the migrant workers' gala and the fame of the host soon helped the event attract widespread public attention. Unlike Spring Festival galas hosted by CCTV and other provincial TV stations that feature professional performers, migrant workers are the main contributors, both as performers and coordinators, to the Dagong gala. MWH has held the gala every year since 2012, and it has become a national cultural event for migrant workers to celebrate the Spring Festival. It has remained an independent and nonprofit event with no commercial sponsorship. Each year, migrant workers from around China perform their original shows as individuals or groups at the gala. They sing songs, recite poems, dance, and perform minidramas. Lailai, a migrant worker, recalled his experiences on the stage: "I feel so honored to recite poems with several other workers [at the gala]. The poems are all written by us. We are acknowledging all the migrant workers who face difficulties but carry on with their lives." In 2015, MWH started to live stream the gala on the internet to reach a wider audience. Since then, the event has received at least ten thousand views per year, sometimes rising to as many as fifty thousand views. Migrant workers' cultural participation in events such as the Dagong gala stands as a marked contrast to the majority of the consumer culture, which privileges representations of urban middle-class life and degrades and marginalizes rural and working-class people.

When I characterize MWH's practices and activities of constructing the new-worker culture as a "working-class cultural production," I mean a nonprofit, grassroots, and collective way of creating cultural content, meanings, and values from a working-class standpoint to resist capitalist ideologies. Working-class cultural production engages in what Stuart Hall conceptualizes as an ideological struggle—an open and continuing process in which ruling ideas can gain hegemonic domination but without guarantees.[19] According to Hall, ruling ideas are not rigid and unchanging. They are not guaranteed to dominate society. Instead, he suggests that the concept of "ideological struggle" recognizes the complexities involved in the formation of ideologies.[20] In other words, Hall believes that the dominance of specific ideas is not solely determined by economic factors. He highlights the dynamic and contested nature of ideological formations. This implies that different ideas and ideologies can emerge and compete for dominance within a society,

FIGURE 3.2 *Dagong Spring Festival Gala, 2014.*
Source: MWH's WeChat public account.

challenging the notion of a fixed and predetermined ideological hierarchy. Hall brings in Gramsci's discussions of common sense. Common sense, as a historical way of popular thinking, is one of the terrains over which ideological struggle intends to occupy.

Capitalist and neoliberal ideas become hegemonic ideologies when moneymaking, profit accumulation, individual competitions, and consumerism become part of a given society's "common sense." The attainment of this kind of hegemony is facilitated by the state, market, and commercial media. As they are elsewhere, ideological struggles in reformist China are dominated by the political and economic elites with the goal of consolidating the legitimacy of the party-state's ruling power and promarket values. By viewing ideological struggle as an open process, social groups can envision possibilities of developing new and different social ideas that challenge the dominant ideologies. Through exposing the social inequalities and injustices concealed by the celebration of China's economic development, working-class cultural production facilitates the formation of counterhegemonic ideologies to imagine and engage new realities.

SINGING FOR RURAL MIGRANT WORKERS

The practices and activities of the New-Worker Troupe (hereafter, the Troupe), MWH's musical band, demonstrate how MWH has challenged dominant ideologies through working-class cultural production. Founded in 2000 by several male migrant workers who shared an interest in singing, the Troupe is the longest-running and most prominent of MWH's various forms of cultural production—even predating the NGO itself. It was the core members of the Troupe who later founded MWH, and they have remained the organization's main staff members ever since. Among them, Sun Heng and Xu Duo were the most influential members in the organization and well known in its networks. The Troupe's activities are a major arm of MWH's regular practices. By producing and distributing advocacy songs, the Troupe has developed and spread anticapitalist and anti-neoliberal ideas and values.

Since the Troupe released its first CD, *Tianxia dagong shi yijia* (天下打工是一家; All migrant workers are a family), in 2003, they have produced ten albums and about one hundred songs. To maintain autonomy from commercial forces, all albums except the first have been independently produced and distributed by the Troupe. Crowdfunding has gradually become the main resource for financing the Troupe's CD productions and live shows. For instance, the cost of its most recent CD, *Hong Wuye* (红五月; Red May), released in May 2017, relied entirely upon crowdfunding. The Troupe sells CDs at MWH's events, but few migrant workers buy them. It is usually scholars and interested members of the public who buy the CDs. To reach wider audiences, particularly migrant workers, the Troupe made the songs available and free to listen and download from the MWH website. I asked Xu Duo if migrant workers listened to their songs. He replied, "Most migrant workers certainly preferred popular songs, and they could be more influenced by mainstream culture. But there were indeed some workers listening to our songs and even singing them. When they heard their lives being represented in songs, they were able to recognize more of the inequalities they deal with. For those migrant workers who already had [class] awareness and consciousness, these songs made strong sense to them." One worker confirmed Xu Duo's views: "I like pop songs. But when I feel down, I like to listen to songs by the New-Worker Troupe. They are different [from pop songs]. The songs are our songs." "Our songs" are those in which migrant

FIGURE 3.3   *A collection of the Troupe's albums, July 2017. Photo by author.*

workers can find representations of their work, life, and feelings.

The Troupe's explicitly articulated goal is to fight against migrant workers' marginalization in mainstream culture, which consistently promotes consumerism and awards an arbitrary distinction of superiority to urban middle-class lifestyles. A song with lyrics written by a migrant worker and music composed by the Troupe narrates the plight of the migrant worker:

> Beijing is so big
> I have not been home for years
> My jobs have been changed one by one
> And I have not earned enough money but lots of
>   grievance
> Beijing is so hot and so cold.[21]

The name of this song, "Beijing, Beijing" (北京,北京; Beijing, Beijing) is the same as a popular rock and roll song by Wang Feng, a well-known Chinese rock singer. Wang Feng's "Beijing, Beijing" was very well received in the mainstream music market. Wang's song, like many other pop songs, expresses an attachment to metropolitan life. The cultural symbols in such songs, like coffee shops, signify an urban middle-class lifestyle that has been promoted as a social distinction to be desired by self-identified bourgeois consumers, regardless of their class status.[22] The distinction promotes middle-class lifestyles and underpins the supremacy of being a member of the urban middle-class in contemporary China. By contrast, the Troupe's "Beijing, Beijing" speaks from the often-neglected perspective of migrant workers. Lyrics in the Troupe's other songs such as "Our material life has become better and better. / Why is our soul becoming emptier and emptier?" and "luxury European lifestyles desired by the middle-class" represent a social and ideological critique of the dominant ideology of consumerism.[23]

Its challenge to middle-class consumer culture makes the Troupe's labor activism different from conventional working-class resistance that seeks substantial improvements in workers' rights, such as protests by laid-off workers in the 1990s and migrant workers' strikes at factories in recent years.[24] Labor activism through cultural production embodies collective resistance to the social reproduction of cultural inequality in urban China. The songs bring critiques to bear on inequalities in regimes of production and distribution, which have been overshadowed by the neoliberal discourse of empowerment through consumption. While workers' strikes resist capitalism on the tangible "battlefield" of labor production itself, working-class cultural production challenges neoliberal hegemony in embodied and narrative ways, such as singing, playing music, and writing articles and poetry. For instance, "Biao ge" (彪哥; Brother Biao) is a song about a construction worker. The first part depicts a typical construction worker's life:

> You work thirteen hours every day.
> You say you are homesick,
> but you have to work hard from day to night
> so that you can earn money for your family.[25]

The second part of the song shifts perspective to issue a critique in the voice of migrant workers themselves:

> You say you hate those who gain without pain,
> and they always look down upon you.
> They do not understand who feeds whom.[26]

Heavy workloads and endless hard work do not improve the living standards of migrant workers; they simply perpetuate the exploitation and discrimination of those workers. Migrant workers sell their labor power to the market in exchange for salaries that are barely enough to cover their basic needs. Migrant-worker wages do not even pay for a small apartment in cities like Beijing.

Cities rely on migrant workers' labor for infrastructure construction, services, and industrial production, but these workers continue to be the deprived poor in prosperous cities. In big cities, like Beijing, most migrant workers live in villages located in suburban areas, where the rent is only about one-tenth of that in urban apartment complexes. In suburban villages, such as Picun, residents are mostly low income, including migrant workers and local working-class people. The dirty streets and shabby buildings appear as ugly scars on the otherwise smooth, glowing body of urban China. One Troupe song, "Zhe ai ai de cunzhuang shi women de jia" (这矮矮的村庄是我们的家; These low-rise villages are our homes in this city), describes migrant workers' living conditions in cities in this way. "Justice" is one of the most frequently used terms in Troupe songs that draw a sharp contrast between the significant contributions of migrant workers to the country's development and their exploitation and marginalization.

In paying tribute to the labor value of migrant workers, the Troupe questions the capitalist ideology that justifies migrant workers as cheap laborers. This labor discourse is simultaneously similar to and different from the way domestic workers call for their labor to be valued in their performances at Didinghua Theater. While Didinghua advocates for workers' labor rights but does not cultivate broad solidarity, the Troupe's activist discourse deploys Mao's state-socialist ideology to question China's more recent embrace of capitalism and neoliberalism. For instance, the phrase *"Dagong* is glorious" is a variation of Mao's political slogan "Labor is glorious." Scholars have been skeptical of the political potential of workers' reappropriation of Mao's socialist discourse in labor strikes, saying that it fails "to challenge directly the legitimacy of a self-proclaimed socialist state" or that workers simply make moral claims to seek protection from the state against capital exploitation.[27] In the case of the Troupe and MWH, the use of socialist discourse in grassroots working-class cultural production should be understood as a political and ideological strategy to earn tolerance from the party-state. The party-state still spouts Maoist, socialist ideas but really is not living up to its own talk. The Troupe is pointing to the hypocrisy of reform-era Chinese policy. The adoption of socialist discourse is making a political demand on the state as well as the public to build an equal and just China.

By destructing the dream discourse that is promoted by the Chinese government, the Troupe's songs reconstruct the political imagination of migrant workers, which is simultaneously detached from and a reconstitution of popular sentiment. The Troupe's song "Women de shijie women de mengxiang" (我们的世界我们的梦想; Our world and our dreams) explicitly lays out the dreams of migrant workers:

Our dreams are to make a living,

to save money and send it back to support families,
to get back wages owed to us, to no longer confront bias,
to have health and security, and to create a new world
    with equality and solidarity.[28]

These dreams are not grandiose desires but grounded wishes to earn a basic living. The irony lies in the disparity between the ordinariness of migrant workers' dreams and the exaggerated prosperity that "dream discourse" often represents. The language of "the dream" frequently appears in official and popular discourses in contemporary societies. For example, the United States is often represented as "a land of opportunities" where immigrants can realize the "American Dream" and acquire affluence through hard work.[29] Since 2012, Xi's government has propagated the "Chinese Dream" as an official discourse. But in contrast to the American Dream that promotes individualized success, the Chinese Dream relies on a collective, nationalist imagination to underpin the legitimacy of the party's leadership. Soon after its introduction into public rhetoric in 2012, the Chinese Dream discourse began to appear widely in mainstream media. The official discourse has generated a nationalist sentiment. Yet in spite of its supposed collectivist ethos, popular dream discourse promotes an individualistic approach to empowerment through consumption. The deployment of the dream discourse by the Troupe is distinct from what dreams symbolize in official and popular narratives. The lyrics of "Our World" reveal the rights migrant workers are deprived of: fair wages, housing, healthcare, and education. "A new world with equality and solidarity" stands for a new political imagination to reconstruct the Chinese Dream.

In its advocacy music, the Troupe also calls for collective action among migrant workers. One typical example is the song "Tuanjie qilai tao gongqian" (团结起来讨工钱; Unite and ask for arrears wages), which directly addresses the issue of the back pay owed to migrant workers. In 2003, the mainstream news media extensively reported on an instance of which the former prime minister Wen Jiabao helped a female migrant worker ask for her back wages. Although this had been a significant issue for migrant workers for years, it previously had attracted little public attention. Since then, the question of unpaid wages has entered the media agenda, yet many news reports only cover the issue when they are able to present a sensationalized story involving tragedy or violence. In this context, the song's emphasis on migrant workers' agency and its call for collective action is trenchant. The Troupe included this song in their 2004 album in response to the 2003 events involving the prime minister.

The song starts with a narrative describing the tricks bosses use to manipulate workers, such as provoking inner conflicts among workers themselves, threatening them, and calling the police. The end of the song calls on workers "to unite" so they can fight for arrears collectively.[30] One member of the Troupe told me that though they have performed this song in some of the Troupe's live shows, tensions often arose when they tried to sing it at production sites, such as factories and construction sites. The administrators of construction sites and factories regard such songs as too "sensitive and agitative," according to an interviewee who is a member of the Troupe. Once, when the Troupe was performing this song at a construction site, they were interrupted and stopped by an angry administrator. Compared with production sites where shows are often monitored by managerial staff, migrant workers' communities

FIGURE 3.4   *New-Worker Troupe singing songs on A Street, 2017. Source: MWH's WeChat public account.*

and universities often provide more open spaces to communicate and embrace radical thoughts.

On May 1, 2016, I attended a gala the Troupe held at Picun. The gala was held in the yard of the Migrant Workers' Home. Labor Day (also known as International Workers' Day) carries political value worldwide as an occasion on which to recognize labor rights and solidarity among workers. However, just as is the case with many other public holidays in China, Labor Day has become a consumerist carnival for the middle classes to shop and travel. Labor Day thus has been a particularly meaningful and important moment for the Troupe to organize celebration galas for migrant workers. In 2016, the stage was small—about thirty square meters—and looked somewhat shabby with little decoration. Around half past six in the evening, community members of Picun started to show up and gather in front of the stage. The gala began at 7:30 p.m., with about three hundred people in attendance. Performers in the gala were all migrant workers. They danced, sang, and recited poems of their own composition. Xu Duo accompanied himself on guitar for a solo rendition of his song "Bu gan le" (不干了; I quit); before he started to sing, he asked the audience, "Do you have time off for the Labor Day holiday? How much more pay do you get for overtime work?"[31] An awkward silence fell among the audience. Then he continued, arguing that "there should be three times the regular wage for overtime work during holidays." Stirred by the song's rock style and strong sense of rhythm, the audience burst into applause when Xu Duo finished singing and shouted out, "We workers have the right to quit."

> The rich in this world still stink of wine and meat,
> and on the bright road,
> there are people frozen to death.
> Thousands of mansions have been built,
> but many poor people are still living on the streets.

These are the lyrics from the Troupe's new song "Hei! Renjian" (嘿!人间; Hey! World) from its latest album, recorded in the summer of 2022.[32] The two sentences are paraphrases from poems by one of the greatest poets in Chinese history, Du Fu, who is well known for his deep concern for the well-being of ordinary people.[33] Du's poems criticize the

FIGURE 3.5   *Audience of Labor Day gala organized by
the MWH at Picun, May 2016. Photo by author.*

extreme wealth gap between the rich and the poor during the Tang dy-
nasty in ancient China. Ironically, his criticisms are equally applicable
more than one thousand years later—a time with waves of rebellions,
reforms, and revolutions. The song's adaptation of the powerful poem
spotlights deepened inequalities in the contemporary world, including in China. Through singing for migrant workers, in the case of the
Troupe, a handful of activists play a leading role in the production of expressive culture—in this case, music—that contests dominant ideologies
of capitalism and neoliberalism and cultivates solidarity among workers. Another of MWH's projects brings in a larger collective of workers
to engage in cultural production: the organization's community media
publication.

COLLECTIVE PRODUCTION OF COMMUNITY-
BASED ALTERNATIVE MEDIA

In April 2017, an autobiographical article titled "I am Fan Yusu," written by a forty-year-old female migrant worker, went viral on Chinese social media. Fan wrote about her life experiences as a girl born into a poor family in a rural village, a battered wife who left her violent alcoholic husband, a single mother raising two teenage daughters, a domestic worker for a wealthy man's mistress and their children, a lifetime devotee of classic and contemporary literature, and a person surviving all the hardships her life has thrown at her. The article was first published in a digital media outlet, known for its nonfiction, with a middle-class readership.[34] In the comment section, many readers expressed their sympathy for Fan's struggles and surprise at her eloquent, crisp, and epigrammatic writing. As the article was widely circulated online, Fan soon gained nationwide fame, and dozens of mainstream-media outlets interviewed her. Two publishers have solicited manuscripts of hers—both a novel and a nonfiction work. Some scholars and media commentators consider the "Fan Yusu phenomenon" to simply be a media fad and criticize the ignorance and arrogance of many middle-class readers who are attracted by the seeming contrast between Fan's humble origins and working-class status and her evident talent and knowledgeability.[35]

In fact, Fan is among a large group of migrant-worker writers at MWH who dedicate their spare time to writing. Some of them believe that reading and writing enrich their spiritual life as they can find temporary respite from their daily difficulties. Some regard it as a crucial mode of self-expression with the political potential to expose and contest inequality and injustice. While these workers have managed to publish their writing in some mainstream and digital media outlets, it usually gains minimal public attention or is subject to a middle-class gaze, as in the case of Fan's article. Access to media produced by and for themselves has significant implications for migrant workers' expression and everyday activism. The aforementioned Picun community newspaper (hereafter, PCN) is just such a communicative space for migrant workers.

MWH founded PCN in 2011 for migrant workers living in Picun to obtain relevant information on current events and also to be able to document their lives. The newspaper is published monthly, and each issue of PCN includes four sections: (1) a front-page news section reporting major events and the activities of the NGO in the past month; (2) Community Culture, which features migrant worker reportage about their lives and commentaries on current events; (3) Social Concerns, offering information and discussions related to migrant workers' concerns, such as labor-policy updates; and (4) a back-page Activities Information section used to introduce the mission of MWH and staff and members, promote membership, and publicize upcoming activities. As a local, community-based publication, PCN has constructed a migrant-worker-community culture by enabling worker residents to narrate their work and lives in Picun. PCN produces what Qiu (Jack) Linchuan identifies as "worker-generated content" that is collective, empowering, and enlivened by advocacy.[36] Through collective production with advocacy goals, PCN allows migrant workers who are virtually invisible and silent in mainstream media to create their own mediated space.

PCN's media-production process is collective, democratic, and inclusive—in line with common characteristics of alternative media. Alternative media are frequently organized in nonhierarchical or collective ways, generally basing themselves on noncommercial interests and favoring inclusive and democratic modes of production.[37] The MWH staff members take turns as editors, with two members serving as editors for each monthly issue. Migrant workers not only are the primary authors of articles but also contribute to the editorial process, with their names then appearing as editors on section headers. Most worker authors live in Picun and are members of MWH. Staff and migrants attend group meetings to decide which articles to publish; every participant expresses opinions during the editorial discussions. Fu, a fifty-year-old male migrant worker, was among the most proactive participants during the late 2010s, when I attended meetings and spoke with the MWH staff and members. Fu has lived in Picun since 2012. He frequently publishes articles in PCN and helps with the editing work. Although Fu only attained a junior high school education, he, like Fan Yusu, is dedicated to writing and continually practices his writing skills and learns new ones.

Most worker authors of PCN have joined a literature-learning and writing group, initiated by MWH in 2012. The group offers free classes, and sometimes instructors organize discussions among workers on a designated social issue. Every Sunday night from 7:00 to 9:00 p.m., a volunteer teacher delivers a class for an hour, and then workers participate in a discussion on the topic.[38] Most of the volunteer teachers are domestic academics, writers, and journalists and a few are international scholars. Each class has about fifteen workers, and more than half of them are regular participants who attend every week. After classes, workers often write about their thoughts. Fan Yusu has been a long-time member of the literature group. Even after her sudden rise to fame, Fan has still attended the group regularly. Fan's fame also attracts some media reports on the literature group.[39] Zhang Huiyu, a university professor, has been a volunteer teacher of the literature group since its initiation. Professor Zhang commented that the classes are not intended to train workers to be professional writers but rather aim to construct a space for workers to reflect on and become storytellers of their own lives. Zhang writes in an article, "Writing is a main way workers can get a temporary release from their alienated life. They can feel empow-

FIGURE 3.6 *Zhang Huiyu (with laptop) teaching at the Picun literature group, 2019. Source: MWH's WeChat public account.*

ered and refreshed from writing."[40] As workers improve their writing skills through their participation in PCN and the literature group, they start to publish in other media outlets, such as literature magazines and social media platforms.

Dedicated to serving the migrant-worker community, PCN embodies a form of citizens' media. The idea of citizens' media emphasizes the capacity of communities and social groups to reshape power relations between agents and media structures.[41] Each Community Culture section contains three to four migrant workers' articles. Workers typically write about their jobs at local factories and shops, their everyday lives and feelings, and their happiness, struggles, and longings and offer their own interrogations of the unfairness and inequalities they encounter. In one article, a migrant worker touchingly describes missing his wife and daughter, who live in his home village, far from Beijing. Some workers describe Picun's small shops, restaurants, dirty streets, and clusters of shabby houses, but regardless of the poor living conditions, many clearly claim Picun as their home community in Beijing. Although migrant workers are highly mobile residents, who may have to relocate continually for work, they are able to build a sense of community when they write about their lives for the Picun community newspaper. The successful, regular nurturing of a community culture affords robust social inclusion to migrants generally marginalized by or excluded from popular culture and urban life. The migrant-worker-community culture distinguishes itself in practice from the consumer culture that characterizes salient urban middle-class lifestyles. Through its regular publication of individual accounts of migrant workers' lives, PCN has created a set of collective storytelling practices closely identified with the migrant workers' community.

PCN also serves MWH's mission of advocacy. In different contexts, civil society organizations, such as NGOs and labor unions, frequently consider alternative media in their strategies to promote social change.[42] In PCN, worker authors write articles to question their low wages, deficient benefits and welfare provisions, and discrimination in general, thus moving them beyond storytelling into a form of communal embodied agency. In addition to PCN's publication of migrant workers' own writing, joint-staff and migrant-worker editorial meetings identify diverse sources of articles for the newspaper's Social Concerns section. This section has featured informative accounts of new policies regarding *hukou* policy and minimum wages, news analyses of cases of migrant-worker wage arrears and work injuries, and identification of social problems, such as migrant children's limited access to local public schools and circumstances of left-behind children. The section also includes scholarly critiques of labor exploitation in the market economy, and ideological domination of capitalism and consumerism in Chinese society. Some articles provide well-elaborated, practical instructions on how migrant workers can respond to labor-rights violations. An article written by a worker to share his experiences of dealing with wage arrears and work injuries encourages the working class to unite in resistance: "If every one of the workers can commit to resistance against inequality, the efforts of three hundred million workers would converge into a huge counterpower. The power could change the world and change lives of every ordinary worker."[43] The author of this article demonstrates a strong sense of class consciousness, and PCN amplifies his voice among the community of migrant workers.

MWH once organized a workshop on strikes. The discussion centered on the feasibility and implications of strikes in China. While the workers all recognized that strikes remain a pivotal tool for collective resistance, they also described the difficulties of collective bargaining and organizing strikes in China. For instance, some workers pointed out that workers with specialized skills—who earn high wages and tend to stand with employers—may not join collective bargaining initiated by assembly-line workers. Due to the lack of laws to protect rights of workers who participate in strikes, individual workers could be fired or punished by employers. Workers also discussed the differences between protests in south China and those in north China. A large number of workers in the South are industrial workers in large-scale manufacturing, and they have more experiences with collective bargaining and strikes. In comparison, workers in the North are concentrated in small-scale production and the service and construction industries, and historically, these industries have been more difficult to organize due to their smaller scale and more dispersed workforces. Realizing the obstacles created by the material conditions and political environment in China, workers emphasize that effective resistance depends upon cultivating class consciousness and building broad forms of solidarity. PCN publicized the workshop with a full-page story in the Community Culture section—a stark contrast to the total lack of coverage that strikes receive in China's mainstream media.

The first and last pages of PCN feature coverage of past and upcoming MWH activities and events, including live performances by the MWH members, social gatherings for community members, and collaborative advocacy events involving MWH and other organizations or institutions. The last section, Activities Information, features upcoming free services and training, activities, and events for migrant workers living in Picun. MWH's social media communication occurs through two WeChat public accounts: Picun gongyou (皮村工友; Picun Workers) and Da di min yao (大地民谣; Earth Folk Music). The content of the WeChat public accounts supplements PCN's print format with an online presence that can reach migrant workers and wider publics who do not reside in Picun. The integration of digital and print media represents a typical pattern of what Clemencia Rodriguez describes as local communities' appropriation of information-communication technologies in citizens' media practices.[44] As migrant workers' use of smartphones and social media have become more common over the past ten years, MWH's use of social media resonates with migrant workers' media-usage habits.[45] The WeChat accounts offer news and notices about the MWH activities occurring outside Picun, including live shows at universities in Beijing and other cities, and call on members and volunteers to join the MWH advocacy programs. The immediacy of social media allows for timely updates about activities and events of MWH to reach its members and, potentially, a wider audience of workers and those sympathetic to labor rights.

In acting as an independent alternative-media outlet that enables the amplification of workers' voices, PCN sustains both the construction of new-worker culture and the building of a migrant-worker community. And both of those processes have contributed to the formation of workers' counterpower.

FORMING COUNTERHEGEMONIC IDEOLOGICAL ALLIES

The explicitly stated working-class standpoint in MWH's labor activism has attracted different social actors to form counterhegemonic ideological allies to advocate for social equality and justice. By "counterhegemonic ideological allies," I mean social groups who unite and build connections based on shared ideologies and political goals against capitalism and neoliberalism. Intellectuals, college students, migrant workers, and journalists maintain long-term relationships with MWH as volunteers, teachers, members, advisory members, and collaborators. These groups do not come from a single class position. Some of them belong to the privileged class while others are among the dominated, but their shared concerns about migrant workers bring them together as a collaborative force. Scholars hold workshops, seminars, and conferences to invite activists, migrant workers, and volunteers to discuss the advocacy of a new-worker culture. Intellectuals, volunteers, migrant workers, and journalists produce writings for domestic academic journals, social media platforms, and media outlets to enhance public understanding of migrant workers' issues. Migrant workers learn Marxist theories on capital and labor exploitation. They also form online groups through social media, where they connect with each other, organize events, and deliberate about issues. These people are what Gramsci describes as organic and traditional intellectuals of the working class.[46]

Ideological alliances in contemporary China are different from social and political alliances, which were formed by intellectuals, students, peasants, and diverse social agents in the country's revolutionary era in the early twentieth century. The two historical moments are obviously quite different. Those social and political alliances were formed to fight against imperialist subjugation and the domination of the old feudal regime and to build an independent and modern China. In the contemporary context, the country has become an active and powerful actor in neoliberal globalization. The state's propagated discourse of rejuvenating the nation appeals to popular nationalist sentiments that celebrate the country's economic growth and emergence as a global influence.[47] Consumerism has filtered into Chinese people's everyday lives to become a dominant ideology through the commercialization of

media and culture.[48] The enthusiastic celebration of national power, the
robust economy, and consumer culture obscures the reality of severe
and growing disparities between the rich and the poor, rural and urban,
and eastern and western regions. The party-state's constant consolidation of its political power and control allows little space for political
or social associations as potential counterforces to its leadership. It is
within such political, ideological, and social conditions that people who
are greatly concerned with increasing inequalities and injustice gather
to promote change. Advocacy for migrant workers has become a shared
cause enabling the formation of ideological alliances across different
classes and sectors of society.

Among the allies, intellectuals play an important role in explain-
ing the relevance of and helping to draw attention to migrant workers' cultural activities. A group of scholars write articles and appear
in news media to identify and acknowledge migrant workers' cultural
production and practices as a means to claim their cultural and political rights. Bu Wei, an esteemed professor from the Chinese Academy
of Social Sciences (Zhongguo shehui kexueyuan; 中国社会科学院), is one
of the most active scholars maintaining a long-term connection with
MWH. In her research articles and media interviews, Bu argues that
the construction of a new-worker culture is fulfilling the cultural rights
of migrant workers who have been deprived of a voice in mainstream
media and culture.[49] In an article published on a news website, she
wrote, "New workers are creators of their own culture, which expresses
their thoughts, aspirations, and feelings."[50] Professor Zhang Huiyu also
endorses migrant workers' cultural practices in his media interviews.[51]
Zhang argues that these practices, such as writing, play an important
role in the formation of a new-worker subject. Scholars have also emphasized the political significance of new workers' collective cultural
production.[52] Wang Hongzhe comments, "New worker culture is not
merely about demanding workers' rights; it articulates a political imagination of China where everyone is equal and free."[53]

In advocating for new workers' equality, scholars reflect upon the
failed promises of the party-state to build a socialist China. In her
second book on new workers, Lü Tu employs the discourses of class conflict and struggles, which were prevalent in Mao's China, to characterize
new workers' forms of resistance through culture making.[54] Class con-

flict and struggles were key ideas promoted by the Communist Party to mobilize the masses and gain popular support in the revolutionary era, but they were dismissed by Deng's administration in the initial era of economic reform in China and have gradually been replaced by the discourse of economic development. The bottom-up forms of workers' resistance in the present era contrast with the top-down mobilization that the government of the past encouraged, revealing that the current-day party-state no longer represents the interests of the working class despite its nominal commitment. Wang Hui, a leading left-wing scholar and well-known public intellectual in contemporary China, presents a similar critique of the party-state in the reformist era in an article. Wang writes, "The absence of new workers in the political field is the most profound symptom of the crisis in China's political system and marks the very beginning of the constitutional principle that the working class as the leading force in the country has disintegrated."[55] The article was published on an independent scholarly website in 2016 and was then widely circulated online. The critique resonates with the growing public outcry, expressed by working people on social media, at the stark inequalities that have been the result of China's economic reform.

Volunteers at MWH come from diverse social groups and include college students and professionals. The most common reason for volunteers to join MWH is their wish to help pursue social justice and care for underprivileged groups. Wu is one such volunteer. Previously a technical worker at a state-owned company, Wu began to volunteer at MWH after retiring in 2012. He served as a volunteer teacher at the primary school established by MWH for migrant children.[56] Wu also participates in and helps with organizing many activities and events at MWH. He is a regular attendee of the literature group and one of the editors of PCN. In his spare time, Wu gives haircuts to workers. In 2018, when Wu turned sixty, he went to Daliang Mountain—a poor rural region in Sichuan Province in southwest China—and became a volunteer teacher at a local school. Almost all the children at the school are left-behind children who live with their grandparents because their parents have had to move to cities for work. Speaking of his experiences, Wu said, "Our society is so unfair. Rural migrant workers work day and night but earn such low wages. [Migrant] children are the poorest. They can't receive the quality education that urban kids do. I am lucky to have had a good job and retirement pay. I just want to do something to make some small changes." A commitment to change is shared among ideological allies. As of 2023, Wu is still a volunteer teacher in Daliang Mountain. He maintains contacts with many workers at MWH and his most recent piece of writing, publicized in MWH's WeChat account, is a poem about Dagong Art Museum.

The ideological allies simultaneously witness and nurture the formation of class consciousness among migrant workers. There have been scholarly debates on whether a shared class consciousness among migrant workers in China actually exists: Pessimistic views argue that workers have shown different types of consciousness, such as subaltern and legal rights, but that class consciousness is generally lacking.[57] Optimistic views either claim that class consciousness is rising among the younger generation or simply consider workers' class consciousness an axiomatic element in labor protests and strikes.[58] But neither camp in these debates pays enough attention to the complex realities of the processes by which migrant workers' class consciousness actually forms. Migrant workers who are active agents among the ideological allies demonstrate a strong sense of class consciousness. They can be considered what E. P. Thompson describes as a "conscious minority."[59] For instance, workers' advocacy articles published by PCN consistently criticize China's embrace of capitalism and labor exploitation in the market economy, vividly demonstrating workers' awareness of class inequalities. In the MWH chat groups on social media, migrant workers—along with other groups—deliberate various political, economic, social, and cultural issues to address structural inequalities. These workers' deliberations go beyond addressing concerns about their own rights.

Some workers involved with MWH actively seek solutions to the inequity they face, and they develop their class consciousness by participating in labor activism. MWH has launched an education program, Worker University (Gongren daxue; 工人大学), that offers free lectures to migrant workers on Marxist theories, China's socialist history, workers' rights, and labor movements in world history. Those who attend Worker University find that the classes help them understand more clearly how the market economy and the state's embrace of capitalism produce their inequalities. One worker said, "When I learned about workers' situations and their protests in the Western countries in the past [nineteenth and twentieth centuries], I could relate so much. Although the government always claims that our country is socialist, I don't find us very different from capitalist countries. I like Marx's [theory] of labor exploitation. Aren't we being exploited every day?"

Although Marxism is one of the compulsory courses in college education in China, it is taught in a distorted form that legitimizes the political leadership of the Chinese Communist Party. Migrant workers' education at Worker University equips them with critical-thinking skills and theories that help them better understand their inequalities and interrogate dominant powers.

Ideology—as a complex system of meanings through which people make sense of their everyday lives—plays a significant role in shaping social formations and struggles.[60] Counterhegemonic allies are engaging in a collective effort of criticism of social inequality in reformist China. Eagerly seeking a newly egalitarian, socialist China, the allies speak to both the general public and the party-state. Their goal is not to overthrow the party-state, as some who support neoliberal democracy would claim; nor do these allies "[lack] interconnective ideological bonds," as some scholarly critiques of resistance in China argue.[61] The allies' agitation over equality urges the party-state to fulfill its socialist promise and intervene in the unequal production and distribution regimes in the market economy.

CONCLUSION

Picun is undergoing demolition, and MWH is closing its offices and moving to Pinggu District, which is in the far eastern area of Beijing. The physical space of Picun may soon be gone, but its legacy as a powerful symbol of the migrant-worker community and culture will endure. MWH's labor activism through cultural production continues. The Dagong Art Museum is being closed, but a staff member told me that they have saved all the collections and hope to find a new space in Pinggu to reopen the museum. PCN stopped publishing, but MWH has started a new, bimonthly magazine titled *Xin gonren wenxue* (新工人文学; New worker literature) that is also collectively produced by migrant-worker members. In Pinggu, the Troupe has performed several concerts to feature its new songs. Although the new location is a two-hour drive from

Picun, MWH continues to receive visits from different social groups, including migrant workers, scholars, students, and concerned publics. But the new distance makes it difficult for migrant workers to visit as public transportation is not reliable in Pinggu District. The weekly literature group still meets in Picun and continues to draw in worker participants. As MWH will eventually relocate all its activities and events to Pinggu, the organization recognizes that its accessibility to migrant workers will be a vital issue. During the COVID-19 pandemic, weekly meetings of the literature groups moved online, and the number of participants even increased. But many workers still prefer offline meetings in order to have face-to-face interactions and discussions with teachers and fellow workers. As one worker said, "I really like the atmosphere of the literature group, and I want to meet them [in person]. I feel everyone is equal here, unlike the rest of society."

What the worker gestures to in his complaint about "the rest of society" is the unequal power relations he constantly encounters in his daily life. In MWH's labor activism, a Marxist critique of class inequality and labor exploitation becomes the key ideological force in organizing workers' collective cultural production through museum displays, music, a community newspaper, etc. Workers' material circumstances are the precondition to their class consciousness and Marxist theory makes migrant workers' material realities more legible to them, in part by demystifying the dominant discourse that champions the achievements of market reform. Enabling multisensory, multimodal forms of labor activism, working-class cultural production is not an abstract expression but rather a process of meaning making using the lived experiences of migrant workers.

In Hall's critique of Britain's transition in the 1980s from social democracy to neoliberalism, he reveals that Thatcherism and the Right struggled to occupy ideological terrain in their project to produce a new consent among the people through education, intellectual work, and popular media.[62] And at the time, the Left had no ideological projects to act as a counterforce: "no journal of opinion, no political education, no organic intellectual base, no alternative reading of popular history to offer."[63] The lessons of such failures are profound. Hall argues that the Left should learn from Thatcherism's hegemonic project and that it should seek to contest Thatcherism's hegemony by developing a coun-

terhegemonic project. Since China's transformation from state socialism to state capitalism, neoliberal discourses of market and economy
have become dominant in the ideological terrain. But working-class
resistance—manifesting in grassroots, collective cultural production—is
in the process of forming an ideological counterforce to capitalism and
neoliberalism. The socialist claims of current-day workers and labor activists are not nostalgic invocations of China's past; they instead are
ideological calls to the state and to the people, and they are invested in
forming a more appealing political imagination that envisions a more
equal and just society.

Yet the orthodox Marxism of MWH's advocacy work has its limitations. While the organization's critique of capitalism and class inequality is robust and well developed, its attention to gender inequalities is
comparatively underdeveloped. In conversation with me, a key member
of the Troupe insisted that class inequality was more important than
gender inequality and should be given priority in workers' collective
resistance projects. The emphasis on class struggles in MWH's labor
activism leads to a marginalization of other forms of oppression and inequality, such as patriarchy and heteronormativity. This single-minded
focus on class struggle as the most, or even only, relevant site of power
closes off the possibility of other interventions that could undermine
intertwined inequalities. The next chapter turns to feminist activists to
consider their intersectional interventions that seek to strengthen and
broaden the scope of labor activism.

FOUR

ARTICULATING FEMINISM

Feminist Labor Activism and Intersectional Interventions

Although gender equality has been incorporated into national policy since the establishment of the People's Republic of China in 1949, feminism, as a social and political ideology, is not as widely embraced as socialism or communism in China. Official discourse stigmatizes feminism as a potential threat to social order and existing power structures. The Chinese government's control over media and public discourse has also limited the visibility and influence of feminist ideas and grassroots feminist activism. Despite these challenges, there are individuals and groups in China who actively advocate for gender equality and women's rights. They work within the existing constraints to push for change and raise awareness about gender issues, such as addressing gender-based violence and harassment. Social media platforms and online communities also provide spaces for individuals to discuss and share feminist ideas and experiences. Online activism and digital campaigns have played a significant role in amplifying feminist voices and fostering a sense of solidarity among activists. At the same time, the burgeoning feminist movements tend to be confined to urban middle-class women and men and lack engagement with rural and working-class people.

This chapter examines two cases of mediated labor activism by feminist activists: Jiu Ye, a feminist band, and Jianjiao buluo, an independent feminist-media platform.[1] Through their cultural and media practices, feminist activists employ an intersectional lens to advocate for equality and rights for working-class women, sexual minorities, and disabled people. I characterize this form of mediated labor activism as feminist labor activism; it prioritizes intersectionality and addresses the needs and rights of those who are often overlooked or excluded. Labor activism often advocates class equality, while contemporary feminist activism has been more middle-class focused. What interventions have this new form of feminist labor activism created to challenge intersected oppressions? In a context where feminism is not a favorable ideology and feminist ideas circulate primarily among the middle class, how does feminist labor activism engage underprivileged and marginalized women and people? How do feminist labor activists make their activism relevant for, inclusive of, and accessible to rural and working-class communities? By addressing these questions, chapter 4 explores the potential of feminist ideas and praxis to become an alternative framework for resistance and liberation that goes beyond a state-sanctioned socialist discourse.

AN INTERSECTIONAL CRITIQUE OF LABOR ACTIVISM AND FEMINIST STRUGGLES IN CHINA

While challenges to capitalism and urban supremacy are central tenets of mediated labor activism, feminist agendas are marginalized, meaning patriarchal power and male domination have been much less contested. The marginalization of feminist struggles in labor activism in China can be attributed to four main reasons. First, the Chinese party-state has a long tradition of discrediting feminism as a Western, bourgeois ideology. While it was a legitimate critique of liberal feminism in the early twentieth century, the party-state's discursive commitment to orthodox Marxism has prohibited the formation of radical feminist forces to dismantle the persistence of patriarchal and heterosexual domination. In Mao's China, female officials within the state cautiously avoided any feminist discourse—to avoid direct confrontations with male officials—while nevertheless successfully promoting gender equality policies.[2] The achievement of state-led women's emancipation in the socialist era has become a vital reference point for the recent official and popular discourses in their project to construct the image of a rejuvenating China and the identity of Chineseness. This celebratory discourse of the socialist past not only circumvents the incomplete task of realizing gender equality, such as challenging misogyny and women's burden of reproductive labor, but also perpetuates the ignorance of a wide range of feminist thoughts and actions with transformative potential toward a genuinely equal and just society.[3] The party-state's demonizing of feminism continues to distort the radical and political potential of feminist ideas, thus allowing it to legitimize its repression of grassroots feminist activism. The state official discourse of labeling feminism a Western liberal ideology manufactures a popular resentment and misunderstanding of feminist ideas and activism in China.[4]

Second, the rise of postfeminism and popular feminism, along with the transnational flow of media and culture in the past decades, has led to contentious interpretations of the term "feminism" in China's public sphere. In global contexts and in China, postfeminist culture advises young middle-class women to achieve empowerment and independence through consumption and constant self-discipline and surveillance.[5] Young women and girls are encouraged by postfeminist discourse to become attractive, heterosexual-desiring subjects to please themselves.[6] While postfeminist media and culture construct an illusion that women are no longer constrained by any inequalities, popular feminist discourse acknowledges the persistent inequalities but primarily focuses on the empowerment of women individually.[7]

The term "popular feminism" refers to the kind of liberal feminist ideas—those that emphasize individual women's equality with men and focuses on elite middle-class women's rights—that have acquired a prevailing presence in the public sphere at the expense of other strains of feminism that more explicitly focus on the predicaments of underprivileged and marginalized women.[8]

In public conversations in China, especially online, "feminism" is a contentious term that frequently sparks intense debates. Feminism is either labeled a consumerism trap or interpreted as the acts of selfish women pursing personal benefits and advantages.[9] Feminist activists face misogynist attacks and are often stigmatized as extremists who cause trouble. The unfavorable and sometimes hostile public attitude toward feminism has caused great obstacles to the dissemination of feminist ideas.

Third, labor activism and working-class resistance both in China and worldwide have historically trivialized or even excluded women's rights and gender equality. In Western developed countries, labor unions and working-class resistance have long been criticized by scholars for sexism, racism, and xenophobia because of a failure to advocate for rights for women, racial minorities, and immigrant workers.[10] Bottom-up, grassroots workers' protests and labor activism in contemporary China have inherited the politics of the state-led labor campaigns of revolutionary and Maoist China, which prioritized class equality over gender equality. The lack of engagement with a feminist ethos in current-day labor activism is therefore a legacy of earlier forms of working-class resistance in history. Migrant workers' strikes and protests have clustered in factories to fight capital exploitation of labor.[11] These collective actions are led by young male migrant workers who demonstrate an emergent class consciousness. In the actual process and practices of resistance, women's access to the labor activist space is constrained and greatly shaped by existing gendered power relations. Women activists find it necessary to form all-women spaces or groups to enable their participation in labor activism.

As we saw in chapters 2 and 3, the cases of MWC and MWH show that gender politics are shaping women's participation in labor activism. MWC is predominately a women's space. All the founders and most of the earlier and current staff members are female. In the 1990s, many young migrant women as well as some young men attended MWC's activities. Migrant-worker participants have all been female since the early 2000s. In contrast, patriarchal gender dynamics have shaped the activities and agenda at MWH. The founders and main staff members of MWH are men, and male power and authority dominate the organization. A few male staff members, who are also founders of the organization, hold the lion's share of power and act like patriarchs of a family.[12] The vast majority of migrant-worker members of MWH are likewise male. Some female migrants are prevented by their husbands from attending MWH's activities and events; as it is a mixed space for women and men, husbands do not want their wives to participate in activities with other men. Conversely, at MWC, some domestic workers say that their husbands encourage and support them to participate at MWC, as it is a women-only space. As one female worker disclosed to me, "My husband never worries about my coming to MWC. There is nothing to worry about, right? All of us here are women." In their different ways, the prevention and encouragement exercise patriarchal power and male control to discipline female workers' body and actions, but these unequal gender relations are not addressed by these two NGOs.

The fourth reason that feminism has typically been marginalized in labor activism has to do with the class position and material circumstances of the leaders of the grassroots radical feminist activism that has flourished in the past two decades in China. Often led and organized by high-profile feminists, this grassroots radical feminism has largely overlooked the disenfranchisement of working-class women and sexual minorities, who face intertwined inequalities due to class, gender, and sexuality and who are struggling to make ends meet in their daily lives.[13] Exemplary efforts include the establishment of the feminist alternative-media outlet Feminist Voices and feminist activists' protests against sexual violence and male privilege in public space.[14] These efforts were later suppressed by the state, with Feminist Voices being shut down and feminist activists being arrested. The Chinese state's suppression of feminist activism was widely criticized by feminists around the globe and by international media. Feminist communities registered their support for Feminist Voices and feminist activists in social media and joined local women's march with posters. International news media reported the arrest of Chinese feminist activists and foreign leaders' calls for the Chinese government to release these activists. The transnational flow of feminist movements, such as MeToo, has become a significant component of feminist struggles in contemporary China. But these domestic forms of grassroots radical feminist activism have been confined almost exclusively to middle-class, educated circles of women and men. And this feminist activism lacks an inclusive agenda to address material disparities between working-class and middle-class, and rural and urban, women.

The lack of antipatriarchy in labor activism and the lack of anticapitalism in grassroots radical feminist activism reveal the unreconciled rifts between feminism and Marxism in contemporary working-class resistance and feminist struggles. Without reconciliation, achieving true liberation and social transformation will not be possible. As Marxist feminist Heidi I. Hartmann argues, "The struggle against capital and patriarchy cannot be successful if the study and practice of the issues of feminism are given up. A struggle aimed only at capitalist relations of oppression will fail, since their underlying supports in patriarchal relations of oppression will be overlooked. And the analysis of patriarchy is essential to a definition of the kind of socialism that would destroy patriarchy, the only kind of socialism useful to women."[15] Capitalism and patriarchy are interlocking and mutually reinforcing systems of oppression: a socialist project without feminism will not emancipate women from patriarchal oppression and male domination, and a feminist project without socialism is not adequate to tackle capitalist exploitation of women's productive and reproductive labor.

The lives of working-class and rural women in China are shaped by gender and class inequalities that work in conjuncture with other forms of oppression. An intersectional lens is needed to perceive and then undermine those multiple forms. The past endeavors of Black feminists in promoting social change are enlightening. In the 1970s in the United States, Black feminist scholars and activists developed a political and conceptual account of interlocking systems of oppression to expose the repressive conditions Black women faced; they then called for individuals, organizations, and movements to combat those interwoven inequalities.[16] For Black women in the United States, the intersection of racism, sexism, heterosexism, and classism constitutes unequal structures in their material and cultural lives and marginalizes them in social movements, such as racial-justice movements led by Black men and feminist movements led by middle-class white women.[17] The contributions of Black feminists in highlighting the interlocking systems of oppression and advocating for a more intersectional approach to social justice have had a profound impact on feminist theory and activism since the 1980s. Their work continues to inspire and inform efforts to challenge and dismantle intersecting forms of oppression and create more equitable and inclusive societies.

By articulating the concept of "intersectionality," Black feminists call for a more inclusive and comprehensive approach to social justice. Legal scholar and Black feminist Kimberle Crenshaw coined the term "intersectionality" in the 1990s to draw attention to the blind spots in the limited categories of "racial justice" and "gender justice" that fail to account for the combinations of racism and sexism that Black women face.[18] Since then, the concept has been broadly adopted by scholars to interrogate entwined unequal power dynamics and encapsulate social-justice movements with intersectional agendas.[19] Sociologist and Black feminist Patricia Hill Collins has developed intersectionality as a theory in the making with an open horizon, and she marks it as a paradigm shift in developing critical theory and praxis concerning power, social inequality, and social transformation. By "open horizon," Collins means that "intersectionality's paradigmatic use . . . constitutes more a starting point for developing a critical social theory."[20] Intersectionality comprises a set of critical tools to expose intersecting systems of power and solve social problems in specific contexts. Here, I suggest that a contextual approach is an important element of intersectional analysis, as it allows ideas of intersectionality to be applied in organic rather than mechanical ways to engage concrete social realities and analyze social actions within specific settings.

An intersectional analysis allows for a deeper understanding of the specific ways in which gender and class inequalities, and other forms of oppression, are intertwined in the Chinese context, and it provides a framework for developing strategies that address these interwoven inequalities. In the following sections, I examine two cases of feminist labor activism to provide insights into how intersectional ideas have been incorporated into their practices. These examples demonstrate how feminist activists have applied intersectionality as a critical theory and praxis to address multiple forms of oppression and promote social justice.

JIU YE: A FEMINIST BAND SINGING FOR WORKING-CLASS WOMEN

In the spring of 2016, three female activists formed a band named Jiu Ye Feminist Band (Jiu ye nüxing zhuyi yuedu; 九野女性主义乐队) to advocate for equal treatment of and rights for female migrant workers. *Jiu* means "nine" and stands for the tripled power of the three members, while the literal meaning of *ye*—"wildness"—connotes the liberation of women. Two members, Duan Yu and Ma Wei are female migrant workers, and the third member, Xiong Ying, is a doctoral student at a domestic research institute. They got to know each other while participating in the Migrant Workers' Home. Having noticed MWH's lack of attention to gender inequalities, the three members decided to form their own activist band—one with a feminist mission. Dedicated to promoting social justice and advocating for women's rights in her research and activism, Xiong Ying elucidates Jiu Ye's feminist objectives: "The equality we aim for is not only gender equality but also encompasses other dimensions, such as class. My feminist agenda responds primarily to patriarchal power, as it is so omnipotent in our society, and I am especially concerned with underprivileged groups, such as female migrant workers and migrant children." Under the supervision of Prof. Bu Wei, Xiong Ying's research focuses on gender and development in China, with particular attention on the well-being of female migrant workers. As Bu Wei maintains a long-term collaboration with MWH, Xiong Ying has also volunteered at the NGO, where she became acquainted with Duan Yu and Ma Wei. Although coming from a middle-class background, Xiong Ying's doctoral study and training enable her to embrace intersectional approaches to examining inequalities.

Female activists' feminist consciousness also arises from their experiences in everyday life and the actual practices of labor activism—sites that are always subject to gendered power relations. Duan Yu, talented in music and composition, was once a member of the New-Worker Troupe. The Troupe's main members have all been men, but several women have been short-term members of the Troupe. Among them, Duan Yu was the longest-serving member. Back then, Duan Yu was the only female member of the Troupe, and she wrote several songs about female migrant workers. Duan Yu came to Beijing in 2004 as a young migrant worker. During her few years in Beijing, she worked as a preschool teacher at a kindergarten, a typist at a small company, and a salesperson at a clothing store. The migrant-worker experience, her interests in music, and her concerns for social justice drove her to join the Troupe in 2005, and she remained in the group until 2008. Unlike other male members who were employed as staff members at the Migrant Workers' Home, Duan Yu spent her spare time working on the Troupe's activities. Although she got along well with other members, she often felt frustrated and found it difficult to "have deep conversations" with them. She recalled, "I did not know why I was not comfortable at the time, but now I can tell it was because they only focused on male workers and all the other members were male and they did not understand me as a female worker and a woman. And they were not interested in women's issues."

Feminist scholar Angela McRobbie's seminal feminist critique of working-class youth rebellion in postwar Britain reminds us that resistance focused on class can perpetuate existing patriarchal structures.[21] Through their subcultural practices of resistance, men had the privilege and power to deploy street life, drugs, rock music, and alcohol to claim a working-class youth culture in opposition to the mainstream, while women hardly had access to, or found pleasure in, those practices and were absorbed into the movement only to serve their working-class male companions.[22] Gendered power dynamics are also present in working-class cultural production in contemporary China. Among over a hundred songs in the Troupe's albums, only a few songs specifically depict female workers, such as "Xiaoshigong" (小时工; Hourly worker), "Dianti guniang" (电梯姑娘; Elevator girl), and "Wo de mingzi jiao Jin Feng" (我的名字叫金凤; My name is Jin Feng), all written and composed by Duan Yu. These songs are narratives about female migrants' experiences as waitresses, domestic workers, and assembly-line workers. Duan disclosed that she also wanted to write about female migrant workers' life struggles as daughters, wives, and mothers and to address all the constraints of being a woman. But her concerns about gender equality did not mesh well with the Troupe's single-minded focus on class equality.

In 2012, Duan Yu got married and left Beijing with her husband; she has been a housewife since then. For a long time, she was depressed by her constant burden of tedious housework. She later joined a local migrant-worker NGO in her new home of Suzhou, Zhejiang Province. At the NGO, female migrant participants shared their life experiences: families were disappointed when they were born; being daughters, they were forced to drop out of school at an early age, migrate to cities to work, and save money for their brothers to go to school; at factories, they did not get equal pay and often faced sexual harassment; in marriage, they were treated like vessels for birthing sons and were always doing all the housework. Duan Yu found that these shared experiences resonated very much with her own. She then became more committed to fight against gender inequality in rural and working-class women's lives. In 2015, she returned to Beijing when her husband's job was relocated. When I met Duan Yu in 2016, she was still a housewife, busy taking care of her three-year-old child, and, at the same time, a feminist labor activist.

Consciousness-raising remains a vital method in feminist movements. Through consciousness-raising, "the impact of male dominance is concretely uncovered and analyzed through the collective speaking of women's experience, from the perspective of that experience."[23] While feminist theories and scholarship are often only accessible to elite circles of educated women in China, feminist activism at labor NGOs facilitates consciousness-raising among working-class women to help them understand and interrogate patriarchy and male domination in their lives.

Ma Wei was also a female member of the New-Worker Troupe, very briefly, and she left for reasons similar to Duan's. Both Duan Yu and Ma Wei told me that their life experiences as women, female migrant workers, and, later, as wives and mothers shaped their motivation and practices in their feminist activism. Ma Wei and her husband have been migrant workers in Beijing for over a decade. At the time when the three members formed Jiu Ye, Ma Wei worked at a small musical-instrument store, selling violins. She is particularly critical of gender norms that perpetuate the assumption that women will bear the burden of domestic work in a household. She said, "Many women like me are busy with work, and their job duties are not lighter than their husbands at all. But it is always women who are doing all the housework and taking care of children."

Gender inequality in domestic division of labor has been among the key issues that feminist scholarship and activism tackle. Under patriarchy, working-class men, like their middle-class counterparts, benefit from women's reproductive labor. Male-centric labor activism rarely provides men with any incentive to combat patriarchal power and norms. In discussing the necessity for women to organize their own resistance, Hartmann contends, "Men's position in patriarchy and capitalism prevents them from recognizing both human needs for nurturance, sharing, and growth, and the potential for meeting those needs in a non-hierarchical, non-patriarchal society. But even if we raise their consciousness, men might assess the potential gains against the potential losses and choose the status quo. Men have more to lose than their chains."[24]

Women are not a homogenous group either. While middle-class women can enjoy class privilege by offloading housework on domestic workers, working-class women face the double oppression of patriarchy and capitalism. Attention to the intersections of gender and class, integrated into Jiu Ye's feminist labor activism, is developed from the members' lived experiences as female migrant workers and feminist activists and one as a critical scholar in training.

Jiu Ye's advocacy songs are meant to appeal to working-class women by offering collective expressions of and feminist critiques by working-class women. The songs also aim to raise awareness of gendered power relations and call on women to take action. "Wo shi nühai" (我是女孩; I am a girl), "Nüren de zibai" (女人的自白; Women's claims), and "Mianbao yu meigui" (面包与玫瑰; Bread and roses) are three exemplary songs. "Wo shi nühai" is a song Jiu Ye produced together with a group of female migrant workers when they participated in an NGO-organized workshop. The song exposes the intertwined inequalities that working-class women face: son-preference culture that deprives them of their education opportunities and creates gendered wage gaps and workplace discrimination. In rural families that can only afford one child's education, it is always daughters who drop out of school and work to support their brothers' education.[25] Factories have a preference for employing young migrant-worker women due to the assumption that they will be submissive and disciplined, while women employees face fewer chances for career advancement compared to their male counterparts.[26]

Duan Yu wrote and composed "Nüren de zibai" during her visit to a local NGO for female workers in Shenzhen in 2016. A group of women workers gathered at the NGO and shared their stories about their difficult lives with Duan Yu. The song's lyrics aggregate these women's voices:

> I think I am still young,
> and I don't want my dream of life to vanish in the
>   persistence of *dagong* [being a migrant worker].
> I don't want to be stuck in kitchens,
> and I want to see the outside world.
> I think I am capable of choosing what I want to do,
> and I don't want others to tell me what to do.

I can take care of children,
but I also have my own ambitions, expectations.
Women should live for themselves.
Our roads are so difficult.
When can we break the chains that have bound women
 for a thousand years? [27]

"When can we break the chains?" questions the long-lasting patriarchal domination that women in China have endured. Duan Yu informed me that the song originates from conversations with female workers. The group hopes that by singing the song, they can reach out to more women and build broader solidarity to advocate gender equality.

In a live show held at Picun on Labor Day, May 1, 2016, Jiu Ye performed "Nüren de zibai." At the beginning of the show, Ma Wei asked the audience, "How many men here have helped their wives with housework?" A few men in the audience reacted or raised their hands. Ma Wei then continued, "I hope men will help do some housework. Please respect your wives. Women are not tools for housework or giving birth."[28] In conversation with me, Wei said that she often employs this kind of interaction with audiences during the group's live shows. She was disappointed but not surprised on the occasion in question that very few men responded that they help with housework at home. She said, "I want to raise these men's awareness of the housework burden and change their minds about housework only being women's work." After the short interaction, Jiu Ye started to sing "Nüren de zibai." Duan Yu sang in a charming mezzo with her guitar; Ma Wei accompanied the singing with her violin; Xiong Ying sang together with Duan Yu while playing a small tambourine for accompaniment. While Jiu Ye were singing, many female migrants were video recording the show with their mobile phones, and some were even wiping away tears.

The song "Mianbao yu meigui" is designed to advocate for female migrant workers' labor rights. The original song, "Bread and Roses," was written and sung by American activist-artists to memorialize and honor immigrant women's struggle for economic and social equality in the United States in the early twentieth century. The song's call for fair wages and dignified lives was composed in the context of capitalist countries' exploitation of immigrants as cheap laborers in the process of industrial development. In Lawrence, Massachusetts, in 1912, working-class immigrant women in the textile industry went on strikes to protest their low wages. The strikes received support from local workers, farmers, and the general public. Workers eventually won the fight with a 15 percent raise and overtime compensation. The victory of Lawrence workers later spread to all the New England textile workers and industries, and millions of workers received raises.[29] The success of strikes in Lawrence demonstrates women workers' leading roles in organizing and sustaining workers' protests and resistance. It also highlights the importance of recognizing the contributions of working-class women in shaping the history of labor movements. "Bread and Roses" elaborates,

> As we go marching, marching,
> we bring the greater days,
> the rising of the women means the rising of the race.
> No more the drudge and idler,
> ten that toil where one reposes,
> but a sharing of life's glories: bread and roses, bread and
>   roses.
> Our lives shall not be sweated from birth until life closes;
> hearts starve as well as bodies;
> bread and roses, bread and roses.[30]

A group of female activists and workers adapted the song and translated it into Chinese.[31] Jiu Ye often sings the song in their live shows. Each time, a band member introduces the background of the song, the Lawrence strikes, to the audience and acknowledges women workers' leadership in labor strikes in history. Jiu Ye spotlights the women workers' strike as a compelling historical example, aiming to empower women and emphasize their strength and determination in working-class resistance and labor movements. The intention is to inspire greater unity among women workers and encourage their participation in collective resistance movements.

Jiu Ye's intersectional feminist activism goes beyond addressing gender and class inequalities and encompasses a broader understanding of power dynamics. For instance, they advocate for people with disabilities, calling for them to receive equal access to working opportunities, services, and resources. They coproduced a song with several people with disabilities titled "Shijie you women butong" (世界有我们不同; Our being makes it a different world). The song aims to raise public awareness about the disadvantaged situations that people with disabilities often face and to promote respect and dignity for all people, regardless of their abilities:

> Dancing with canes,
> beauty is confidence.
> Expressing with hands,
> beauty is elegance.
> Showing prostheses without disguise,
> beauty is full acceptance.
> Running in wheelchairs,
> beauty is feeling the speed.[32]

Jiu Ye also advocates for rights for migrant workers' children in some of their songs. Duan Yu wrote the song "Ertong de huayuan" (儿童的花园; Children's garden) to shed light on the disparities and challenges faced by migrant workers' children, such as limited access to education, healthcare, and social opportunities:

> Every child deserves a garden of health and medicine.
> Bathe in the sun and rain and get the nourishment of
>   education.
> Every child should grow up with safety and equality.[33]

Jiu Ye has performed these songs at NGO-sponsored workshops and events. The power of music connects people at an emotional level and can foster empathy and understanding, inspiring listeners to see these people as whole individuals deserving of equal opportunities and rights.

Jiu Ye maintains close relationships with the Migrant Workers' Home, other local NGOs, activist groups, and academics. They have participated in dozens of workshops and live shows at community spaces and universities to advocate for equality and rights for female migrant workers. In the summer of 2019, I attended an academic workshop on migrant workers' labor rights in Beijing where Jiu Ye was invited to perform. They featured their song "Zaijian yinghuochong" (再见,萤火虫; Bye, fireflies), based on a true, tragic story. In 1993, a toy factory caught fire in a coastal city in southern China. More than eighty women workers died in the fire. The song narrates the story of one survivor, a teenage girl named Xiao Ying. The first half of the song describes Xiao Ying's heavy workload on the assembly lines and poor dormitory conditions. Xiao Ying, together with other teenage-girl workers, produced "cute toys for European children" in the factory. The song's second half describes the difficulties of Xiao Ying's life when she returned to her home village after being seriously injured in the fire. Living with disabilities in a rural village, Xiao Ying was struggling with daily life and often countered judgmental attitudes and prejudiced views from others. "Zaijian yinghuochong" is a touching song that vividly reveals the precarious living and exploitative working conditions of young women migrant workers in factories in the 1990s.

FIGURE 4.1 *Duan Yu performing Jiu Ye's advocacy songs in the workshop, June 2019. Photo by author.*

Jiu Ye's presence and participation at the workshop enhanced the visibility and engagement of feminist ideas and actions in labor activism. After performing their advocacy songs, Duan Yu introduced their band and activist missions. There was a Q&A following the performance. Scholars responded enthusiastically and spoke highly of Jiu Ye's intersectional feminist activism. Some scholars and students expressed appreciation and commented that Jiu Ye's practices enrich the academic conversations on migrant workers' labor rights by providing practical examples and insights from their feminist activism. The high regard toward Jiu Ye demonstrates the recognition of their valuable contributions to bridging labor movements with feminist movements in contemporary China.

In mid-2017, Jiu Ye changed the band's name to Jiu Ye Female Folk Band (Jiu Ye nüxing minyao yuedui; 九野女性民谣乐队) and deliberately dropped the word "feminist." I asked Xiong Ying about the name change. She explained that in their on-site activism, when they introduce the band, the term "feminism" often invokes confusion among audiences and that "feminism" is a term "too academic to resonate with ordinary people." Given the stigmatization of feminism and the misogyny prevalent in the Chinese political and social context, as outlined earlier in this chapter, it is not surprising that Jiu Ye strategically decided to downplay the discourse of feminism.[34] But the name change does not alter the advocacy agenda of the band. They continue to advocate gender and class equality and to engage working-class women through songs and live shows. To the present, Jiu Ye has created more than twenty advocacy songs covering the themes of female migrant workers' rights, migrant children's rights, antibullying, and stopping sexual violence. Compared with members of the New-Worker Troupe, who have institutional support from MWH to enable them to dedicate themselves to full-time activism, members of Jiu Ye are more constrained. Since they do not enjoy the kind of institutional funding that the Troupe receives, the Jiu Ye project must be relegated to the members' spare time. So far, Jiu Ye has relied on crowdfunding as the primary source for covering their travel expenses when they take their activities outside Beijing.

By recognizing that underprivileged and marginalized groups face different forms of oppression and that their struggles are nevertheless

FIGURE 4.2 *Jiu Ye singing with female migrant workers at a festival to celebrate Women's Day organized by a local NGO in Shenzhen, 2019. Source: Jiu Ye's WeChat public account.*

interconnected, the feminist activists of Jiu Ye strive for a more comprehensive and inclusive vision of equality and liberation for all. Their songs can encourage people to engage in activism, support organizations working on these issues, and push for systemic change.

JIANJIAO BULUO: AN INDEPENDENT WORKING-CLASS FEMINIST-MEDIA OUTLET

A registered NGO, Jianjiao buluo runs as an online-media nonprofit advocacy organization promoting equality, diversity, and social inclusion for female migrant workers while opposing sexism, homophobia, and class inequality. When Jianjiao was seeking to hire a new editor, it made its requirements clear in the job listing it posted: "We expect that you are a feminist, can analyze issues through the lens of class, and will advocate for gender equality and labor rights in straightforward and understandable language."[35] Such a clearly articulated inclusive and intersectional agenda is rare in migrant workers' labor activism. Jianjiao was established by several feminist activists in 2014 as the first independent media platform for female migrant workers. It publishes narratives, poems, commentaries, analyses, and discussions written by workers and activists, many of which expose and critique the structural inequalities female migrant workers face in the prevailing economic and cultural regimes in reformist China. Arguments against patriarchal power relations and class inequality are often presented through specific cases of women trafficking, gender stereotypes, domestic violence, unequal pay, labor exploitation, and violations of labor rights. Jianjiao is also a unique media outlet to present writings by working-class lesbians. Self-identified lesbian workers write of subjective experiences and struggles in their everyday lives. As queer activism is predominately led by middle-class people in China, Jianjiao provides pivotal, inclusive spaces for working-class queer people.[36]

Jianjiao's practices embody both a form of women's media action and labor activism. Feminist-media scholars Carolyn M. Byerly and Karen Ross propose a model of "women's media action" to account for media activism among feminists, including feminist-media production and the creation of feminist public spheres in different countries in Europe, South Asia, and Latin America.[37] In this model, feminist-media activists are mostly educated, middle-class women who self-identify as feminists and are politically motivated.[38] The establishment of Jianjiao represents an instance of feminist action within the realm of contemporary media to promote gender equality in China. And what differentiates Jianjiao's feminist-media activism from radical feminist activism, such as the MeToo movement and Feminist Voices is its focus on the intertwined gender and class inequalities at stake in the fight for working-class women's labor rights.[39] Jianjiao can thus be characterized as an independent working-class feminist-media outlet.

Jianjiao's production and distribution is internet based, largely through social media, catering as it does to migrant workers as a highly mobile group who are increasingly engaged with social media. An inclusive mode of production is part of Jianjiao's mobilizing strategy. Individual authors submit articles to Jianjiao for publication, some using pen names, and all introduce themselves with a brief biography. The most frequently mentioned self-identities are "feminist," "migrant worker," "female worker," and "rural woman." The editors maintain flexible standards for migrant-worker submissions; they intentionally do not select pieces on the basis of the author's writing skills or literary style. Jianjiao deliberately decided to adopt the QQ and WeChat social media platforms in response to migrant workers' common and frequent use of these two social media platforms. To encourage more workers to express themselves and share their experiences, Jianjiao holds periodic online thematic-writing contests, offering cash and gift prizes. Themes range from migrant workplace and life experiences to narratives of emotional life to women's rights advocacy. The contests encourage participants to use diverse formats, welcoming narratives, pictures, videos, songs, poems, and so forth.

Three social media platforms—WeChat, QQ, and Weibo—are Jianjiao's main distribution channels. About 70 percent of its readership are female migrant workers, and the remaining 30 percent are male workers and concerned members of the public. QQ and WeChat host online deliberation sessions, where migrant workers interact with each other to discuss various issues. Jianjiao's uses of social media platforms construct what media scholar John D. H. Downing usefully characterizes as plural deliberative spaces. Within a deliberation space, "numerous challenges, like climate change, women's subordination, digital surveillance, can be addressed with collective wisdom, insight, and argument."[40] In the plural deliberative spaces, migrant workers, Jianjiao staff, and concerned members of various publics congregate to consider issues of equality and justice. Gender stereotypes and bias are frequent topics of discussion. Writers and readers raise awareness of women's excessive burden of housework, gender discrimination in labor markets, and sexual objectification in popular media. In addition, individual workers sometimes consult Jianjiao staff through the online platforms when they encounter problems or want advice. Jianjiao also designs dynamic offline activities to expand their audience. Collaborations with other NGOs, individual activists, advocacy groups, and scholars result in workshops, live musical shows, and other performances promoting gender equality and advocating for female workers' rights. Women workers participate in such events with full-time activists and scholars.

As female workers' voices are hard to find in mainstream media, Jianjiao creates a hospitable mediated space through which female work-

FIGURE 4.3 *Jianjiao's media page on WeChat, April 2018. Source: Jianjiao WeChat public account.*

ers define their voices and articulate their realities. This assembly of voices constitutes collective action by previously silenced groups, communicating and acting in ways that challenge the unequal power relations of institutionalized media.[41] While middle-class LGBTQ groups enjoy a certain social and cultural visibility due to their power as consumers, sexual-minority migrant workers are marginalized due to their economic position.[42] Jianjiao's online spaces allow lesbian workers to write about their particular experiences as members of a working-class sexual minority. One wrote that she did not dare reveal her sexuality at her workplace for fear of discrimination or even overt aggression, with the result that she was socially isolated in both the factory and the dorm. Others have written about their peer workers', friends', and families' difficult social experiences as gay people.

The narratives Jianjiao circulates expose the gender inequalities widely prevalent in Chinese society. They tell of how son-preference culture deprives women of educational opportunities, fosters precarious working and living conditions in cities, and implicitly condones the trafficking of women. Among the many such stories Jianjiao has published, one uses the example of the author's aunt who was sold to be the wife of the author's uncle as the starting point for a broader consideration of the prevalence of trafficking. In the author's village, there have been many trafficked women, most of them from rural communities and many of whom had been victims of domestic violence and sexual assault. Many women tried to escape but rarely succeeded. Those who did were often urged by their original families to simply settle in and accept life with their buyer husbands. Discriminated against and excluded by local women who regarded them as outsiders, trafficked women resisted by refusing to learn local dialects, and some even committed suicide. At the end of the article, the author writes, "As a woman growing up in rural areas, I feel responsible for writing the true stories of people who were neglected by the media and the public. Writing stories about rural trafficked women focuses on women themselves, to reveal the difficulties of rural women and to reflect on the gender oppression that all women face."[43] In a milieu where mainstream news media report female trafficking simply as discrete, individual crimes without acknowledging it as a systemic issue of gendered violence, Jianjiao's articles draw attention to the lived experiences of trafficked women and critique trafficking as the consequence of hegemonic patriarchy.

Through contesting mainstream news media, Jianjiao embodies a form of alternative journalism. Alternative journalism not only has different values about what should be considered news but also adopts different approaches to gathering, writing, and presenting news, often referencing nonofficial sources in news stories.[44] For instance, one female worker wrote an article sharply criticizing a mainstream-news report on the sexual assault of a female janitor in a subway station, which used the suggestive headline "La yanjing" (辣眼睛; Making your eyes spicy) and reported the assault as out of the ordinary and mocked the janitor as an old working-class woman. The migrant writer observed that mainstream media reporting on sexual assault and harassment treats female victims as sexualized objects and reproduces patriarchal forms of inequality and objectification. Jianjiao, as an independent media platform for workers, enables the visibility of critiques made by workers in response to the problematic reports of mainstream media. Establishment of migrant workers' community / alternative media, such as Jianjiao buluo and Picun community newspaper (PCN) discussed in chapter 4, has emerged as a significant and effective approach to labor activism in China. Unlike PCN, which focuses on reaching migrant workers living in a specific physical community, Jianjiao takes a different approach by transcending spatial boundaries and building online communities for migrant workers. Through the use of digital platforms and social media, Jianjiao creates virtual spaces where migrant workers can connect, share resources, and support each other regardless of their physical location.

Many of Jianjiao's articles address the issue of domestic violence. One article by a Jianjiao editor enumerates factors that perpetuate domestic violence in China: longstanding patriarchal norms that maintain male supremacy and legitimize men's violence toward women; women's more limited education and employment options, making them more likely to be vulnerable subjects; and lack of social support for female victims of domestic violence. The article also incorporates comments by readers on Jianjiao's previous published articles about domestic violence, who shared their experiences and observations of domestic violence in their lives.

Mainstream-media news stories of domestic violence usually render women as voiceless victims, although the articles themselves sometimes include disturbing and tragic stories to increase their sensationalist appeal to audiences. Both types of representation commodify women's victimhood as a media product for consumption and fail to offer any critical reflections upon the patriarchal power structures that normalize violence against women. Jianjiao's articles, on the other hand, interrogate the unequal power relations undergirding domestic violence and advocate for action toward change. One migrant author argues that families, friends, neighbors, and relevant institutions should intervene to protect and help victims, thus countering a reluctance to get involved based on the common perception of domestic violence as a private issue between couples. One migrant worker's story of her colleague who suffered from multiple incidents of domestic violence is typical. When the victim was forced by her abusive husband to return home after escaping from a rural village, many of the workers shamed or blamed her for not being a good wife.

As contemporary Chinese society still lacks a general understanding of domestic violence as a structural problem, Jianjiao's advocacy content represents an important intervention. The intersectional lens of gender and class, present in Jianjiao's articles, underlines that the vulnerabilities of working-class women, exacerbated by their economic disadvantage, pose significant obstacles in addressing domestic violence. As one women worker said to me during an interview, "I can't simply get divorced because my salary is so low, and I can't afford to raise my child by myself." While ending a marriage is often seen as a solution to escape domestic violence, it is not a simple option for working-class women due to financial concerns.

"What Jianjiao does is so important to female [migrant] workers. It provides a platform for us to express our voices," writes one reader in response to a Jianjiao WeChat article celebrating the organization's third anniversary. Other workers are similarly enthusiastic about Jianjiao. Workers' and activists' online deliberations, campaigns, and activities through Jianjiao can be characterized as digital working-class feminist activism. Media scholars often attribute the rise of contemporary feminist movements and activism to the internet and social media, such as the transnational flow of the MeToo movement.[45] But I suggest that technological affordances are not necessarily sufficient to facilitate activism and social movements in contemporary societies. In the case of Jianjiao, the crucial element is the workers and activists who are focused on addressing structural inequalities; they use digital technologies to help them drive transformative actions. Jianjiao's digital activism is not merely an aggregation of individuals sharing their experiences in digital space; rather, it is online collective action informed by an intersectional feminist-advocacy agenda that invites people to engage labor activism against intertwined power structures of patriarchy, capitalism, and heterosexuality.[46]

Migrant workers have welcomed Jianjiao as an independent workers' media platform for empowerment and advocacy, yet it is clear that such content only circulates among a relatively small audience. In commercialized social media, popular WeChat articles usually receive more than one hundred thousand page views; many of these popular sites are entertainment-based or gear content toward middle-class audiences, and most feature advertising on their pages. By contrast, a Jianjiao article typically draws about one thousand page views, with view numbers varying little between articles. Most draw fewer than ten comments, usually from migrant workers relating their own experiences, questioning inequalities, or expressing the sense of helplessness they feel as female workers. On Weibo, the number of pages views, reposts, and comments for Jianjiao's posts were even fewer than those for WeChat. One of the main limitations of alternative media is that they do not reach the large, broad audiences as mainstream commercial media do.[47] Whereas popular social media public accounts rely heavily on marketing strategies to increase readership and thus attract more advertising, the promotion of Jianjiao remains primarily interpersonal, accomplished through small networks of migrant workers. Considering the large number of rural migrant workers in China, the small readership of Jianjiao reveals that because audiences are used to commercial media and culture, the capacity of independent media to attract workers as readers and participants is rather constrained.

At the same time, the low profile of Jianjiao prevents it from being targeted for censorship by the party-state. The ban of Feminist Voices by the Chinese government in 2018 can be attributed primarily to its increased visibility and impact, which was demonstrated by its active presence with a substantial number of followers on social media. The reality of constant censorship and surveillance makes the editorial team of Jianjiao cautious about circulating any direct critique of the government or comments on China's political affairs. Even with this level of caution, editors disclosed articles with discussions of political events, such as workers' strikes in other countries, were often deleted due to online censorship. In China's context, the biggest threat to the survival of independent media is the political environment. Whereas media-policy activists may successfully lobby for changes to benefit the development of alternative and independent media in democratic countries, media activism in China is less able to intervene in the policymaking process.[48] Media scholar Arne Hintz offers a thorough review of media-policy activism in different countries and identifies two approaches for policy-activist practices: first, civil society organizations, lobby groups, and coalitions engage with policymakers directly to advocate for policy change; second, offline and online campaigns and protests demand changes to media policies.[49] But in China's context, the political system does not allow bottom-up collective action to intervene in the state policymaking process. As a result, NGOs, activists, and workers cannot turn to advocacy of media-policy change as a feasible way to protect independent media.

CONCLUSION

The two cases of Jiu Ye and Jianjiao buluo embody what I characterize as feminist labor activism. Feminist labor activism is an intersectional intervention into labor activism that typically prioritizes class struggles and middle-class-oriented radical feminist activism in contemporary China. It takes the standpoint of working-class women to advocate for both gender *and* class equality. Working-class women are not *either* individuals who are subjected to male dominance *or* workers who face capitalist exploitation. They encounter the intertwined structures of patriarchy and capitalism that control and exploit women's bodies and labor. Because of their subject positions, they possess the capacity and have the potential to emerge as the primary driving force in challenging patriarchy and capitalism. By recognizing and addressing the specific challenges and experiences faced by female migrant workers, feminist labor activism amplifies their voices within the broader labor movement. By engaging female migrant workers, a significant portion of China's population of working-class feminist labor activism establishes a crucial connection between working-class resistance and feminist activism. Activist projects like Jiu Ye and Jianjiao buluo carry potentials to reconcile the concerns of Marxist class struggle with those of feminist struggle.

Feminist labor activism embraces an open horizon of intersectionality to expose and combat interwoven inequalities and injustice. Equipped with intersectional feminist ideas and practices, Jiu Ye's and Jianjiao buluo's advocacy efforts are crucial in highlighting the experiences and struggles of underprivileged and marginalized people in China. An inclusive, intersectional advocacy agenda goes beyond single-issue activism and recognizes that different forms of oppression are interconnected and reinforce each other. This approach acknowledges that the struggles of underprivileged and marginalized people are interconnected and that collective action is needed to dismantle the intersecting systems of power and domination. By centering intersectionality, feminist labor activism works toward a more inclusive and equitable society for all.

Feminist activists adopt different mediated forms, such as music and alternative journalism, to reach and mobilize migrant workers both offline and online. Similar to the New-Worker Troupe, music is a powerful medium for the feminist activists of Jiu Ye to challenge inequalities and convey messages of empowerment, solidarity, and social justice. A strong appeal to migrant workers' emotions is enabled through sonic resonance, critical lyrics, and face-to-face interaction in live shows. Workers' feelings of anger, frustration, sadness, empathy, motivation, and solidarity are evoked through listening and singing advocacy songs. In Jianjiao's alternative journalistic space, similar emotions are also expressed through workers' shared experiences, reflections, and deliberations. These collective experiences help build a sense of community and support, reinforcing the idea that they are not alone in their struggles.

Compared with labor activism and workers' resistance, which often draw upon state-sanctioned socialist discourse, feminist labor activism takes intersectionality as an alternative, inclusive framework for grassroots resistance. Although activists still cautiously avoid direct confrontation with the party-state, they no longer seek legitimacy from the state or regard the state as a potential agent for change. Instead, they confront the party-state's attempts to discredit feminist beliefs and actions. The activism recognizes women as independent political actors who exercise their agency to fight intertwined power structures. It rejects the notion that women need to be liberated by a patriarchal, socialist state, as is often suggested in official narratives. Women's emancipation was once an important index to measure the achievements of state socialism in Mao's China. For instance, subsuming women into the production force was considered the main way to empower women in state-led women's emancipation projects. During that time, a substantial number of women from rural and urban areas were mobilized to enter the workforce, resulting in a noticeable improvement in their social status.[50] But these projects left patriarchal power and male privilege intact, and they were premised on preserving the primacy of the party-state's authority.[51]

Feminist labor activism breaks from the state's top-down approach to women's emancipation and does not seek validation or legitimacy from the state's discursive commitment to gender equality. It carves out

grassroots, autonomous, and inclusive spaces to incorporate intersectional feminism and combat interwoven inequalities in every aspect of
women's lives, including reproductive rights, education, employment,
and social norms. Moreover, the spaces it creates invite women, migrant workers, LGBTQ groups, and people with disabilities to join in
collective resistance. True change comes from these collective efforts of
people driven by shared goals and values to oppose oppressive systems
and ideologies. In this sense, feminist labor activism embraces possibilities to grow into an independent resistance force for transformative
changes.

Mediated labor activism facilitated by NGOs and activist groups has
embraced multiple agendas with varied focuses, missions, and goals. It
creates multifaceted activist spheres and spaces where different social
actors are appealed to join and form coalitions, alliances, and networks.
The next chapter will delve into the complexities of forming connections and networks and politics of participation among social actors in
labor activism, shedding light on the power dynamics, challenges, and
opportunities social actors encounter when they work together in the
context of mediated labor activism toward equality and justice.

FIVE

BUILDING ALLIANCES

Pluralistic Counterpublics and Networks of Labor Activism

In authoritarian regimes like China, people are still able to find ways to resist by navigating different spaces and exploring various possibilities even under the constant threat of political repression. Varied forms of resistant action, such as protests and demonstrations, strikes, and online activism, address issues of workers' rights, environmental protection, and gender equality. In contrast to Mao's era, when non-state-affiliated civil organizations hardly existed, China has seen the growth and development of nongovernmental organizations, advocacy groups, and human rights organizations in recent decades. These organizations have played a significant role in promoting bottom-up changes and advocating for human rights and social justice in reformist China, often with affordances of ICTs. Meanwhile, the Chinese government still maintains a high level of control and oversight over civil society organizations. NGOs and other civil organizations must operate within certain limitations, and those involved in sensitive issues face potential surveillance, restrictions, or even crackdowns. The survival and precarity of migrant-worker NGOs and activist groups are situated in ever-evolving negotiations and tensions between the authoritarian state and grassroots actions.

During my in-person fieldwork in Beijing and digital ethnography on social media platforms, I encountered a diverse group of people all concerned with the well-being of rural migrant workers. These individuals engage in a wide range of practices and activities to support and advocate for the rights and equality of migrant workers. They often bring different perspectives to bear on the current circumstances. Shaped by the individuals' personal backgrounds, experiences, values, and ideologies, the varying perspectives influence their actions and practices in specific ways. Engaging theories of the "counterpublic," I map out these social-actor participants in the context of mediated labor activism and pay attention to the generational differences among migrant workers—in particular, the younger generation's lack of interest in the sociality that NGO activities offer. Explicating the politics of participation is to avoid romanticizing resistance and assuming it is frictionless and to allow for critical analyses of the complexities and power dynamics at play in bottom-up struggles and resistance.

Although mediated labor activism has not yet grown into or yielded a large-scale labor or social movement in contemporary China, it nevertheless embraces a key element of movement building: informal networks. Mario Diani conceptualizes "informal networks" as a distinctive characteristic of social movements to differentiate them from collective actions taking place within the boundaries of organizations.[1] In the forming process of movements, individuals, social groups, and organizations are involved in constant negotiations and coordination.[2] While labor NGOs and activist groups do play an essential role in mediated labor activism, informal networks also emerge and thrive in the process, going beyond the boundary of specific organizations. I attend to offline and online connections in mediated labor activism, including the alliances, coalitions, and networks that have been formed through the participation of varied social actors.

Seeking to understand how mediated labor activism has arisen as a particular way of doing activism in the current historical moment of China, this chapter asks the follow questions: Why do differently positioned social actors become interested in labor activism? How does mediated activism allow for a fluidity in the construction of activist groups and practices? How have informal networks been facilitated in

the process of mediated labor activism? What is the relationship between online and offline practices and connections?

CONTENTIOUS POLITICS AND THE POLITICAL
ECONOMY OF NGOS IN POSTSOCIALIST CHINA

Since the fierce suppression of the 1989 Tiananmen Square protests,
the Chinese government has been vigilant in responding to signs of any
mass protests, demonstrations, or movements developing. Although
there have been few large-scale social movements in the post-1989
period—due to a highly sensitive political environment—smaller-scale
protests, demonstrations, and activist efforts persist.[3] These actions
often emerge in response to specific issues or events, such as labor
rights, environmental concerns, human rights violations, or gender
inequality.[4] Actions range from individual resistance on a daily basis
to collectively mobilized actions and the establishment of civil society
organizations. For instance, in the late 1990s, laid-off urban workers
from former state-owned factories protested their disenfranchisement
due to the economic reforms.[5] The market economy has eliminated the
job security, guaranteed benefits, and welfare that urban workers could
expect in Mao's planned economy. In the post-Mao era, laid-off state
workers have also relied on collective actions to gain more bargaining
power. They have turned to sit-ins and demonstrations to demand substantial rights.[6] In coastal cities, urban residents and environmental
activists protested local factories and successfully made the factories
terminate their projects that caused pollution.[7]

   In the past two decades, there has been an ever-increasing use of
information-communications technologies (ICTs) in resistance and activism by ordinary citizens, activists, and NGOs. Despite the government's political control and online censorship, the internet does provide
avenues for cultivating activism and resistance movements. There have
been numerous online actions by individuals, groups, and organizations
to address such issues as HIV/AIDS, environmental protection, wom-
en's rights, and religious freedom, to name a few.[8] Dispersed individuals are able to engage in grassroots activism via social media to expose
misconduct by individuals and government officials.[9] Online platforms

also facilitate the dissemination of uncensored information, bypassing the traditional media channels that are typically subject to government control. In postsocialist China, bottom-up, grassroots rebellions that challenge various forms of injustice have been vibrant.

Contrary to the popular belief that an authoritarian state is repressive toward any type of collective resistance, the relationship between the Chinese government and protestors is complex and multifaceted. The government's response to protests and collective resistance can vary depending on various factors, such as the nature of the issue, the scale of the protest, the location, and the potential impact on social stability. The Chinese government's reaction to opposition can be characterized as a responsive authoritarianism that involves selective accommodation and repression of grievances, protests, and dissent.[10] Cai Yong-shun's extensive analysis of collective resistance in China reveals that protestors can often gain leverage against local governments by seeking intervention from the upper levels of government, and the national government is more accepting of non-regime-threatening protests.[11] In other words, successful protest/resistance that leads to problem-solving or even policy changes must occur within the legitimate political framework of the party-state.

In their critique of contemporary protests and resistance in China, Elizabeth J. Perry and Mark Selden argue that the single-issue conflicts fail to form a collective counterpower to overthrow the party-state.[12] But their view overlooks the fact that the authoritarian party-state is one factor among several that constitute hegemonic power in contemporary China. Transnational and domestic capital, urban middle-class-oriented consumerist culture, and heterosexual-patriarchal power interlock to form hegemony in the contemporary conjuncture. Also, it is important to take into consideration that any direct confrontation with the party-state's political power faces brutal repression. To simply discredit resistant actions because their primary goal is not the overthrow of the state is to fall into a liberal trap that does not recognize the potential and politics of forming various types of counterpower.

In Mao's China, the government tightly controlled all aspects of society, and there was little political space in which non-state-affiliated organizations could exist. Since the economic reform, the Chinese government has recognized civil society organizations as a vital force in reducing the state's own burden, and many NGOs have been founded in the areas of education, disaster relief, and social welfare.[13] While acknowledging the significance of NGOs in dealing with social problems that the state or market are unable or unwilling to solve, the government is nevertheless quite aware of NGOs' potential to organize and mobilize bottom-up collective actions that could threaten the dominance of the party-state. Since the 1990s, the government has set up strict regulations covering all forms of social organizations, mobilizations, and movements for the purpose of maintaining political stability. Official policy toward NGOs is comprehensively regulatory.[14] Registration is the main way for the government to control NGO development. The policy sets a bar for social organizations to register as NGOs, requiring a minimum of fifty members and ¥10,000 for operating funds, and the policy allows the government to eliminate NGOs by shutting down registered ones that it regards as badly managed or engaging in illegal actions.[15]

Given the authoritarian regime in China, scholars have agreed that NGOs' autonomy from the state should not be the only standard by which to evaluate their democratic potential for constituting civil society and the public sphere.[16] Instead, scholarly attention has shifted to the following areas: the benefits NGOs derive from their close relations with municipal governments, the micropolitics of their actual practices and influences, and the particular configurations of civil society and the public sphere in China. Those NGOs that maintain close relationships with the government have successfully brought their agendas into the official policymaking process.[17] Other benefits of maintaining close relationships with local governments include easier access to registration, political protection, approval of activities, and grant funding.[18] Wang Jing suggests that NGOs' provision of social services is a form of "nonresistant activism" that offers possibilities for sustainable social change in authoritarian China.[19]

While there is general agreement that civil society cannot gain autonomy from the state in China, this does not preclude civil and social forces from being able to penetrate the totalitarian power of the party-state.[20] Based on research about services that a NGO provided to rural women and migrant workers in the 1990s, Tamara Jacka points out that although the organization's activities fit with the state's agenda for self-development and self-governance and were not directed against the power of the state, they did contribute to a more egalitarian public sphere in China.[21] The public sphere is not separate and completely independent from the state but is in constant interaction with the state. Wang Hui usefully describes the unique nature of the public sphere in China: "The public sphere is not a mediating space between state and society; rather, it is the result of the penetration of society into a certain space of the state."[22] In China's authoritarian context where an independent civil society hardly exists, the capacities of NGOs and grassroots initiatives to carve out a space for change should not be underestimated.

NGOs in China can be categorized into two types: service oriented, which provide services to underprivileged and disadvantaged groups; and advocacy oriented, which seek to effect legislative and policy changes.[23] In Hu's regime from 2002 to 2012, the state was cautious of advocacy NGOs; since 2013, Hu's principle of "maintaining social stability" has been replaced by Xi's "consolidating state security," and repression of both types of NGOs has expanded and intensified.[24] The service and advocacy NGOs that have been suppressed during Xi's regime cover a wide range of areas, including rural education, disability rights, LGBT rights, labor, environmental rights, AIDS, and gender equality, and the state has claimed that its crackdowns aim to prevent Western influence and avoid a latter-day color revolution (uprising to overthrow the existing political regime) that would erode national security.[25] Like NGOs worldwide, Chinese NGOs often get funding from Western charities and civil organizations, such as Oxfam and the Ford Foundation. In the 1990s and early 2000s, the Chinese government held a favorable view of the potential of foreign funders and international NGOs to help deal with social problems in China, even as it remained wary of Western influence on and erosion of Chinese society.[26] This caution has escalated in the period of Xi's regime. In 2017, the state launched the Overseas NGOs Law to cut foreign funding, which has made the already precarious financial condition of many NGOs even worse.[27] Many grassroots NGOs have turned to crowdfunding and social entrepreneurship to maintain financial sustainability, however fragile. The hope is that social entrepreneurship will cultivate economic independence of nonprofit organizations, like development NGOs, so that they do not merely rely on grant writers for economic survival.

Labor NGOs, such as the Migrant Women's Club and Migrant Workers' Home, discussed in chapters 2 and 3, respectively, often embrace both service and advocacy agendas. Not only do labor NGOs' service provision embody what Wang Jing characterizes as "non-resistant activism," but also these NGOs were able to become an organizational force to bring together workers, activists, and concerned publics and create spaces for resistance and collective action. By emphasizing their service-providing functions, MWC and MWH have been able to strategically frame their activities in a way that is perceived as nonthreatening to the regime. This approach has allowed them to navigate the political landscape and gain a certain level of political tolerance from the state. But if this approach allows labor NGOs to operate within the existing system, it can also result in constraints and compromises. Labor NGOs face restrictions on the scope of their advocacy work or face pressure to align their activities with the state's agenda. This can limit their ability to address systemic issues or engage in more directly confrontational forms of activism.

The political tolerance granted by the state can be conditional and subject to change. As political dynamics and government priorities have gradually shifted under Xi's regime, labor NGOs find themselves facing increased pressure or even repression. This has required them to constantly adapt and carefully navigate the political landscape. For instance, in May 2022, the New-Worker Troupe changed the band's name to Gucang (谷仓), literally meaning "barn." One of the members explained that a primary reason for the change is the increasing political hostility toward labor activism. The old name with its reference to the "new worker" and their focus on class inequalities could be politically risky. The new name caters to the current government's official focus on the rehabilitation of the Chinese countryside.[28] MWC and MWH have also been financially affected by policy changes. The prior funding sources for MWC and MWH from Oxfam were terminated shortly after the state policy to restrict foreign fundings was implemented. In 2018, the Didinghua performance program at MWC was ended due to the lack of financial support and the departure of a core staff member. Since then, MWC and MWH, like many labor NGOs, have turned to social entrepreneurship and crowdfunding for financial independence.

Labor NGOs that primarily focus on activism, without engaging in much service provision, may face greater challenges in maintaining their survival when political tolerance decreases. For instance, in the summer of 2021, Jianjiao buluo permanently shut down its online account, and the NGO was closed as the result of a police crackdown. The events leading to Jianjiao's shutdown began with a former staff member who, involved in a labor dispute with Jianjiao, disclosed some essential inside information online, including details about a key member being a high-profile feminist activist and Jianjiao receiving funding from foreign recourses. The disclosure generated heated discussions on several social media platforms, and conspiracy theories about Jianjiao posing a political threat were widely circulated online. In the current political environment, many NGOs and advocacy groups face increased political suppression, and so the online discussions about Jianjiao soon attracted police attention. The local police went to the office of Jianjiao, confiscated the organization's documents and materials and interrogated its key staff members. On August 9, 2021, Jianjiao buluo officially announced its closure. Labor NGOs maintain a delicate balance between continuing their activism and avoiding actions that could be perceived as threatening to the regime, and the biggest challenge of their survival is precisely the mercurial nature of the state's political tolerance.

Mediated labor activism, which has made a substantial contribution to the growth and development of contentious action and resistance culture in reforming China, embodies a particular sustainable form of collective resistance that labor NGOs and activist groups engage to navigate the unpredictability of state scrutiny and repression. By harnessing the power of cultural expression and community embedded in migrant workers' everyday lives, mediated labor activism is less susceptible to state repression than large-scale labor strikes or public protests, as they may not initially appear as overt political threats. Taking expressive forms appealing to migrant workers' longing for equality and justice, such as performance, music, and alternative media, among others, mediated labor activism is able to create a sense of collectivity and solidarity and effectively mobilize and organize migrant workers.

In the process of mediated labor activism, labor NGOs and activist groups play a crucial role in creating spaces for collaboration and fostering solidarity among migrant workers and other social groups. In the next section, I discuss how varied social actors participating in mediated labor activism form what I call pluralistic counterpublics.

PLURALISTIC COUNTERPUBLICS IN MEDIATED LABOR ACTIVISM

Participants in mediated labor activism come from a diverse range of social groups and backgrounds. Despite their varied social statuses, they all recognize how urban middle-class consumer culture and media in tandem with government policy and political economy cause the exclusion of rural migrant workers from the dominant public sphere. Such recognitions lay out a foundation for the formation of what Robert Asen defines as "counterpublics."[29] A counterpublic is defined by its participants' recognition of the exclusionary nature of dominant publics and their goal of articulating alternatives to engage wider publics.[30] To clarify just what the *counter* in "counterpublics" means, Asen reminds us of the reductionist tendency in the counterpublics theory: "Proceeding not from exclusion but the recognition of exclusion situates counter as a constructed relationship. Foregrounding its construction offers some critical resistance against explicitly fixing or implicitly relying on particular persons, places, or topics as necessary markers of counter status."[31] In other words, people from subordinate groups do not belong to counterpublics by default; they do once they recognize or contest the exclusions. And those from privileged backgrounds may become part of counterpublics when they challenge the inequality embedded in the dominant public sphere. To characterize these counterpublics thus requires close examination of the participants and their discourse and practices in relation to the hegemonic power.

I categorize social actors and their participation into four types of counterpublics: (1) subaltern counterpublics, (2) proletariat counterpublics, (3) feminist counterpublics, and (4) nonresistant counterpublics. "Subaltern counterpublics," as defined by Nancy Fraser, refers to discursive arenas for marginalized and disadvantaged groups, such as women, workers, racial minorities, and LGBT people, who face inequalities, oppression, and exclusion to claim power.[32] Drawing upon Fraser's concept, I see subaltern counterpublics in the context of mediated labor activism as collectives of social actors who both recognize migrant workers' exclusion and participate in discourses and practices that challenge that subordination. Alexander Kluge and Oskar Negt pioneered the framework of counterpublic and proletarian public spheres as a critical response to Jürgen Habermas's bourgeois public sphere, which to them excludes the interests and voices of working-class people.[33] Kluge and Negt contend that the goals of the proletarian public sphere are to develop counterideas, counterlanguages, and counterpublicity to cultivate collective awareness about labor exploitation and oppression and inspire collective action for liberation and emancipation.[34] In the context of mediated labor activism, proletarian counterpublics arise from the type of participation that produces distinctive working-class counterlanguages and counterpractices. Rita Felski elaborates on a feminist public sphere in which women can express gender-specific concerns, share experiences of gender subordination, and develop a collective feminist consciousness and solidarity.[35] Within the realm of mediated labor activism, feminist counterpublics refer to forms of participation that embrace feminist discourse and agendas. In line with Wang Jing's view of characterizing NGOs' service provisions as "non-resistant activism," I define nonresistant counterpublics as participation in NGOs' activities and events with a recognition of migrant workers' exclusion but without an adoption of alternative political discourses and practices.

The coexistence of the four types of counterpublics constitutes what I call pluralistic counterpublics in mediated labor activism. I use the term "pluralistic counterpublics" to recognize the diversity of perspectives and practices of social actors who participate in labor activism and NGOs' services based on a common understanding of the inequality migrant workers face. These four categories of counterpublics cannot be reduced to the identity of the social-actor participants. Having a privileged social status does not exclude participants from forming counterpublics, and meanwhile, having a disadvantaged position does not necessarily make participants part of the counterpublics. It is the participants' actual discourse and practices that determine their relationship to specific kinds of counterpublics. The difference between subaltern and proletarian counterpublics depends on whether there are clearly articulated discourses and practices against labor exploitation and the domination of capital inherent in capitalist systems—in the case of proletarian counterpublics, there are. The distinctiveness of feminist counterpublics lies in their specific focus on feminist agendas and intersectional approaches to challenging interconnected forms of oppression and multiple forms of discrimination. These features set them apart and highlight their unique contributions within the broader labor activism landscape.

Examples of the formation of subaltern counterpublics can be seen in female migrant domestic workers' participation in Didinghua Theater at the Migrant Women's Club, migrant-worker participation in the Migrant Workers' Home's collective cultural production, the practices of migrant workers, women, and people with disabilities who attend Jiu Ye's workshops and live shows, and workers and working-class sexual minorities writing and publishing stories and essays through Jianjiao buluo. Dominant public spheres exclude or silence these subordinate groups, leading to a lack of representation and a perpetuation of power imbalances. By sharing their stories, these people challenge prevailing narratives that may overlook or misrepresent their experiences. By occupying alternative spaces where their voices can be heard, recognized, and validated, they engage in dialogue, advocacy, and activism to break down stereotypes and misconceptions, fostering a more nuanced understanding of their realities. In an illuminating study on migrant workers' engagement with a wide range of mainstream and alternative media and culture, Sun Wanning argues that migrant workers' oppositional stance and defiance are rooted in their subaltern consciousness rather than class consciousness.[36] Subaltern consciousness is formed in subordinate groups' relationship to the elites.[37] While class consciousness and feminist consciousness often entail mobilizing efforts, subaltern consciousness arises from migrant workers' everyday encounters of marginalization and social exclusion in urban life. It is the subaltern consciousness that drives migrant workers to participate in varied forms of mediated labor activism in the first place.

What differentiates proletariat counterpublics from subaltern counterpublics is the clear demonstration of class consciousness, the occupation of a working-class standpoint, and the development of anticapitalist ideas and discourses. Proletariat counterpublics are formed by a diverse range of individuals who are actively engaged in labor activism with a shared goal of critiquing, resisting, and eventually overthrowing capitalism and neoliberalism. As discussed in chapter 3, activists, migrant workers, student volunteers, and scholars who actively participate in MWH's labor activism and form ideological allies are key examples of participants in proletariat counterpublics. They come together to challenge the exploitative nature of the capitalist system and advocate for social and economic justice for the working class. Through their activism, proletariat counterpublics aim to raise awareness, mobilize support, and push for systemic changes that address the concerns and rights of the working class.

Feminist activists play a crucial role in forming feminist counterpublics within the realm of mediated labor activism. By exposing and then opposing intersecting forms of oppression based on gender, class, sexuality, and ability, the feminist activists of Jiu Ye and Jianjiao buluo create inclusive spaces for women, migrant workers, working-class sexual minorities, and people with disabilities to develop an intersectional feminist consciousness, counterdiscourses, and practices. In these spaces, enabled by advocacy music, shows, and performance, online writing and publishing, and group deliberations, individuals acquire a more comprehensive understanding of intertwined inequalities. These spaces encourage reflexivity, collaboration, and collective effort needed to challenge and dismantle multiple and interconnected systems of oppression.

Nonresistant counterpublics are mainly formed by participants who have been driven by moral imperatives to join in providing services or taking part in activism. Discourses of inequality and social justice are not often used among these participants, and therefore class consciousness is not a motivating factor for them. They tend to see their participation as "doing the right thing." Here, rightness assumes an ostensibly "apolitical" moral guise—the show of empathy and/or sympathy toward subaltern people—rather than a political endeavor to resist inequality and injustice. Moral motivations are attached to a humanitarian value of "being a good and noble man," a Confucian morality widely promoted in China's official discourse as part of moral education.[38] For instance, Lu, a new staff member at MWH, said in conversation, "I joined the organization because I believe they are doing good things, and I want to be part of it. We need to help migrant workers."

Previously, Lu had worked at a state-owned coal mine for over twenty years in a small city in Shandong Province. In 2014, Lu happened to attend a local performance that the New-Worker Troupe held in a town in Shandong and learned about MWH's service and activism. He became acquainted with a key member of the Troupe and was considering joining them. Lu's twenty-year working experience as a mine worker and his musical talents made him an ideal new member. The Troupe welcomed him warmly. But nonetheless, quitting his job and joining MWH was not an easy decision for Lu as it meant leaving his wife and daughter, living alone in Beijing, and starting a completely new career. The motivation to "do some good things," in Lu's own words, finally drove him to make the decision. In 2015, Lu quit his job, went to Beijing, and became a staff member at MWH and a singer of the Troupe.

Lu's understanding of NGOs' service and activism as "doing good things" is common among other social-actor participants. Zhensheng, a journalist who has reported on MWC and its advocacy work, said that she is sympathetic toward domestic workers and finds it very unfair that they often face bias and disrespect. After graduating from college, Zhensheng started working for a news-media outlet run by a municipal government, reporting on social issues and the lives of members of marginalized groups. By the time I interviewed her, she had already left the media, due to the shrinking institutional support for journalists to report social-issue stories. Zhensheng was unambiguous in her support of MWC: "I think the advocacy work at the Migrant Women's Club is very important and much needed in our society, for nowadays people look down upon the poor and have little respect or mercy toward the disadvantaged. Most people only care about making money. This is very problematic, and we should change people's views."

The emphasis on an apolitical morality, particularly evident in the popular conception of viewing NGOs' work as *gong yi* (公益), which literally translates to "public interests and charity," has characterized the formation of nonresistant counterpublics among participants whose discourse and practice do not explicitly contest established power relations. Since the economic reform, the government, recognizing the need for social-support structures beyond the state, has begun to encourage and regulate charitable activities. *Gong yi* gained prominence in the 1990s and 2000s as China experienced rapid economic growth and urbanization. The emergence of a more affluent middle class, along with an increasing awareness of social issues, contributed to the growth of philanthropy and charitable activities. With its connotations of philanthropic principles, *gong yi* has become a depoliticized concept that is invoked to acknowledge the good will of the givers without suggesting that those charitable acts pose any challenge to the status quo. Large corporations, domestic and transnational, have become a major force in initiating *gong yi* projects, largely to meet their corporate social-responsibility requirements. These projects are mainly charitable in that they rely on donations and purchases from the wealthy and the middle class to help the poor and underprivileged people.

Both MWC and MWH have adopted the discourse of *gong yi* to describe some of their services, such as collecting donations of clothes from urban dwellers and offering free technology classes for middle-aged rural migrants. There is a clear distinction constructed in the moral discourse of *gong yi* between the status of "helping" and that of "being helped." Participants believe that they are assisting migrant workers who are underprivileged people in need of help. Liu has been a volunteer lawyer offering legal consultations to migrant workers at MWC for several years. Growing up in a rural village herself, Liu is very concerned about migrant workers' well-being. She said, "Though I became a lawyer, I feel I am still part of them [rural people], and I want to do something with my knowledge to help them." Ke was a corporate-employee volunteer for MWC for several years, and he was responsible for a charitable program for a transnational company. The program collaborated with MWC to offer free training classes to migrant workers to use smartphones. During an eight-week training period, every Sunday or Saturday, Ke and his colleagues taught a group of middle-aged female migrants how to use maps, buy train tickets, and search the web through their smartphones. Ke referred to these female migrants as "old sisters" and said he really enjoyed this volunteer work and felt very fulfilled when he received thanks from these old sisters for his help. To "help" those who "need help" is driven by a recognition of migrant workers' subordination, but the discourse and practices of "help" do not necessarily aim to resist the structural power and values that sustain and normalize the subordination.

POLITICS OF PARTICIPATION AMONG MIGRANT
WORKERS IN LABOR ACTIVISM

Migrant-worker participants, who are driven by social and cultural needs to join labor NGOs, are a main component of nonresistant counterpublics. Socializing was the primary focus of migrant worker activities at MWC in the 1990s. In the early days, migrant workers came to

Beijing without families and friends; meeting people, especially other migrant workers, and making friends were important ways to cope with the loneliness, severe social exclusion, bias, and prejudice they experienced in the city. After staying in the city for years, migrant workers gradually develop their own social networks and become less motivated to participate in NGOs for social purposes. But for domestic workers, socialization is still a key factor in their participation. These domestic workers are mostly female migrants who have come to Beijing for the first time, and they face an isolated existence similar to that of the migrant workers in the 1990s. The majority are live-in maids who have hardly any private space or social life when living with employer families. MWC is one of the few places where domestic workers can spend their leisure time.

When I first met some domestic-worker participants at MWC in 2016, they expressed a strong sense of belonging to the NGO. One worker told me on our way to the subway station after MWC's activities on a Saturday, "Living in with my employer's family, I feel myself a stranger and need to be cautious all the time, but here [at MWC], I am relaxed and comfortable, and we are like a family." Others have told similar stories. Many of the workers need to take a bus for more than an hour to go to MWC, but this inconvenience does not stop them from going. Another worker explained to me, "I don't mind the long distance because I really enjoy staying here [at MWC]. I am always counting the days until I can come [to MWC] and have fun on Saturdays. Even if I do not usually participate in any formal activities, just sitting there and chatting with sisters [other female workers] makes me joyful."

At MWC, in addition to the main program of performance, discussed in chapter 2, middle-aged female migrants do dance and fashion shows over the weekend. A staff member proposed the idea of fashion shows and explained that it aims to improve female migrants' self-confidence and has turned out to be an effective way to do so. One participant, a fifty-year-old domestic worker, told me, "I don't have opportunities to wear beautiful clothes and make-up when I am working in my employers' house on weekdays, but what woman doesn't love dressing up? So I really enjoy doing fashion shows with my sisters [other female workers] here [at the Migrant Women's Club]." Dancing and fashion shows are well received as forms of activity among female migrant participants.

These activities enable broader and easier participation since they demand less skill and preparation than musical or theatrical performance.

MWH has also served as a community space for migrant workers to spend their downtime in the evenings and on weekends. During my visits to MWH in Picun, I observed workers coming to borrow books, attend galas for holidays, watch films, or just gather in small groups to chat. Workers and their children borrow books from MWH's library and watch outdoor movies that MWH shows in their office yard on summer weekends. The movies are mostly commercial ones for entertainment. On holidays, MWH organizes galas in which staff members and migrant workers perform various shows. Often, several hundred community residents attend as audiences. Lei, a thirty-eight-year-old migrant worker who was a regular participant in MWH's activities, said, "We workers also need spiritual [and cultural] life, but it is too expensive to do these activities [such as going to movie theaters and attending concerts] in cities." Lei worked in a furniture factory near Picun, and he had lived in Beijing for almost ten years. Like many other middle-aged migrant workers, Lei has worked in different industries and at various kinds of workplaces, such as factories, restaurants, and manual workshops. MWH's various cultural activities motivated Lei to live in Picun, where he rents a small room.

Wei, a forty-three-year-old migrant worker, moved to Picun where he encountered MWH in 2014. Initially, Wei was attracted to the NGO's free library, though he gradually became a regular participant in various activities. By the time I met Wei at the NGO in May 2016, he had become one of its most active participants. Wei told me that it was the feeling of equality and respect at the organization that appealed to him most. Staff members, some of whom are migrant workers themselves, maintain close relationships with migrant-worker participants. The mutual support and trust among migrant workers at the NGO made Wei feel at home, especially since he found that it was often hard to develop trust and friendship with his migrant-worker colleagues at his place of work.

The social activities and cultural services at labor NGOs hold greater appeal for first-generation rural migrants than for the younger ones. Though younger migrants are also exploited as cheap laborers, they have lighter economic burdens and more financial freedom compared to their parents' generation; due in part to their relative economic stability, the younger generation feels more affinity with urban life and consumer culture. In contemporary China, middle-class consumer culture dominates urban cultural life; going to theaters, coffee shops, trendy restaurants, and shopping malls are key markers of an urban middle-class lifestyle. Such a lifestyle is usually not appealing to first-generation migrant workers, nor is it affordable to those who need to provide financial support for their families. Comparatively, the younger migrants are much more integrated into urban consumer life, and they do not carry the same economic burden of supporting families. The younger generation of migrant workers can be more "individualist, consumeristic, and prone to seduction."[39] When the first-generation migrant workers entered cities in the 1980s and 1990s, urban exclusion was severe and there was little public space for these workers to spend leisure time. Since the late 1990s, as China accelerated market reforms, much more commercialized space has been developed.

In my conversations with several young migrant workers who work in beauty and hair salons, they revealed that they spent most of their leisure time on the internet. Like their urban counterparts, these young workers also hang out with friends in commercial spaces, going to movie theaters and having meals in restaurants. Xiaodan, a twenty-two-year-old female migrant worker, disclosed, "I just do what others do, otherwise, what else can I do for fun? I like to shop on Taobao [China's largest retailer website], but I don't have much money, so I just lurk online or watch dramas and videos. Nor do I go out to eat very often." Xiaodan came from a rural town in Sichuan Province. She attended a professional beauty school after graduating from high school. As a second-generation migrant, Xiaodan has a much lower economic burden than her parents did. She said she was not good at studying and had little chance to pass the national entry exams for college, so her family decided to let her learn some professional skills. "Factory work is too grueling," she said. "Doing beauty work is a better fit for us girls." But even if the working environment in a beauty salon is much better than that in a factory, the workload is not much lighter: Xiaodan often has to work more than ten hours per day and does not get holiday breaks.

Xiaodan is typical of second-generation migrant workers, who are employed in the service industry and are burdened with heavy work-loads. In cities with few factories, younger migrants often work in low-end service sectors, such as waiting tables in restaurants or working in beauty or hair salons. They find housing in widely dispersed areas of the city and therefore cannot assume they will be able to enjoy proxim-ity to their fellow workers. Their busy work schedules leave them few rest days. Xiaotian is a nineteen-year-old male migrant worker from a rural village in Hebei Province, near Beijing. His story is very similar to Xiaodan's. Ruling out factory work as too dirty and tedious, Xiaotian went to work at a hair salon in Beijing. When I asked about his work and leisure time, he complained, "I have to work till midnight every day and don't have regular rest days. During holidays, when there are usually many more customers coming to have their hair done, we are even busier. We have to work from early morning to late at night and stand all day. On busy days, we don't even have time for meals. I just want to lie in bed when I don't need to work. I'm already so exhausted. I don't want to go anywhere." Second-generation migrant workers are habituated to urban consumer spaces, but they are also typically too exhausted by their work schedules to be motivated to socialize much in their downtime. And so the social and cultural services and activities at labor NGOs are not as appealing to them as to older migrant workers.

Differing from earlier scholarly observations that origins of place play a vital role in the formation of migrant workers' social networks, identification with NGOs as members of a community becomes prom-inent in forming social bonds among migrant workers spanning both generations.[40] For instance, female migrant domestic workers strongly identify with MWC and its current advocacy mission of domestic work-ers' rights. When they participate in MWC's activities in public spaces, they often proudly introduce themselves as members of the NGO. Tamara Jacka's study of MWC in the 1990s reveals that, at that time, the NGO created a subjective position of *dagongmei* (打工妹; young female migrant workers) for female migrants and focused on improving their *suzhi* through self-development, but many female migrant members were dissatisfied with the judgmental discourse that saw them as lack-ing *suzhi*.[41] My analysis shows that female migrant participants started to embrace an organizational identity as the NGO shifted from being a mere service provider to an advocacy force.

Migrant-worker participants at MWH are also closely bonded through their identification with the organization. The membership is more like a community than an organization. Whereas organizational membership tends to be a professional relationship driven by shared goals, a feeling of community constitutes social inclusion and belonging among migrant workers themselves. Migrant workers at MWH hold a variety of jobs, including working as contract workers at small factories, self-employed carpenters, and domestic workers, among others. These workers develop a strong sense of solidarity through frequent participation in MWH's social/cultural and activist activities. Staff members of NGOs serve as key coordinators, maintaining close relationships and connections with migrant-worker participants. Some early female migrant participants at MWC in the 1990s still retain connections with MWC staff from that time. Many migrant-worker participants at the two NGOs told me that some staff members are kind and attentive to them, and their close relationships with staff constitute one of their primary motivations for attending NGO activities.

The form and nature of migrant workers' participation at labor NGOs are not static and may change over time. While many workers are initially attracted to NGOs because of their activities and services, they may develop a stronger interest in social-justice advocacy and activism later on. In other words, workers can move across the boundaries of different types of counterpublics as they develop a new consciousness, embrace new discourses, and adopt new practices over the course of their participation in NGOs' activities, interaction with other workers, and comprehension of systemic issues. Workers join subaltern counterpublics when they resist their subordination and social exclusion through performance, writing, and deliberations. As workers develop an understanding of their shared experiences of exploitation and oppression under capitalism, they become a significant component of proletariat counterpublics, defined by a cultivated class consciousness and a commitment to collective actions. Workers' engagement with Jiu Ye and Jianjiao buluo's feminist labor activism makes them part of feminist counterpublics, which strengthens their awareness of the intersecting forms of subordination they face.

Wei's experiences and participation at MWH is such an example. Although his initial interest was simply borrowing books from the library as part of MWH's cultural service, he progressively began participating in more activities ranging from literature groups to Worker University. Eventually, he became a consistent contributor, publishing stories about migrant workers and critiquing labor exploitation and capitalism in the Picun community newspaper and Jianjiao buluo. Wei expressed the evolution of his thoughts, stating, "Initially, I was frustrated and angered by the circumstances of rural migrant workers. However, at MHW, through participating in classes and engaging in discussions with fellow workers, we cultivated a robust working-class consciousness and gained the language to critique capitalist exploitation. We also aspire to take action and bring about change. I believe in the power of writing. The more we write about our experiences, the greater awareness we can generate about inequalities." Wei's transformation is a common occurrence among migrant-worker participants, who shift from being part of the subaltern counterpublics to embracing proletarian counterpublics, characterized by a strong sense of class consciousness.

Some migrant-worker writers and readers of Jianjiao buluo also exhibit an evolving mode of participation time. One female migrant worker, Nuo, shared that she initially perceived Jianjiao as merely an online media platform for female migrants. She enjoyed reading articles published on Jianjiao and occasionally wrote her own pieces, submitting them to the platform. She particularly appreciated articles that analyzed how the intersection of gender and class influences the lives of rural and migrant women. Nuo remarked, "It is through reading these articles that I developed a feminist consciousness and became acquainted with the term 'patriarchy.' I started to reflect on and question all my past experiences with gender inequality: the disparate treatment from my parents toward me compared to my younger brothers and the harassment I faced in factories and restaurants where I've worked. It is all because I am a woman from a poor rural family." The transition from subaltern counterpublics to feminist counterpublics is an enlightening process.

An NGO's activist agenda is particularly important for engaging the younger generation of migrant workers. Young migrant workers may not be attracted to the services or social and cultural activities an NGO offers, but they can be in fact more interested in activist events and practices. For instance, the anticapitalist and anti-neoliberal agenda of MWH's mediated labor activism has mobilized many young migrant workers, along with the older generation, to participate in the collective working-class cultural production. The vision of a genuine socialist China resonates with young migrant workers who wish for an equitable future and motivates them to join the collective resistance to work toward achieving this vision. As twenty-seven-year-old male worker Xiaohe, an active member of MWH, said, "Our fellow workers are protesting labor exploitation and capital in factories in the South [of China], and we are resisting capitalist, neoliberal, and consumerist ideologies and discourses by telling our own stories and envisioning our own future. We are fighting together, though in different places and in different ways." Generational differences can be overcome when migrant workers develop a sense of solidarity among workers in the process of participating in activism.

Beyond their examples of how generational differences can be transcended, the cases of Jiu Ye and Jianjiao buluo make it evident that an inclusive and intersectional activist agenda can foster a sense of solidarity among migrant workers and other marginalized and underprivileged groups, transcending differences of gender, sexuality, place of origins, and other power dynamics. Working together on activism projects, these people realize that they are all fighting against common systems of oppression. Consciousness-raising happens concurrently with the process of politicization and mobilization as workers navigate various forms of counterpublics. The acknowledgment of interlocking systems of oppression allows for a more nuanced analysis of power dynamics and helps to bridge gaps between different subordinate groups. The solidarity is based on shared struggles and the understanding that their liberation is interconnected.

BUILDING COALITIONS AND NETWORKS

In the sphere of grassroots labor activism in China, coalitions have formed among a range of nonprofit and nongovernmental organizations, individuals, and social groups. As two pioneering and influential migrant-worker NGOs, MWC and MWH have formed alliances with both well-established and grassroots foundations, local and international NGOs, activists, and advocacy groups. International charities and foundations, such as Oxfam and the Ford Foundation, have remained the main sources of funding for Chinese NGOs over the past three decades. Both MWC and MWH have received financial support from Oxfam. The passing of the Overseas Foreign NGOs Law in 2017 caused a sharp reduction in NGOs' funding: a staff member of MWC revealed that all of Oxfam's funding for the organization's rural programs was cut off as a result of the new law. MWC and MWH maintain connections and communication with NGOs, activists, and advocacy groups in mainland China, Hongkong, Taiwan, and foreign countries. They pay visits to other NGOs and host visits from other NGOs, individual activists, and groups, organizing workshops and cultural and social events. For example, during 2016 and 2017, staff members and female migrant participants from MWC visited two local domestic-worker NGOs in Xi'an and Jinan. MWH frequently organizes events with other local grassroots labor NGOs and activist groups.

As discussed in chapter 4, Jiu Ye, as a working-class feminist activist group, also maintains close connections and collaborations with varied NGOs, institutions, and advocacy groups for labor rights, women's rights, and disability rights. These collaborations foster the formation of transnational and translocal networks, through which knowledge and resources are shared. Migrant workers actively navigate the landscape of these coalitions and proactively participate in coordinated activities and events. For instance, after attending live shows co-organized by MWH and Jiu Ye, some members and participants of MWH developed interest in Jiu Ye's activist agendas, and they started to participate in Jiu Ye's advocacy workshops. Domestic workers in MWC's Didinghua Theater performed with workers from MWH in the events co-organized by the two organizations. Participants at MWH regularly publish their articles at Jianjiao buluo to reach a broader community of migrant workers.

China's government can play a role beyond that of a regulatory or repressive force in its relationship with migrant-worker NGOs. Perspectives that are critical of labor NGOs that cultivate relationships with the state do not take into account the multiple layers of these relationships.[42] It is true that NGOs can face severe surveillance and regulation from the state, but maintaining a good relationship with the government can bring labor NGOs benefits in terms of resources, support, and legitimacy.[43] A credible public image is particularly important for migrant-worker NGOs, as some scholars observe that Chinese migrant workers often do not trust labor NGOs and their "free services."[44] In the 1990s, MWC collaborated with local women's federations and the labor department of the local government to successfully reach out to migrant workers and provide them with services. When it lacked public recognition and credibility in its early days, MWC's collaboration with a municipal government and its first leader's background in governmental work helped build migrant workers' trust in the organization.

Organizing events in a government-sponsored space can grant NGOs symbolic legitimacy, making them appealing to migrant-worker participants and attracting public attention. For instance, MWH held one of its early *dagong* spring galas at Chaoyang Cultural Center (Chaoyang wenhua zhongxin; 朝阳文化中心), a municipal governmental space. This type of collaboration helped the grassroots cultural event enhance its influence among both migrant workers and the general public. MWH has been given an award by Beijing City Hall as "Beijing top 10 volunteer groups" (Beijing shida zhiyuan tuanti; 北京十大志愿者团体) in 2005, and the New-Worker Troupe received the honor of National Advanced Group to Serve Farmers and Promote Grassroots Culture (Quanguo fuwu nongmin fuwu jiceng wenhua gongzuo xinajin jiti; 全国服务农民服务基层文化工作先进集体) from China's Ministry of Culture in the same year.[45] Sun Heng, MWH's founder, has received several honorary titles from the government. Anthony J. Spires developed the concept of "contingent symbiosis" to characterize this type of relationship in which there is a mutual need between the government and NGOs: while the government may take credit for the work NGOs do, such as providing services to underprivileged groups, NGOs nevertheless need support and resources from the government.[46]

Chinese NGOs often make allies with particular government officials.[47] MWC and MWH have adopted this strategy. Key NGO staff members and government officials serve indispensable roles in maintaining the relationship between the two entities. When MWC was founded by Xie Lihua in 1996, Xie's status as a retired senior government staff member and connections with the government provided crucial resources and support for the organization's establishment and development. A municipal governmental official provided tremendous support to MWC and MWH during Xie's term of office. Even though the leaders and staff members of MWH did not have the same privileged background as Xie, they received substantial support from MWC when the organization was founded in the early 2000s. As they emerged as the top two prominent NGOs for migrant workers in Beijing, the two organizations maintained strong connections, which eased the sharing of resources. Staff members from both NGOs recalled that the local official was very concerned about migrant workers' issues and generously supported the two NGOs' events and activities.

Despite the conditional support NGOs may receive from the state, it should be noted that the power relationship between the government and NGOs remains extremely unequal. Not only do NGOs face a constant threat of repression (as can be seen in the crackdown of Jianjiao buluo), but the recent shift in the central state's attitude toward NGOs has created growing tensions between municipal governments and NGOs. MWH's being forced to leave its facilities in Picun is a recent example: On a freezing and gloomy afternoon in December 2016, about fifty officials entered one of the two Migrant Workers' Home's quarters, where its staff lived, and smashed the winter-heating boilers. The group of fifty was drawn from the police, urban-management department, fire department, bureau of trade, township government, and the village committee of Picun. They destroyed the boilers in the name of preventing potential security risks, but no prior notice or contact had been made with MWH. Two months earlier, officials of Picun Village demanded that MWH move out without giving any specific reason. Since the organization held a legal lease with the landlord, they refused to do so. One day, their two premises suddenly had all their power cut off. More than twenty staff members made do without electricity for two months afterward. The situation got very tense after the government raid that destroyed MWH's boilers. The average temperature of winter in Beijing is around minus ten degrees Celsius, and it would be extremely hard to live without heating.

In this moment of crisis, the networks and coalitions that MWH had established and maintained became crucial not only to the well-being of the organization but to the very survival of its staff and worker participants. MWH announced a call for fundraising through its WeChat public accounts. The call described the incident and itemized the financial aid the organization needed to buy thirty sets of insulated quilts and a large diesel generator. The fundraising post received over ten thousand page views and quickly attracted wide attention.[48] It was widely shared across social media platforms. Several mainstream-media outlets reported the story. Well-known scholars, migrant workers, NGOs, activists, and members of the public expressed their support for MWH by writing and sharing articles and commentaries through social media platforms. Although the voices and discourses deployed in the articles varied in that some were centrist while others were radically left-wing and interpretations of the events were also shaped by different perspectives, this reportage did direct public attention toward MWH's difficult situation and led to further discussions in some news-media outlets and social media among concerned publics on social equality and underprivileged groups.

By the end of December, MWH had raised $10,000 from crowdfunding which enabled them to purchase a diesel generator for electric heating. On January 2, the power supply for MWH was restored after seventy-eight days of power outage. MWH's crisis reveals the persistently precarious conditions of labor NGOs in China. On the other hand, the organization's survival demonstrates that symbolic power accumulated through the building of sustained coalitions and networks can have concrete results. The support and actions that were mobilized within a rather short period of time should be attributed to the influence and credibility that MWH has gained through its decades-long efforts in labor activism.

The ordeal MWH experienced in late 2016 also shows how ICTs have gradually become a vital component of participation and network formation in labor activism in the past decade and a half. Virtual access is a critical counterpart to in-person participation, which is often constrained by distance and time availability. The increasing use of smartphones among migrant workers provides them access to technology that then enables greater participation in NGOs and activism efforts. In the early 2000s, QQ was the most popular internet-communication tool among migrant workers.[49] In recent years, WeChat has become the main social media network used by migrant workers. It has also become a prominent communicative platform for labor NGOs and advocacy groups. Jianjiao primarily relies on WeChat as an online platform. Staff members of MWH and MWC have also established several chat groups on WeChat. Each organization has one main chat group with around three hundred to four hundred people, and these people include participants from the different social groups discussed above.

In the main MWH chat group, daily discussions usually focus on social and political issues, such as government policies and labor exploitation. There has often been harsh criticism toward China's embrace of capitalism. MWC's main chat group focuses more on information sharing and social networking. Job-recruitment information is often shared among domestic-worker participants. In the group, female migrants chat with friends from MWC about their lives. MWH and MWC also set up separate chat groups for their different programs. There are usually dozens of participants in the programs, including staff members, migrant workers, scholars, volunteers, and some visitors who have attended past organization events. The use of social media facilitates communication and interaction among participants. For those who do not live in Beijing or cannot attend NGO activities regularly, online chat groups are a means of remaining connected to the NGOs and other participants.

Digital media are undoubtedly beneficial to labor activism in China, but we should not fall into a technological determinism that views ICTs as the decisive factor in mobilizing resistance. Online labor activism through the internet and social media is built upon existing offline alliances and advocacy efforts to cultivate collective awareness, identities, and networks among migrant workers and other social actors. To demystify the transformative potential of technologies, Nick Couldry reminds us that technologies in themselves cannot guarantee that people's voices will be valued.[50] Similarly, Jo Tacchi suggests that there should be a decentering of ICTs in order to deconstruct the functionalist interpretation of ICTs and to locate their impact in larger social, cultural, economic, and political processes.[51] In the course of daily labor activism, ICTs do provide opportunities for migrant workers to amplify their voices and document their lives and experiences, but making those voices heard and matter to other workers and the general public requires much more work than the mere adoption of technologies. It is imperative to integrate online activism into sustaining efforts of offline mobilizing, organizing, and networking.

CONCLUSION

Mediated labor activism has become a significant component of contentious actions contesting different forms of power domination and inequalities in contemporary China. Labor NGOs are a main actor facilitating mediated labor activism, and their survival is mainly subject to the political tolerance of the state, which is constantly changing and unpredictable. Although labor NGOs continuously navigate and adapt to changing political dynamics, the extreme power imbalance between labor NGOs and the state renders their survival precarious and contingent. Chinese civil society has indeed gone through a rapid development and growth in the past four decades of reform, yet civil society in China is never fully independent of the state, which exercises control over civil society and civil society organizations through coercive means, including laws, policies, and police violence. Contestations and struggles do not take place in an independent public sphere outside the state's power; rather, they occur within the realm of ostensible containment and stabilization exerted by state power. These struggles challenge and push against the constraints imposed by the state, seeking to expand the space for dissent and alternative voices within the existing political framework.

The formation of pluralistic counterpublics among social actors complicates the conventional understanding of power dynamics as a simple binary between domination and resistance. It underscores the fluidity and contradictions of power relations in the sphere of mediated labor activism. Power relations in mediated labor activism are not fixed or predetermined. They are constantly negotiated, contested, and reconfigured by various social actors. Within these pluralistic counterpublics, different perspectives, interests, and strategies for labor activism coexist. This diversity can lead to inconsistencies and tensions among social actors, who may have different goals or visions for labor rights and social justice. Power dynamics can shift as a result of changes in government policies, economic factors, or shifts in public opinion. It thus requires continuing dialogues, negotiations, and coalition building among social actors within pluralistic counterpublics. The circumstances and perspectives of second-generation migrant-worker participants, as well as nonparticipants, reveal that the mobilization and organization efforts of labor NGOs and activists should focus more on activism, rather than merely providing services, in order to engage more workers.

The alliances and networks of mediated labor activism are built at both organizational and individual levels. At the organizational level, it is mostly civil society organizations that share and exchange experiences, resources, and expertise and coordinate advocacy efforts. Meanwhile, individual connections and collaborations are built between labor NGOs and activist groups and people from established institutions, such as governmental officials, scholars, and journalists, the concerned publics, and migrant workers. At the present stage of mediated labor activism, leading labor NGOs and activists are still playing pivotal roles in the process of facilitating and sustaining informal networks.

Within China's neoliberal era, the historical moment of the early twenty-first century presents a cluster of social factors that may in fact be conducive to the formation of a broader counterhegemonic movement. While NGOs must continue to work "within the system"—that is, within existing structures of discourse and action allowed by the state—their work makes possible the formation of coalitions across various social strata and markers of identity: rural and urban, blue- and white-collar, young and old, hetero and queer, female and male. Along with NGO efforts, the increasing centrality of ICTs in contemporary life has also enabled the formation of these various coalitions—these informal networks. ICTs sustain the offline activities, practices, and networks while also facilitating the establishment of new connections in the process of mediated labor activism. With the growth and consolidation of these networks, mediated labor activism can gain momentum, broaden its impact, and bring about concrete change in the realm of labor rights and social justice.

CONCLUSION

ANOTHER WORLD IS INDEED POSSIBLE

In a media-saturated world, media and communication technologies are sites of struggles—places where hegemonic powers seek to maintain their dominance but also places that provide opportunities for resistance and contestation. Mediated activism emerges as a critical domain where prevailing ideologies can be challenged and transformative social ideas can be formed and articulated. Mediated activism, therefore, represents a nexus where social ideas connect with social forces. It serves as a conduit for the amplification of dissenting voices, compelling narratives, and calls to action; it facilitates the organization of online and offline movements to transform social ideas into tangible forces that can challenge existing power structures.

Even in authoritarian contexts with ever-increasing political suppression, such as China, bottom-up interventions and changes can be realized and achieved: mediated activism can become a cornerstone of workers' collective resistance and a driving force with transformative potential in the landscape of labor activism. And therefore, mediated labor activism can become a long-term, collective, multifaceted form of working-class resistance. The preceding chapters have provided evidence of a new kind of activism emerging in contemporary China. This new activist agenda begins with but goes beyond merely addressing rural migrant workers' labor rights. Recognizing that the struggles of workers are deeply intertwined with broader systems of oppression and discrimination, some mediated labor activists have begun to incorporate intersectionality into their work.

The forms of mediated labor activism emerging in twenty-first-century China can help create new subjectivities. Participating in performance as a critique of the bias and discrimination against reproductive labor, domestic workers become resistive laboring subjects, working collectively to change their labor conditions and societal perceptions of their work. By participating in working-class cultural production, rural migrant workers spanning two generations develop their class consciousness, thereby forming a critique of capitalist exploitation and neoliberal ideologies and building a working-class community. Through advocacy music and online feminist media, intersectional feminist labor activism invites migrant workers, women, and other marginalized people to detach from the state-sanctioned version of socialism and instead create and embody an independent feminist subjectivity.

The particular power of various mediated-labor-activist practices lies in their ability to engage both the emotional and intellectual dimensions of social issues. Embodied and expressive practices such as theater, music, and creative writing promote understanding and solidarity across differences and foster a shared sense of humanity. Within these diverse media, cultural, and communicative practices, mediated labor activism has articulated a series of counterdiscourses to expose, criticize, and oppose dominant values and ideologies in contemporary China, including urban supremacy and discrimination against rural migrants, capitalist and neoliberal ideologies of free market doctrines and consumerism, heterosexual patriarchal power and norms, and institutional and informal practices of ableism. By occupying the physical and symbolic spaces of local communities, civil institutions, mainstream media, and social media, these counterdiscourses reshape or at least penetrate those spaces to reach more workers and a broader public. The enhanced presence and visibility of counterdiscourses transform spaces that previously excluded or marginalized rural migrant workers into spaces of contestations where struggles for recognition and rights occur.

Throughout this book, I have taken pains to show that the decentralized nature of mediated labor activism is in fact one of its key strengths. In contrast to labor movements that are often led by labor unions, mediated labor activism is mainly facilitated by labor NGOs, independent activists, and migrant workers. Its decentralized approach fosters collaboration, alliances, and networks among diverse social actors. Despite the varied motivations, discourses, and practices of participants, pluralistic counterpublics share a recognition of rural migrant workers' plight and a concern for their well-being. The distinctive characteristics of mediated labor activism in contemporary China are a result of the interplay between China's authoritarian political system and grassroots responses to it. Mediated activism serves as a way for workers, activists, and a range of social actors to work within the constraints of the existing political system toward a reform or even a transformation of that system.

THE DAUNTING FORCES PERSIST

Since the collapse of the Soviet Union, Marxism and socialism in Western countries either have occupied a marginal position in a continuum of political philosophies or have been rejected altogether as failed political systems. But in China, Marxism and socialism have remained fundamental to the party-state's ideological framework, and officially, China is still a communist state. From state socialism in Mao's era to "socialism with Chinese characteristics" in the economic-reform era, the Communist Party has consistently emphasized its commitment to these ideologies as a legitimizing force for its rule. While Marxism's critique of capitalist labor exploitation and socialism's ideals of equality have effectively mobilized rural migrant workers to join collective resistance in the form of mediated labor activism, these political ideas are paradoxically co-opted by the party-state to maintain its hegemonic power. Challenges to the authoritarian state face not only a response of political coercion but also the risk of conflating the socialist principles that inspire grassroots, bottom-up resistance with the state's distorted, propagandized version of socialism.

The emphasis on the importance of class struggle and the overthrow of capitalist systems instilled by Mao's regime provide a foundation for activists and protesters to advocate for social equality and justice, with a particular focus on workers' rights. Workers' collective resistance, from laid-off state workers' protests in the 1990s to migrant workers' labor activism in the twenty-first century, often deploys aspects of Maoist socialist discourse—such as the notion that proletariats are the masters of the country—to legitimize their actions. Mao's ideology centered the role of the state and regarded the party-state as the vanguard of the revolution and the protector of the interests of the working class. Such an ideology has shaped workers' ambivalent and even contradictory attitudes toward the party-state in the reforming era. On one hand, workers are not unaware of the state's discriminatory policies that make them susceptible to capitalist exploitation, and they also fully realize the state's suppression, harassment, and violence toward their varied forms of resistance. On the other hand, workers are still inclined to count on the party-state to combat the domination of capital.

The reliance on the party-state is divided into two types. The first type is strategic: workers hope to gain legitimacy for their resistance against capitalist exploitation and avoid confrontation with state power. The second type encompasses some genuine faith in the party-state's commitment to socialism and communism. Attitudes like these have a concrete impact on workers' acts of resistance. In their protests of labor exploitation and urban residents' prejudice and advocacy efforts for equal rights, many rural migrant workers regard the state as the main agent that can promote change, circumventing the state's authoritarianism and its complicity with transnational and domestic capital.

Rising nationalist and anti-Western sentiments are key among the sociopolitical conditions in China that prevent mediated labor activism from expanding into a broader, more impactful movement. Nationalism has surged in China over the past decade, driven by a series of state and popular discourses: the official and commercial media, through news, TV shows, and films, glorify the purportedly extraordinary civilization and history of China, celebrate the remarkable accomplishments of the country's economic reform, and salute the current-day leadership of the Communist Party. A cohesive narrative that emphasizes national pride and achievements has generated a strong sense of nationalism among vast portions of the Chinese populace. This nationalist narrative aims to secure Chinese citizens' loyalty to the party-state by positioning the state as the protector of their well-being, security, and interests.

Central to the party-state's official discourse of nationalism is a portrayal of Western ideas and culture as threats to Chinese culture, tradition, and social norms. And recent geopolitical tensions between China and the United States have only exacerbated the anti-Western sentiment, which the state then exploits to gain public support for its suppression of dissidents. When the state arrested feminist activists in 2015, permanently shut down all LGBTQ student organizations and their social media accounts in major universities in 2021, and forcefully crushed the street protests against COVID-19 lockdowns in December 2022, it claimed these measures would prevent Western influence and interference and maintain Chinese social stability.

The authoritarian state with its repressive political power remains the most daunting obstacle to mediated labor activism, preventing it from developing into a large-scale resistance movement. In addition to the party-state's program of propagating its distorted version of socialism and its hegemonic power of mainstream Chinese media, the Chinese government retaliates against social movements in more direct ways: by cracking down on labor actions and protests and surveilling and proscribing the work of some NGOs, the party-state creates an omnipresent atmosphere of fear and intimidation. In this atmosphere, workers, activists, and other social actors are compelled to constantly monitor and self-regulate their actions to avoid any potential confrontation with state power, and many may be discouraged from participating in activism and collective resistance. As one migrant worker reflected, "Compared with what we want to do, what we can do is so limited. After all, we can't march in Tiananmen Square." The image of "marching in Tiananmen Square" expresses not only the worker's conflicting sentiments but the contradictory meanings Chinese people attach to the 1989 protests: on one hand, a longing for the groundswell of political conviction that led to the heroic mass protests; on the other, a bitter recollection of the brutal violence with which the state responded to the protests, leading to deaths, arrests, and the forced exile of many individuals. The worker was not referring to limitations enforced by policies or laws but by the state's use of pervasive and often oblique intimidation tactics meant to discourage dissenting views before they can even develop into organized actions.

Mass commercialism has also been decisive in limiting or slowing the formation of a broader resistance movement. The dominant power of commercial culture remains intact in the majority of rural migrant workers' lives, shaping their media and cultural habitus. It is true that migrant workers across two generations are participating in mediated labor activism, but the number of participants is low relative to the large number of migrant workers in China. The top-down depoliticizing of contemporary Chinese culture has resulted in subdued political discourse and engagement among the public. Most people accept societal and economic disparities as a natural consequence of the country's path of economic development. Collective actions and values are replaced by a neoliberal ethos of individual competition and achievement. Under these circumstances, migrant workers, like their urban middle-class counterparts, have become more accustomed to engaging with commercialized media and culture. As I have noted in the preceding chapters, both generations of migrant workers prefer activities such as listening to popular music, watching blockbuster films, and engaging in online entertainment over spending time and effort to organize and plan resistance actions.

The question remains how to find ways to involve a greater number of workers in mediated labor activism, in its diverse forms. Material disparities between middle-class professionals and rural migrant workers impede the formation of a broader sense of solidarity. While a notable number of middle-class individuals, including scholars, journalists, and volunteers, have demonstrated their concern for the well-being of migrant workers and actively participate in mediated labor activism, a broader sense of solidarity is still in the process of development. For instance, in recent years, there has been a growing trend of online public discussions among middle-class professionals about labor exploitation and capital dominance in varied Chinese social media sites. These discussions have particularly centered on issues such as the prevalent practice of overtime work (referred to as "996," indicating working twelve hours per day, six days per week) in the information-technology (IT) industry and the difficulty of obtaining affordable housing in major metropolitan cities, like Beijing and Shanghai. But these public discussions are largely disconnected from critiques of the disenfranchisement and exploitation experienced by rural migrant workers. Portions of China's middle class have recognized their exploitation by capital, yet they remain ignorant of how the country's working class has been similarly, or more severely, exploited for far longer. After all, IT programmers earn salaries ten times greater than those of migrant workers.

Ironically, current-day China is a supposedly communist state in which the reality of class disparity has become almost totally obscured. But when we look at social-justice struggles around the globe, it becomes obvious that class still matters. It matters because material inequalities persist in contemporary societies in the face of rapid technological advancement and vast accumulation of wealth. Various financial crises, along with the precarity exposed and exacerbated by the global pandemic have broken down the promise of neoliberalism to bring prosperity to people's lives. From the Seattle World Trade Organization protests in 1999 and the Occupy movements in 2011 to Amazon warehouse workers establishing their first union in the United States in 2022, class struggles have been haunting world centers. In countries where neoliberalism has been incorporated into existing political and economic systems, workers organize to resist severe exploitation. Yet the centrality of class does not mean that resistance efforts should stick to an orthodox Marxist approach to liberation exclusively focused on class struggles. New waves of transnational feminist movements, racial-justice movements, and LGBTQ movements provide evidence of continuous collective efforts to combat other systems of oppression in addition to capital domination. The slogan "Another world is possible," proposed at the World Social Forum in 2001, is the sentiment that has been at the heart of this book. Another world is indeed possible, but there is a long journey ahead. Envisioning and building another world, one free from exploitation, domination, exclusion, and discrimination, necessitates forging deep connections between class struggles and other resistance movements.

EMBRACING DEMOCRATIC SOCIALIST AND FEMINIST AGENDAS

Part of my argument in this book has been that mediated labor activism holds a distinct potential to effect broad societal change within China, but my argument hinges on a crucial qualification: the transformative potential of mediated labor activism can only become true social transformation under certain conditions. It is imperative for Chinese activists to transcend the state-sanctioned discourse of socialism and embrace democratic socialist and feminist agendas. Democratic socialism depends on workers' democratic control over production and the overthrow of capitalist control of the means of production—these facets mark the difference between democratic socialism and social democracy, the latter of which, despite implementing a robust welfare state, maintains reliance on the capitalist mode of production.[1] Democratic socialism advocates for the democratization of the state and supports political pluralism, individual freedoms, and civil liberties, which distinguishes it from the state socialism in the former Soviet Union and Mao's China, where the authoritarian state exerted totalitarian control over political, economic, social, cultural, and personal spheres. The successful pursuit of democratic socialism will involve not only domestic changes but also a revival of international alliances, cooperation, and solidarity among workers. Transnational worker coalitions could overcome nationalist divisions and counteract the capitalist class's deliberate fragmentation of global working populations.

I remain convinced that if labor activism has a future, it must be a fundamentally intersectional future. By incorporating feminism, democratic socialism can create an integrated framework to undermine the deeply intertwined structures of capitalism, authoritarianism, patriarchy, heteronormativity, racial hierarchy, and ableism. A feminist democratic socialism is, paraphrasing bell hooks's words, a commitment to equality and justice for all.[2] This type of integrated framework advocates structural changes at both symbolic and material levels; it challenges free market doctrines, the ideology of authoritarianism, patriarchal and heterosexual norms, white supremacy, and discrimination against people with disabilities.

In her critique of disability politics, feminist scholar Rosemarie Garland-Thomson suggests that "social justice and equal access should be achieved by changing the shape of the world, not changing the shape of our bodies."[3] Put another way, we must recognize that inaccessible public spaces and unwelcoming environments create misfits, that existing social systems actively exclude people with disabilities. An embrace of intersectional democratic socialism involves dismantling the gendered and racial divisions of labor that have historically underpinned and sustained labor exploitation in capitalism. All workers, irrespective of their gender and race, should have equal access to democratic control over the means of production. As Black feminists assert in the "The Combahee River Collective Statement," "We realize that the liberation of all oppressed peoples necessitates the destruction of the political-economic systems of capitalism and imperialism as well as patriarchy. We are socialists because we believe that work must be organized for the collective benefit of those who do the work and create the products, and not for the profit of the bosses. Material resources must be equally distributed among those who create these resources. We are not convinced, however, that a socialist revolution that is not also a feminist and anti-racist revolution will guarantee our liberation."[4] I, too, believe that a true socialist revolution shall be a holistic transformation that addresses the root causes of all systemic forms of injustice.

An intersectional form of democratic socialism must also include the democratization of reproduction. Reproduction has persisted as a key domain where patriarchy exerts control over women's bodies and sexuality, while capitalism benefits from women's unpaid or underpaid reproductive labor.[5] Democratization of reproduction thus seeks two types of social change. First, it demands that everyone have the ability to make autonomous decisions about their reproductive lives through making reproductive rights, choices, and healthcare more accessible, inclusive, and equitable for all individuals regardless of factors such as gender, class, race, sexuality, or other forms of identity and through challenging existing inequalities and barriers that may limit certain groups' access to reproductive resources and healthcare. Second, it seeks to dismantle the notion that reproductive tasks are solely the responsibility of families or individuals, especially women, and promote a collective approach to caregiving and reproductive responsibilities, contributing to more equitable and supportive societies. It advocates gender equality to challenge traditional gender roles and expectations, emphasizing that both men and women can participate equally in caregiving and reproductive responsibilities.

The type of inclusive, intersectional framework I am describing has the potential to rally more extensive collaborations among agents of change. Though individuals are always subject to the historical conditions into which they're born, they possess the potential to reshape those conditions and become antagonist subjects. My book demonstrates that an effective social-change project starts with locating these antagonist subjects in specific conjunctures. By developing a nuanced and contextualized comprehension of the interplay among diverse and evolving forces at a particular historical juncture, we can gain valuable insights into the motivations, grievances, and aspirations that propel individuals toward antagonistic positions.[6] By recognizing and understanding the various motivations and aspirations of antagonist subjects, it is possible to construct more effective strategies for engaging with and mobilizing them in the pursuit of societal transformation.

Collective resistance arises when antagonist subjects unite to form social groups, organizations, and communities that can then cultivate and attract more antagonist subjects, extending beyond the confines of the initial group. Continuous expansion can ultimately enhance the scalability and durability of resistance movements as forces for social change at local, national, and transnational levels. The consistent efforts of rural migrant workers and diverse social actors engaged in mediated labor activism, despite fluctuations, stand out as a significant form of collective resistance within the unequal social structure of China. The present upswing in working-class resistance underscores the interconnectedness of class struggles and intersectional feminist activism. These connections leave us with hope for the ongoing development of counterhegemonic power, contributing to the pursuit of a more equal, just, and inclusive world.

Notes

Introduction

1. National Bureau of Statistics of China, *2022 Annual Report of Rural Migrant Workers*, April 2023, https://www.stats.gov.cn/sj/zxfb/202304/t2023042 7_1939124.html.

2. Chris King-chi Chan and Ngai Pun, "The Making of a New Working Class? A Study of Collective Actions of Migrant Workers in South China," *China Quarterly* 198 (June 2009): 287-303; Jenny Chan, "Jasic Workers Fight for Union Rights," *New Politics* 17, no. 2 (Winter 2019): 84-89; Jenny Chan and Mark Selden, "China's Rural Migrant Workers, the State, and Labor Politics," *Critical Asian Studies* 46, no. 4 (2014): 599-620; Taihui Guo, "Rights in Action: The Impact of Chinese Migrant Workers' Resistances on Citizenship Rights," *Journal of Chinese Political Science* 19 (2014): 421-34; Parry P. Leung, *Labor Activists and the New Working Class in China: Social Movements and Transformation* (New York: Palgrave Macmillan, 2015).

3. Jennifer Jihye Chun, "The Contested Politics of Gender and Irregular Employment: Revitalizing the South Korean Democratic Labour Movement," in *Labour and the Challenges of Globalization: What Prospects for Transnational Solidarity?*, ed. Andreas Bieler, Ingemar Lindberg, and Devan Pillay (London: Pluto, 2008), 23-42; Sara Duvisac, "Reconstituting the Industrial Worker: Precarity in the Indian Auto Sector," *Critical Sociology* 45, no. 4-5 (2019): 533-48.

4. Rachel K. Brickner and Meaghan Dalton, "Organizing Baristas in Halifax Cafes: Precarious Work and Gender and Class Identities in the Millennial Generation," *Critical Sociology* 45, no 4. (2019): 485-500.

5. J. Chan, "Jasic Workers."

6. Dan Clawson, *The Next Upsurge: Labor and the New Social Movements* (Ithaca, NY: Cornell University Press, 2003); Laurence Cox and Alf Gunvald Nilsen, *We Make Our Own History: Marxism and Social Movements in the Twilight of Neoliberalism* (London: Pluto, 2014); Ernesto Laclau and Chantal Mouffe, *Hegemony and Socialist Strategy: Towards a Radical Democratic Politics* (London: Verso Books, 2014); Peter Waterman, "Social-Movement Unionism: A New Union Model for a New World Order?" *Review* 16, no. 3 (Summer 1993): 245-78.

7. David Kerr, "Theater for Development," in *The Handbook of Development Communication and Social Change*, ed. Karin Gwinn Wilkins, Thomas Tufte, and Rafael Obregon (Malden, MA: Wiley Blackwell, 2014), 207-25.

8. Kate Winskell and Daniel Enger, "Storytelling for Social Change," in *The Handbook of Development Communication and Social Change*, ed. Karin Gwinn Wilkins, Thomas Tufte, and Rafael Obregon (Malden, MA: Wiley-Blackwell, 2014), 189-206.

9. Mark McLell, "Art as Activism in Japan: The Case of a Good-for-Nothing Kid and Her Pussy," in *The Routledge Companion to Media and Activism*, ed. Graham Meikle (London: Routledge, 2018), 162-70.

10. Ron Eyerman and Andrew Jamison, *Music and Social Movements: Mobilizing Traditions in the Twentieth Century* (Cambridge: Cambridge University Press, 1998); Rob Rosenthal and Richard Flacks, *Playing for Change: Music and Musicians in the Service of Social Movements* (New York: Routledge, 2011).

11. Lina Dencik and Peter Wilkin, *Worker Resistance and Media: Challenging Global Corporate Power in the 21st Century* (New York: Peter Lang, 2015).

12. Bart Cammaerts, Alice Mattoni, and Patrick McCurdy, introduction to *Mediation and Protest Movements*, ed. Bart Cammaerts, Alice Mattoni, and Patrick McCurdy (Bristol: Intellect, 2013), 5.

13. WeChat is one of the most popular social media platforms in China.

14. Cammaerts, Mattoni, and McCurdy, introduction; Donatella della Porta, "Bridging Research on Democracy, Social Movements and Communication," in *Mediation and Protest Movements*, ed. Bart Cammaerts, Alice Mattoni, and Patrick McCurdy (Bristol: Intellect, 2013), 21-39; Donatella della Porta and Elena Pavan, "The Nexus between Media, Communication and Social Movements: Looking Back and the Way Forward," in *The Routledge Companion to Media and Activism*, ed. Graham Meikle (London: Routledge, 2018), 29-37.

15. Todd Gitlin, *The Whole World Is Watching: Mass Media in the Making and Unmaking of the New Left* (Berkeley: University of California Press, 1980); Dieter Rucht, "The Quadruple 'A': Media Strategies of Protest Movements since the 1960s," in *Cyberprotest: New Media, Citizens, and Social Movements*, ed. Wim van de Donk et al. (London: Routledge, 2004), 25-48.

16. Stephen Coleman and Karen Ross, *The Media and the Public: "Them" and "Us" in Media Discourse* (Malden, MA: Wiley-Blackwell, 2010).

17. Rucht, "Quadruple 'A.'"

18. Coleman and Ross, *Media and the Public*.

19. Rucht, "Quadruple 'A.'"

20. Rucht, "Quadruple 'A'"; Anna Feigenbaum, "Can the Women's Peace Camp Be Televised? Challenging Mainstream Media Coverage of Greenham Common," in *The Routledge Companion to Media and Activism*, ed. Graham Meikle (London: Routledge, 2018), 47-56.

21. Coleman and Ross, *Media and the Public*; Rucht, "Quadruple 'A.'"

22. Diana Fu, *Mobilizing without the Masses: Control and Contention in China* (Cambridge: Cambridge University Press, 2018); Wanning Sun, "Inequality and Culture: A New Pathway to Understand Social Inequality," in *Unequal China: The Political Economy and Cultural Politics of Inequality*, ed. Wanning Sun and Yingjie Guo (New York: Routledge, 2013), 27-42.

23. Scholars have developed concepts of "alternative media" (Chris Atton), "citizens' media" (Clemencia Rodriguez), and "social movement media" (John D. H. Downing) to refer to this specific form of mediated activism. See Chris Atton, *Alternative Media* (Thousand Oaks: SAGE, 2002); Chris Atton, "Alternative Media," in *Encyclopedia of Social Movement Media*, ed. John D. H. Downing (Thousand Oaks: SAGE, 2011), 15-19; Chris Atton, "A Reassessment of the Alternative Press," *Media, Culture and Society* 21, no. 1 (1999): 51-76, https://doi.org/10.1177/016344399021001003; Clemencia Rodriguez, "Citizens' Media," in *Encyclopedia of Social Movement Media*, ed. John D. H. Downing (Thousand Oaks: SAGE, 2011), 98-102; Clemencia Rodriguez, "Civil Society and Citizens' Media: Peace Architects for the New Millennium," in *Redeveloping Communication for Social Change: Theory, Practice, and Power*, ed. Karin Gwinn Wilkins (Lanham, MD: Rowman and Littlefield, 2000), 147-62; John D. H. Downing, "Social Movement Media in the Process of Constructive Social Change," in *The Handbook of Development Communication and Social Change*, ed. Karin Gwinn Wilkins, Thomas Tufte, and Rafael Obregon (Malden, MA: Wiley-Blackwell, 2014), 331-50.

24. Chris Atton, *Routledge Companion to Alternative and Community Media* (New York: Routledge, 2015); Gabriele Hadl, "Alternative Media: Policy Issues," in *Encyclopedia of Social Movement Media*, ed. John D. H. Downing (Thousand Oaks: SAGE, 2011), 33-35; Martha Fuentes-Bautista and Gisela Gil-Egui, "Community Media and the Rearticulation of State-Civil Society Relations in Venezuela," *Communication, Culture and Critique* 4, no. 3 (2011): 250-74.

25. Bingchun Meng, *The Politics of Chinese Media: Consensus and Contestation* (New York: Palgrave Macmillan, 2018); Yuezhi Zhao, *Media, Market, and Democracy in China* (Urbana: University of Illinois Press, 1998); Yuezhi Zhao, "Neoliberal Strategies, Socialist Legacies: Communication and State Transformation in China," in *Global Communications: Toward a Transnational Political Economy*, ed. Paula Chakravartty and Yuezhi Zhao (Lanham, MD: Rowman and Littlefield, 2008) , 23-55.

26. Wanning Sun, "Indoctrination, Fetishization, and Compassion: Media Construction of the Migrant Women," in *On the Move: Women and Rural-to-*

Urban Migration in Contemporary China, ed. Arianne M. Gaetano and Tamara Jacka (New York: Columbia University Press, 2004), 109-30; Wanning Sun, *Subaltern China: Rural Migrants, Media and Cultural Practices* (London: Rowman and Littlefield, 2014).

27. Manuel Castells, *The Rise of the Network Society* (Hoboken, NJ: John Wiley and Sons, 1996); Manuel Castells, *Communication Power* (Oxford: Oxford University Press, 2009); Manuel Castells, *Networks of Outrage and Hope-Social Movements in the Internet Age* (Cambridge: Polity, 2012).

28. W. Lance Bennett, "Communicating Global Activism: Some Strengths and Vulnerabilities of Networked Politics," in *Cyberprotest: New Media, Citizens and Social Movements*, ed. Wim van de Donk et al. (London: Routledge, 2004), 128.

29. W. Lance Bennett and Alexandra Segerberg, *The Logic of Connective Action: Digital Media and the Personalization of Contentious Politics* (London: Cambridge University Press, 2013).

30. Graham Meikle, "Introduction: Making Meanings and Making Trouble," in *The Routledge Companion to Media and Activism*, ed. Graham Meikle (London: Routledge, 2018), 7.

31. Paolo Gerbaudo and Emiliano Trere, "In Search of the 'We' of Social Media Activism: Introduction to the Special Issue on Social Media and Protest Identities," in "Social Media and Protest Identities," ed. Paolo Gerbaudo and Emiliano Trere, special issue, *Information, Communication and Society* 18, no. 8 (2015): 865-71.

32. Christian Fuchs, "Critique of the Political Economy of Informational Capitalism and Social Media," in *Critique, Social Media and the Information Society*, ed. Christian Fuchs and Marisol Sandoval (New York: Routledge, 2013), 48-63.

33. Christian Fuchs, *Social Media: A Critical Introduction* (Thousand Oaks: SAGE, 2014).

34. Dencik and Wilkin, *Worker Resistance and Media*.

35. Maria Rovisco and Jonathan Corpus Ong, introduction to *Taking the Square: Mediated Dissent and Occupations of Public Space*, ed. Maria Rovisco and Jonathan Corpus Ong (New York: Rowman and Littlefield, 2016), 5.

36. John D. H. Downing, "Looking Back, Looking Ahead: What Has Changed in Social Movement Media since the Internet and Social Media?," in *The Routledge Companion to Media and Activism*, ed. Graham Meikle (London: Routledge, 2018), 19-28; Fuchs, *Social Media*.

37. Antonio Gramsci, *Antonio Gramsci: Selections from Political Writings, 1910-1920*, trans. John Mathews (New York: International Publishers, 1977).

38. David Harvey, *A Brief History of Neoliberalism* (Cary, NC: Oxford University Press, 2006); David Harvey, "Neoliberalism as Creative Destruction," *Annals of the American Academy of Political and Social Science* 610, no. 1 (2007): 22-44; Jason Hickel, *The Divide: A Brief Guide to Global Inequality and Its Solu-*

tions (London: William Heinemann, 2017); Ellen Wood, *Empire of Capital* (London: Verso Books, 2005).

39. Angela Davis, *Women, Race and Class* (New York: Random House, 1981); Julia Sudbury, "A World without Prisons: Resisting Militarism, Globalized Punishment, and Empire," *Social Justice* 31, no. 1 (2004): 9–30; Bryan Warde, "Black Male Disproportionality in the Criminal Justice Systems of the USA, Canada, and England: A Comparative Analysis of Incarceration," *Journal of African American Studies* 17, no. 4 (2013): 461–79.

40. Aihwa Ong, *Neoliberalism as Exception: Mutations in Citizenship and Sovereignty* (Durham, NC: Duke University Press, 2006); Immanuel Ness, *Southern Insurgency: The Coming of the Global Working Class* (London: Pluto, 2016).

41. Stuart Hall, *The Hard Road to Renewal: Thatcherism and the Crisis of the Left* (London: Verso Books, 1988).

42. Hall, *Hard Road*.

43. Harvey, *Brief History of Neoliberalism*.

44. David Harvey, "Universal Alienation," *Triple C: Communication, Capitalism and Critique* 16, no. 2 (2018): 424–39.

45. Ong, *Neoliberalism as Exception*, 14.

46. Richard Stahler-Sholk, "Resisting Neoliberal Homogenization: The Zapatista Autonomy Movement," *Latin American Perspectives* 34, no. 2 (2007): 48–63.

47. Donatella della Porta and Mario Diani, *Social Movements: An Introduction*, 2nd ed. (Malden, MA: Blackwell, 2006).

48. Andreas Bieler, Ingemar Lindberg, and Devan Pillay, "The Future of the Global Working Class: An Introduction," in *Labour and the Challenges of Globalization: What Prospects for Transnational Solidarity?*, ed. Andreas Bieler, Ingemar Lindberg, and Devan Pillay (London: Pluto, 2008), 1–11.

49. Iris M. Young, "Five Faces of Oppression," *Philosophical Forum* 19, no. 4 (1988): 276.

50. Maria Mies, *Patriarchy and Accumulation on a World Scale: Women in the International Division of Labour* (New York: Zed Books, 2022); Heidi I. Hartmann, "The Unhappy Marriage of Marxism and Feminism: Towards a More Progressive Union," *Capital and Class* 3, no. 2 (1979): 1–33.

51. Karl Marx, *Capital: A Critique of Political Economy*, vol. 1, *The Process of Production of Capital* (1867; repr., London: Penguin Classics, 1990).

52. bell hooks, *Feminism Is for Everybody: Passionate Politics* (New York: Routledge, 2000); Davis, *Women, Race and Class*; Audre Lorde, "Age, Race, Class and Sex: Women Redefining Difference," in *Campus Wars: Multiculturalism and the Politics of Difference*, ed. John Arthur and Amy Shapiro (Boulder, CO: Westview, 1995), 191–98.

53. Kumari Jayawardena, *Feminism and Nationalism in the Third World* (1986; repr., London: Verso Books, 2016).

54. Kristen Ghodsee, *Socialist Women's Activism and Global Solidarity during the Cold War* (Durham, NC: Duke University Press, 2019).

55. Laclau and Mouffe, *Hegemony and Socialist Strategy*, xviii.

56. Xueguang Zhou, *The Logic of Governance in China: An Organizational Approach* (Cambridge: Cambridge University Press, 2022). Zhou provides a comprehensive analysis of the Chinese party-state's authoritarian governance.

57. Harvey, *Brief History of Neoliberalism*, 120.

58. Ngai Pun, *Made in China: Women Factory Workers in a Global Workplace* (Durham, NC: Duke University Press, 2005); Hui Wang, *The End of the Revolution: China and the Limits of Modernity* (New York: Verso Books, 2011); W. Sun, *Subaltern China*; B. Meng, *Politics of Chinese Media*; Y. Zhao, "Neoliberal Strategies."

59. Lisa Rofel, *Desiring China: Experiments in Neoliberalism, Sexuality, and Public Culture* (Durham, NC: Duke University Press, 2007).

60. Zheng Wang, *Finding Women in the State: A Socialist Feminist Revolution in the People's Republic of China, 1949-1964* (Oakland: University of California Press, 2016); Siyuan Yin, "Re-articulating Feminisms: A Theoretical Critique of Feminist Struggles and Discourse in Historical and Contemporary China," *Cultural Studies* 36, no. 6 (2022): 981-1004.

61. Bingchun Meng and Yanning Huang, "Patriarchal Capitalism with Chinese Characteristics: Gendered Discourse of 'Double Eleven' Shopping Festival," *Cultural Studies* 31, no. 5 (2017): 659-84, https://doi.org/10.1080/09502386.2017.1328517; Tamara Jacka, *Creating a Public Sphere: A Case Study of a Rural Women's NGO in Beijing* (Canberra: Australian National University, 2004); Pun, *Made in China*; Hairong Yan, *New Masters, New Servants: Migration, Development, and Women Workers in China* (Durham, NC: Duke University Press, 2008).

62. Louis Althusser, *On Ideology* (1971; repr., London: Verso Books, 2008), 47.

63. Althusser, *On Ideology*, 56.

64. Michel Foucault, "The Subject and Power," in *Michel Foucault: Beyond Structuralism and Hermeneutics*, ed. Hubert Dreyfus and Paul Rabinow (Chicago: University of Chicago Press, 1983), 208-26.

65. Kathi Weeks, *Constituting Feminist Subjects* (London: Verso Books, 2018), 43.

66. E. P. Thompson, *The Making of the English Working Class* (New York: Random House, 1966).

67. Catherine A. MacKinnon, "Feminism, Marxism, Method, and the State: An Agenda for Theory," *Signs* 7, no. 3 (1982): 515-44.

68. Sandra Lee Bartky, *Femininity and Domination Studies in the Phenomenology of Oppression* (Oxfordshire: Routledge, 1990), 15.

69. Frantz Fanon, *Black Skin, White Masks* (New York: Grove Press, 1952), 48. Exposing the impacts of colonialism on colonized people, Fanon's concept of "psychic alienation" refers to the psychological and emotional consequences of being subjected to systemic oppression, discrimination, and the devaluation of one's identity and culture.

70. Gramsci, *Antonio Gramsci*, 11.

71. Della Porta and Diani, *Social Movements*.

72. Feminist Voices is an independent feminist-media outlet in China. It was established by a feminist activist in 2009 and was permanently shut down by the government in 2018.

73. Linda Briskin and Patricia McDermott, eds., *Women Challenging Unions: Feminism, Democracy, and Militancy* (Toronto: University of Toronto Press, 1993); Ann Shirley Leymon, "Unions and Social Inclusiveness: A Comparison of Changes in Union Member Attitudes," *Labor Studies Journal* 36, no. 3 (2011): 388-407.

74. International Labor Organization, *Domestic Workers Organize—but Can They Bargain?* February 2015, https://www.ilo.org/publications/domestic-workers-organize-can-they-bargain.

75. Evelyn Encalada Grez, "Justice for Migrant Farm Workers: Reflections on the Importance of Community Organising," *Relay: A Socialist Project Review* 12 (2006): 23-25; Adriana Paz Ramirez and Jennifer Jihye Chun, "Struggling against History: Migrant Farmworker Organizing in British Columbia," in *Unfree Labour? Struggles of Migrant and Immigrant Workers in Canada*, ed. Aziz Choudry and Adrian Smith (Oakland, CA: PM Press, 2016), 87-104.

76. Ngai Pun and Huilin Lu, "Unfinished Proletarianization: Self, Anger, and Class Action among the Second Generation of Peasant-Workers in Present-Day China," *Modern China* 36, no. 5 (2010): 493-519; T. Guo, "Rights in Action"; Ching Kwan Lee, *Against the Law: Labor Protests in China's Rustbelt and Sunbelt* (Berkeley: University of California Press, 2007).

77. The connection and networks of the founder have facilitated the later development of MWC, including funding from several international foundations, municipal governments' support, and media reports. Many scholars have written about RWKA and MWC to recognize their contribution to the advocacy of rural women's and female migrants' rights and well-being through providing a range of services. Scholars also address limitations in serving as a radical and transformative force to contest structural inequalities. See, e.g., Jacka, *Creating a Public Sphere*; Tamara Jacka, *Rural Women in Urban China: Gender, Migration, and Social Change* (New York: Routledge, 2006); Diana Fu, "A Cage of Voices: Producing and Doing *Dagongmei* in Contemporary China," *Modern China* 35, no. 5 (2009): 527-61; Siyuan Yin, "Producing Gendered Migration Narratives in China: A Case Study of *Dagongmei Tongxun* by a Local NGO," *International Journal of Communication* 10 (2016): 4304-23.

78. George E. Marcus, "Ethnography in/of the World System: The Emergence of Multi-sited Ethnography," *Annual Review of Anthropology* 24 (1995): 105-7.

79. This type of activist group, such as Jiu Ye, is different from underground labor NGOs as organizations without legal registration. See Diana Fu, "Disguised Collective Action in China," *Comparative Political Studies* 50, no. 4 (2017):

499–527. Unlike registered labor NGOs with full-time staff members and underground labor NGOs with migrant workers as activist, members of Jiu Ye all have their own full-time study or work.

80. Sandra Harding, *Whose Science? Whose Knowledge? Thinking from Women's Lives* (Ithaca, NY: Cornell University Press, 1991); Patricia Hill Collins, "Some Group Matters: Intersectionality, Situated Standpoints, and Black Feminist Thought," in *A Companion to African-American Philosophy*, ed. Tommy Lee Lott and John Pittman (Hoboken, NJ: Blackwell, 2003), 205–29.

Chapter 1

1. Andreas Bieler, Ingemar Lindberg, and Devan Pillay argue that a "new historical subject" is required to contest capitalist domination in the era of neoliberal globalization, at a time when the global working class is ever more fragmented and subject to the power of transnational capital. The emergence of the new historical subject will correspond to the rising precarity of workers and other structural inequalities that affect women and minority groups. See Andreas Bieler, Ingemar Lindberg, and Devan Pillay, eds., *Labour and the Challenges of Globalization: What Prospects for Transnational Solidarity* (London: Pluto, 2008).

2. David Harvey, *The Condition of Postmodernity: An Enquiry into the Origins of Cultural Change* (Cambridge, MA: Wiley-Blackwell, 1989); Harvey, *Brief History of Neoliberalism*; Harvey, "Neoliberalism as Creative Destruction"; Ong, *Neoliberalism as Exception*.

3. Harvey, *Condition of Postmodernity*; Geoff Bickerton and Jane Stinson, "Challenges Facing the Canadian Labour Movement in the Context of Globalization, Unemployment and the Casualization of Labour," in *Labour and the Challenges of Globalization: What Prospects for Transnational Solidarity?*, ed. Andreas Bieler, Ingemar Lindberg, and Devan Pillay (London: Pluto, 2008), 161–76; Heiner Dribbusch and Thorsten Schulten, "German Trade Unions between Neoliberal Restructuring, Social Partnership and Internationalism," in *Labour and the Challenges of Globalization: What Prospects for Transnational Solidarity?*, ed. Andreas Bieler, Ingemar Lindberg, and Devan Pillay (London: Pluto, 2008), 178–96; Wakana Shutŏ and Mac Urata, "The Impact of Globalization on Trade Unions: The Situation in Japan," in *Labour and the Challenges of Globalization: What Prospects for Transnational Solidarity?*, ed. Andreas Bieler, Ingemar Lindberg, and Devan Pillay (London: Pluto, 2008), 139–58; Neil H. Spencer et al., *Work in the European Gig Economy: Research Results from the UK, Sweden, Germany, Austria, the Netherlands, Switzerland and Italy* (Brussels: Foundation for European Progressive Studies, 2017); Niels van Doorn, Fabian Ferrari, and Mark Graham, "Migration and Migrant Labour in the Gig Economy: An Intervention," *Work, Employment and Society* 37, no. 4 (2023): 1099–111.

4. Niels van Doorn, "Platform Labor: On the Gendered and Racialized Exploitation of Low-Income Service Work in the 'On-Demand' Economy," *Information, Communication and Society* 20, no. 6 (2017): 901.

5. Workers' Action Center, *Still Working on the Edge: Building Decent Jobs from the Ground Up*, March 2015, https://workersactioncentre.org/wp-content/uploads/2016/07/StillWorkingOnTheEdge-Exec-Summary-web.pdf. See also David Weil, *The Fissured Workplace: Why Work Became So Bad for So Many and What Can Be Done to Improve It* (Cambridge, MA: Harvard University Press, 2014).

6. Economic Policy Institute, *National Survey of Gig Workers Paints a Picture of Poor Working Conditions, Low Pay*, June 2022, https://www.epi.org/publication/gig-worker-survey/.

7. Barbara Harriss-White, *India Working Essays on Society and Economy* (Cambridge: Cambridge University Press, 2002); Anne Posthuma and Dev Nathan, *Labour in Global Production Networks in India* (New Delhi: Oxford University Press, 2010).

8. Ness, *Southern Insurgency*.

9. Jonathan Unger, *The Transformation of Rural China* (New York: Routledge, 2016), https://doi.org/10.4324/9781315292052.

10. Pun, *Made in China*; Ong, *Neoliberalism as Exception*; Harvey, *Brief History of Neoliberalism*.

11. As the national household-registration policy implemented in the 1950s, *hukou* policy requires individual citizens to register in one place, and their access and eligibility to social welfare and services, such as public education and medical care, depend on their *hukou* status.

12. Unger, *Transformation of Rural China*; Andrew G. Walder, *China under Mao: A Revolution Derailed* (Cambridge, MA: Harvard University Press, 2017).

13. Chris King-chi Chan, Ngai Pun, and Jenny Chan, "The Role of the State, Labour Policy and Migrant Workers' Struggles in Globalized China," *Global Labour Journal* 1, no. 1 (January 2010): 132–51, https://doi.org/10.15173/glj.v1i1.1068; Shi Li, "The Economic Situation of Rural Migrant Workers in China," *China Perspectives* 4 (2010): 4–15, https://doi.org/10.4000/chinaperspectives.5332; Pun, *Made in China*; Cara Wallis, "Technology and/as Govermentality: The Production of Young Rural Women as Low-Tech Laboring Subjects in China," *Communication and Critical/Cultural Studies* 10, no. 4 (2013): 341–58; Feng Xu, *Women Migrant Workers in China's Economic Reform* (London: Palgrave Macmillan, 2000); Pengyu Zhu, "Residential Segregation and Employment Outcomes of Rural Migrant Workers in China," *Urban Studies* 53, no. 8 (2015): 1635–56.

14. All translations are by the author.

15. Migrant workers' children are those who live in cities with their parents without an urban *hukou*.

16. Hongwei Hu, Shuang Lu, and Chien-Chung Huang, "The Psychological and Behavioral Outcomes of Migrant and Left-Behind Children in China," *Children and Youth Services Review* 46 (2014): 1–10, https://doi.org/10.1016/j.childyouth.2014.07.021; Xiaodong Zheng, Yue Zhang, and Wenyu Jiang, "Inter-

nal Migration and Depression among Junior High School Students in China: A Comparison between Migrant and Left-Behind Children," *Frontiers in Psychology* 13 (2022): 811617, https://doi.org/10.3389/fpsyg.2022.811617.

17. Zai Liang et al., "Choices or Constraints: Education of Migrant Children in Urban China," *Population Research and Policy Review* 39 (2020): 671-90.

18. Jessica L. Montgomery, "The Inheritance of Inequality: *Hukou* and Related Barriers to Compulsory Education for China's Migrant Children," *Pacific Rim Law and Policy Journal* 21, no. 3 (2012): 591-622, https://digitalcommons. law.uw.edu/wilj/vol21/iss3/7; Yang Xiao and Yanjie Bian, "The Influence of *Hukou* and College Education in China's Labour Market," *Urban Studies* 55, no. 7 (2017): 1504-24; Shou Zhou and Monit Cheung, "*Hukou* System Effects on Migrant Children's Education in China: Learning from Past Disparities," *International Social Work* 60, no. 6 (2017): 1327-42.

19. Migrant children's schools are private schools set up in big cities for migrant workers' children who cannot attend public schools or afford elite private schools. But these schools usually lack qualified teachers and resources for utilities, and many unlicensed schools are subject to crackdowns by local governments. See China Labor Bulletin, *Migrant Workers and Their Children*, September 2023, https://clb.org.hk/en/content/migrant-workers-and-their-children.

20. Mary Beth Mills, "Gender and Inequality in the Global Labor Force," *Annual Review of Anthropology* 32 (2003): 41-62.

21. Bridget Anderson, "Just Another Job? Paying for Domestic Work," *Gender and Development* 9, no. 1 (2001): 25-33.

22. Li Zhang, *Strangers in the City: Reconfigurations of Space, Power, and Social Networks within China's Floating Population* (Stanford: Stanford University Press, 2001).

23. Harald Bauder, "Foreign Farm Workers in Ontario (Canada): Exclusionary Discourse in the Newsprint Media," *Journal of Peasant Studies* 35, no. 1 (2008): 100-118.

24. Michelle Ye Hee Lee, "Donald Trump's False Comments Connecting Mexican Immigrants and Crime," *Washington Post*, July 8, 2015, https://www .washingtonpost.com/news/fact-checker/wp/2015/07/08/donald- trumps -false-comments-connecting-mexican-immigrants-and-crime/.

25. Tom Vickers and Annie Rutter, "Disposable Labour, Passive Victim, Active Threat: Migrant/Non-migrant Othering in Three British Television Documentaries," *European Journal of Cultural Studies* 21, no. 4 (2018): 486-501.

26. Hsin-I Cheng, "On Migrant Workers' Social Status in Taiwan: A Critical Analysis of Mainstream News Discourse," *International Journal of Communication* 10 (2016): 2509-28.

27. Siyuan Yin, "'Patriotic Heroes' and 'Foreign Laborers': Politics of Media and Public Discourses on Essential Workers and Migrant Workers in Canada during the COVID-19," *International Journal of Communication* (forthcoming).

28. Wanning Sun, *Maid in China: Media, Morality and the Cultural Politics of Boundaries* (New York: Routledge, 2009).

29. Yu Shi and Francis L. Collins, "Producing Mobility: Visual Narratives of the Rural Migrant Worker in Chinese Television," *Mobilities* 13, no. 1 (2018): 126–41.

30. Sun, "Indoctrination."

31. Y. Zhao, *Media, Market, and Democracy.*

32. Althusser, *On Ideology,* 16.

33. Y. Zhao, "Neoliberal Strategies"; B. Meng, *Politics of Chinese Media.*

34. Y. Zhao, "Neoliberal Strategies."

35. Jack Linchuan Qiu, *Working-Class Network Society: Communication Technology and the Information Have-less in Urban China* (Cambridge, MA: MIT Press, 2009).

36. Qiu, *Working-Class Network Society*; Wallis, "Technology and/as Governmentality."

37. Ann Anagnost, "The Corporeal Politics of Quality (*Suzhi*)," *Public Culture* 16, no. 2 (2004): 189–208; Tamara Jacka, "Cultivating Citizens: *Suzhi* (Quality) Discourse in the PRC," *Positions Asia Critique* 17, no. 3 (2009): 523–35, https://doi.org/10.1215/10679847-2009-013; Andrew Kipnis, "*Suzhi*: A Keyword Approach," *China Quarterly* 186 (2006): 295–313, https://doi.org/10.1017/S0305741006000166; W. Sun, *Maid in China*; Hairong Yan, "Neoliberal Governmentality and Neohumanism: Organizing *Suzhi*/Value Flow through Labor Recruitment Networks," *Cultural Anthropology* 18, no. 4 (2003): 493–523; Yan, *New Masters.*

38. Yan, *New Masters,* 115.

39. Jacka, *Rural Women,* 33.

40. Pierre Bourdieu, *Distinction: A Social Critique of the Judgement of Taste* (London: Routledge, 1984).

41. Sun, "Indoctrination."

42. Chun, "Contested Politics of Gender."

43. Brickner and Dalton, "Organizing Baristas."

44. Jamie Woodcock, *The Fight against Platform Capitalism: An Inquiry into the Global Struggles of the Gig Economy* (London: University of Westminster Press, 2021).

45. Isabel Rauber, "The Globalization of Capital and Its Impact on the World of Formal and Informal Work: Challenges for the Responses from Argentine Unions," in *Labour and the Challenges of Globalization: What Prospects for Transnational Solidarity?*, ed. Andreas Bieler, Ingemar Lindberg, and Deven Pillay (London: Pluto, 2008), 98–111.

46. Kjeld Jakobsen and Alexandre de Freitas Barbosa, "Neoliberal Policies, Labor Market Restructuring and Social Exclusion: Brazil's Working-Class Response," in *Labour and the Challenges of Globalization: What Prospects for Trans-*

national Solidarity?, ed. Andreas Bieler, Ingemar Lindberg, and Devan Pillay (London: Pluto, 2008), 115-30.

47. Pauline Dibben, "Trade Union Change, Development and Renewal in Emerging Economies: The Case of Mozambique," *Work, Employment and Society* 24, no. 3 (2010): 468-86; Pauline Dibben and Sara Nadin, "Community Unionism in Africa: The Case of Mozambique," *Industrial Relations* 66, no. 1 (2011): 54-73.

48. Jorg Nowak, "Strikes and Labor Unrest in the Automobile Industry in India: The Case of Maruti Suzuki India," *Working USA: The Journal of Labor and Society* 19, no. 3 (2016): 419-36.

49. J. Chan and Selden, "China's Rural Migrant Workers," 614.

50. Jack Linchuan Qiu, *Goodbye iSlave: A Manifesto for Digital Abolition* (Urbana: University of Illinois Press, 2017), 88.

51. In 2010, both the central government and the municipal government of Shenzhen declared that they paid high attention to the case and sent investigation teams to Foxconn factory. The municipal government promised to find solutions to prevent the tragedy in the future. International and domestic news reports on the Foxconn tragedy. See "Shenzhen dangju beizhi hushi fushikang shijian" 深圳当局被指忽视富士康事件 [Shenzhen government was criticized of neglecting the Foxconn instance], BBC (China edition), May 27, 2010, https://www.bbc.com/zhongwen/trad/world/2010/05/100527_foxconn_shenzhen; Lan Fang, "Zhongyang diaochazu ganfu Shenzhen fushikang" 中央调查组赶赴深圳富士康 [The investigation team of the central government arrived at Foxconn in Shenzhen], Sina 新浪财经, May 28, 2010, http://finance.sina.com.cn/roll/20100528/13208019636.shtml.

52. Stella Yifan Xie and Liyan Qi, "Zhongguo gongchang zaoyu yonggonghuang" 中国工厂遭遇用工荒 [Chinese factories are facing labor shortage], *Wall Street Journal*, August 28, 2021, https://cn.wsj.com/articles/中国工厂遭遇用工荒.

53. C. Chan and Pun, "New Working Class"; J. Chan and Selden, "China's Rural Migrant Workers"; T. Guo, "Rights in Action"; Qiu, "Social Media."

54. QQ is an instant-message app and a social media platform. Qiu, *Goodbye iSlave*.

55. Qiu, *Goodbye iSlave*.

56. C. Chan and Pun, "New Working Class"; Manfred Elfstrom, "Two Steps Forward, One Step Back: Chinese State Reactions to Labour Unrest," *China Quarterly* 240 (2019): 855-79, https://doi.org/10.1017/S0305741019000067.

57. J. Chan and Selden, "China's Rural Migrant Workers," 609.

58. Elfstrom, "Two Steps Forward"; Chun Lin, *Revolution and Counterrevolution in China: The Paradoxes of Chinese Struggle* (London: Verso Books, 2021).

59. Elfstrom, "Two Steps Forward."

60. J. Chan and Selden, "China's Rural Migrant Workers"; Ching Kwan Lee and Yuan Shen, "The Anti-solidarity Machine? Labor Nongovernmental Organizations in China," in *From Iron Rice Bowl to Informalization: Markets, Work-*

ers, and the State in a Changing China, ed. Sarosh Kuravilla, Ching Kwan Lee, and Mary E. Gallagher (Ithaca, NY: ILR Press, 2011), 173-87; Yi Xu, "Labor Non-governmental Organizations in China: Mobilizing Rural Migrant Workers," *Journal of Industrial Relations* 55, no. 2 (2013): 243-59.

61. C. Lee, *Against the Law*; Eli Friedman, *Insurgency Trap: Labor Politics in Postsocialist China* (Ithaca, NY: Cornell University Press, 2014); Fu, *Mobilizing without the Masses.*

62. W. Sun, *Maid in China*, 48.

63. Maghiel van Crevel, "Misfit: Xu Lizhi and Battlers Poetry (*Dagong Shige*)," *Prism* 16, no. 1 (2019): 85-114; Wanning Sun, "Narrating Translocality: *Dagong* Poetry and the Subaltern Imagination," *Mobilities* 5, no. 3 (2010): 291-309; W. Sun, *Subaltern China.*

64. W. Sun, *Subaltern China*, 220.

65. W. Sun, *Subaltern China*, 226.

66. W. Sun, *Subaltern China.*

67. Min Zhou and Shih-Ding Liu, "Becoming Precarious Playbour: Chinese Migrant Youth on the Kuaishou Video-Sharing Platform," *Economic and Labour Relations Review* 32, no. 3 (2021): 322-40.

68. Rebecca Gumbrell-McCormick and Richard Hyman, *Trade Unions in Western Europe: Hard Times, Hard Choices* (Cary, NC: Oxford University Press, 2013).

69. Zaad Mahmood, "Trade Unions, Politics and Reform in India," *Indian Journal of Industrial Relations* 51, no. 4 (2016): 531-49; J. S. Sodhi, "Trade Unions in India: Changing Role and Perspective," *Indian Journal of Industrial Relations* 49, no. 2 (2013): 169-84.

70. Ness, *Southern Insurgency.*

71. Jenny Chan, Manjusha Nair, and Chris Rhomberg, "Precarization and Labor Resistance: Canada, the USA, India and China," *Critical Sociology* 45, no. 4-5 (2019): 469-83.

72. Chun, "Contested Politics."

73. Duvisac, "Reconstituting the Industrial Worker."

74. Dencik and Wilkin, *Worker Resistance and Media*; Waterman, "Social-Movement Unionism"; Peter Waterman, "A Trade Union Internationalism for the 21st Century: Meeting the Challenges from Above, Below and Beyond," in *Labour and the Challenges of Globalization: What Prospects for Transnational Solidarity?*, ed. Andreas Bieler, Ingemar Lindberg, and Devan Pillay (London: Pluto, 2008), 248-61.

75. Jane Wills and Melanie Simms, "Building Reciprocal Community Unionism in the UK," *Capital and Class* 28, no. 1 (2004): 59-84.

76. Cynthia Cranford and Deena Ladd, "Community Unionism: Organising for Fair Employment in Canada," *Just Labour* 3 (Fall 2003): 46-59; Steven Tufts, "World Cities and Union Renewal," *Geography Compass* 1, no. 3 (2007): 673-94.

77. Kim Scopes, "Understanding the New Labor Movements in the 'Third

World': The Emergence of Social Movement Unionism," *Critical Sociology* 19, no. 2 (1992): 81–101.

78. Dencik and Wilkin, *Worker Resistance and Media*.

79. Annelies Moors et al., "Migrant Domestic Workers: A New Public Presence in the Middle East?" in *Publics, Politics and Participation: Locating the Public Sphere in the Middle East and North Africa*, ed. Seteney Shami (New York: Social Science Research Council, 2009), 151–76.

80. Ng Sek Hong and Malcolm Warner, *China's Trade Unions and Management* (London: Palgrave Macmillan, 1998); Malcolm Warner, "Trade Unions in China: In Search of a New Role in the 'Harmonious Society,'" in *Trade Unions in Asia: An Economic and Sociological Analysis*, ed. John Benson and Ying Zhou (New York: Routledge, 2008), 140–56.

81. Ying Zhu, Malcolm Warner, and Tongqing Feng, "Employment Relations 'with Chinese Characteristics': The Role of Trade Unions in China," *International Labor Review* 150, no. 102 (2011): 127–43.

82. Feng Chen, "Between the State and Labour: The Conflict of Chinese Trade Unions' Double Identity in Market Reform," *China Quarterly* 176 (2003): 1006–28.

83. Feng Chen, "China's Road to the Construction of Labor Rights," *Journal of Sociology* 52, no. 1 (2015): 24–38; Friedman, *Insurgency Trap*.

84. Au Loong Yu, "The Jasic Mobilisation: A High Tide for the Chinese Labour Movement?" in *Dog Days: Made in China Yearbook 2018*, ed. Ivan Franceschini et al. (Canberra: Australian National University Press, 2018), 12–16.

85. Chris King-chi Chan, "Community-Based Organizations for Migrant Workers' Rights: The Emergence of Labour NGOs in China," *Community Development Journal* 48, no. 1 (2012): 6–22.

86. China Labor Bulletin is a NGO based in Hong Kong, and its main mission is to support and facilitate labor movements in China. The Chinese Working Women Network is a labor NGO founded in 1996 in Hong Kong, and they pioneered establishing a community-based service center for migrant women in mainland China in the 1990s. Labor scholar Jenny Chan wrote a short piece introducing the history and activism of the Chinese Working Women Network. See Jenny Wai-Ling Chan, "Chinese Women Workers Organize in the Export Zone," *New Labor Forum* 15, no. 1 (2006): 19–27.

87. Lee and Shen, "Anti-solidarity Machine?"; C. Chan, "Community-Based Organizations"; Fu, *Mobilizing without the Masses*.

88. Ivan Franceschini, "Labour NGOs in China: A Real Force for Political Change," *China Quarterly* 218 (2014): 474–92.

89. Jacka, *Rural Women*; Cara Wallis, *Technomobility in China: Young Migrant Women and Mobile Phones* (New York: New York University Press, 2013).

90. Wallis, *Technomobility in China*.

91. Lee and Shen, "Anti-solidarity Machine?"

92. Fu, *Mobilizing without the Masses*.

Chapter 2

1. Besides our structured interview, I often chatted informally with Chengmei to discuss her work at Didinghua, and we remain in close contact to the present day.

2. Dechao Yao, Lin Zhang, and Weiquan Zou, *Nongcun liudong nüxing chengshi shenghuo fazhan baogao* 农村流动女性城市生活发展报告 [Report on development of rural-to-urban female migrants] (Beijing: Social Sciences Academic Press, 2014).

3. The convention calls upon countries to implement labor laws and policies to protect labor rights of domestic workers, recognize their special working conditions, and campaign against discrimination. International Labor Organization, Domestic Workers Convention, C189, no. 189 (2011), https://www.ilo.org/dyn/normlex/en/f?p=NORMLEXPUB:12100:0::NO::P12100_ILO_CODE:C189.

4. I remain in contact with two staff members of MWC and most of the domestic workers I got to know during the fieldwork. We sometimes chat via WeChat and talk about recent events in our lives.

5. Silvia Federici, "Social Reproduction Theory: History, Issues and Present Challenges," *Radical Philosophy* 204 (2019): 55–57; Hartmann, "Unhappy Marriage"; Mies, *Patriarchy*.

6. Evelyn Nakano Glenn, *Issei, Nisei, War Bride: Three Generations of Japanese American Women in Domestic Service* (Philadelphia, PA: Temple University Press, 1986); Mary Romero, *Maid in the U.S.A.* (New York: Routledge, 2002).

7. Shirlena Huang and Brenda S. A. Yeoh, "Maids and Ma'ams in Singapore: Constructing Gender and Nationality in the Transnationalization of Paid Domestic Work," *Geography Research Forum* 18 (1998): 21–48.

8. Nicole Constable, *Maid to Order in Hong Kong: Stories of Migrant Workers*, 2nd ed. (Ithaca, NY: Cornell University Press, 2007).

9. Yan, *New Masters.*

10. Yan, *New Masters.*

11. Arianne M. Gaetano, "Filial Daughters, Modern Women: Migrant Domestic Workers in Post-Mao Beijing," in *On the Move: Women and Rural-to-Urban Migration in Contemporary China*, ed. Arianne M. Gaetano and Tamara Jacka (New York: Columbia University Press, 2004), 41–79; Yan, *New Masters.*

12. Yan, *New Masters.*

13. See, e.g., Minghui Liu, *Migrants and Cities: Research Report on Recruitment, Employment, and Working Conditions of Domestic Workers in China*, Conditions of Work and Employment Series 92, International Labor Organization (Geneva: International Labor Office, 2017); Yao, Zhang, and Zou, *Nongcun liudong nüxing.*

14. Yao, Zhang, and Zou, *Nongcun liudong nüxing.*

15. Pun, *Made in China*; Wallis, "Technology and/as Govermentality"; F. Xu, *Women Migrant Workers.*

16. Yao, Zhang, and Zou, *Nongcun liudong nüxing*; Liu, "Migrants and Cities."

17. International Labor Organization, Domestic Workers Convention.

18. Dwight Conquergood, "Performance Studies: Interventions and Radical Research," *Drama Review* 46, no. 2 (2002): 145–56.

19. Zhiyong Zhao, "Wenhua shijian shouhu diceng quanyi yu zunyan" 文化实践守护底层权益与尊严 [To protect rights and dignity of the underprivileged through cultural practices], *Refeng xueshu* 热风学术 10 (2016): 168. See also Augusto Boal, *Theatre of the Oppressed* (Toronto: Pluto, 1979).

20. D. Soyini Madison, "Performance, Personal Narratives, and the Politics of Possibilities," in *The Future of Performance Studies: Visions and Revisions*, ed. Otis J. Aggert Festival and Sheron J. Dailey (Annandale, VA: National Communication Association, 1998), 276–86.

21. On "new subjectivities" as a practice of challenging capitalism, see J. K. Gibson-Graham, *A Postcapitalist Politics* (Minneapolis: University of Minnesota Press, 2006).

22. Weeks, *Constituting Feminist Subjects*, 7.

23. Gibson-Graham, *Postcapitalist Politics*.

24. Graziano Battistella, "The Human Rights of Migrant Workers: Agenda for NGOs," *International Migration Review* 27, no. 1 (1993): 191–201; C. Chan, "Community-Based Organizations"; Jacka, *Rural Women*; Piya Pangsapa, "When Battlefields Become Marketplaces: Migrant Workers and the Role of Civil Society and NGO Activism in Thailand," *International Migration* 53, no. 3 (2015): 124–49.

25. Wanning Sun documents individual domestic workers' various forms of transgressive action, including talking back to the urban-centric media gaze and gossiping with other workers. See W. Sun, *Maid in China*. Arianne Gaetano also reveals the individual strategies that domestic workers have adopted to improve their working conditions, such as forging kinship-like ties with employers and switching employers strategically to earn higher wages. See Gaetano, "Filial Daughters." Nicole Constable acknowledges the political potential of collective action among Filipino, Indonesian, Thai, and Malaysian domestic workers in Hong Kong. Constable argues that such protest is not possible in mainland China. See Nicole Constable, "Migrant Workers and the Many States of Protest in Hong Kong," *Critical Asian Studies* 41, no. 1 (2009): 143–64. While her argument is partially right, considering China's political environment, it is based on a conventional understanding of collective resistance that prioritizes protests and strikes.

26. In the United States, enslaved people's singing performances expressed pain and protest against the oppression of the slavery system. See Frederick Douglass, *My Bondage and Freedom* (1855; repr., New York: Dover, 1969). As enslaved people's access to literature was forbidden, singing became their powerful articulation. More contemporary examples include performances by Aboriginal theater people to demand indigenous rights in Australia and indige-

nous theaters fighting against racism in Canada and Australia. See, respectively, Fiona Magowan, "Dancing with a Difference: Reconfiguring the Poetic Politics of Aboriginal Ritual as National Spectacle," *Australian Journal of Anthropology* 11, no. 2 (2000): 308-21; Helen Gilbert, "Black and White and Re(a)d All over Again: Indigenous Minstrelsy in Contemporary Canadian and Australian Theatre," *Theatre Journal* 55 (2003): 679-98.

27. I watched the performance and its rehearsals many times at MWC, a university, and a gala organized by a domestic-service company.

28. On narratives, see Kagendo Mutua and Beth Blue Swadener, introduction to *Decolonizing Research in Cross-Cultural Contexts: Critical Personal Narratives*, ed. Kagendo Mutua and Beth Blue Swadener (Albany: State University of New York Press, 2004): 1-23. On counternarratives, see Norman K. Denzin, "Emancipatory Discourses and the Ethics and Politics of Interpretation," in *The SAGE Handbook of Qualitative Research*, ed. Norman K. Denzin and Yvonna S. Lincoln (Thousand Oaks: SAGE, 2005), 933-58.

29. *Wo de laodong, zunyan yu mengxiang* 我的劳动,尊严与梦想 [My labor, dignity, and dream], dir. Zhiyong Zhao and Chengmei Yan, Didinghua Theater, MWC's Twentieth Anniversary Gala, Beijing, China, April 9, 2016. This play is hereafter referred to as *Wo de laodong*.

30. *Wo de laodong*, Didinghua Theater, rehearsal, Beijing, China, April 4, 2016.

31. See, e.g., Anderson, "Just Another Job?"

32. *Wo de laodong*, Didinghua Theater, Shoujie ayijie shenban wanhui 首届阿姨节申办晚会 [The First Domestic Workers' Festival Gala], Beijing, China, July 21, 2016.

33. *Wo de laodong*, Didinghua Theater, rehearsal, Beijing, China, April 4, 2016.

34. *Wo de laodong*, Didinghua Theater, Shoujie ayijie shenban wanhui.

35. *Wo de laodong*, Didinghua Theater, Beijing waiguoyu daxue北京外国语大学 [Beijing Foreign Studies University], Beijing, China, May 2, 2016. The story was also performed at Shoujie ayijie shenban wanhui on July 21, 2016. I watched this part of the performance twice at a university and a gala. Both times, the moment brought me to tears out of feelings of anger at and sympathy for the systematic inequality and injustice these women have suffered.

36. Norman K. Denzin, *Performance Ethnography: Critical Pedagogy and the Politics of Culture* (Thousand Oaks: SAGE, 2003); Denzin, "Emancipatory Discourses"; D. Soyini Madison and Judith Hamera, eds., *The SAGE Handbook of Performance Studies* (Thousand Oaks: SAGE, 2006).

37. Feifei Festival is a nonprofit event for nonprofessional groups to present performances on diverse themes, and it has been held from May to June every year since 2009.

38. Madison, "Performance," 282.

39. Franceschini, "Labour NGOs."

40. "Didinghua de chuntian" 地丁花的春天 [Didinghua's spring], *Jiaodian fangtan* 焦点访谈, January 7, 2016, http://www.cctv1.tv/jiaodianfangtan/3965.html.

41. "Didinghua jushe" 地丁花剧社 [Didinghua Theater], *Xinwen Diaocha* 新闻调查, April 22, 2017, https://tv.cctv.com/2017/04/22/VIDEm5u6mbFP33ViLZZZ84Gc170422.shtml.

42. Sun, "Indoctrination," 112 .

43. Ye Zhang, "Chengzhongcun wenyi" 城中村文艺 [Art in urban villages], *Pengpai* 澎湃, March 29, 2018, https://www.thepaper.cn/newsDetail_forward_2046443.

44. Henan is a province located in central China. Dongbei refers to all three provinces in northeastern China: Liaoning, Jilin, and Heilongjiang. People often identify those from the three provinces as Dongbei *ren* (folks).

45. On "enabling ground," see Weeks, *Constituting Feminist Subjects*, 129.

Chapter 3

1. On gentrification in China, see Hyun Bang Shin, "Economic Transition and Speculative Urbanisation in China: Gentrification versus Dispossession," *Urban Studies* 53, no. 3 (2016): 471–89; Weixuan Song and Xigang Zhu, "Gentrification in Urban China under Market Transformation," *International Journal of Urban Sciences* 14, no. 2 (2010): 152–63; Qinran Yang, Yang Liu, and Linchuan Yang, "Commercial Gentrification in China and Its Distribution, Development, and Correlates: The Case of Chengdu," *Frontiers in Environmental Science* 10 (August 2022): 1–15.

2. Raymond Williams, *The Long Revolution* (London: Chatto and Windus, 1961), 328.

3. On interpellation, see Althusser, *On Ideology*.

4. Harvey, "Neoliberalism as Creative Destruction," 148.

5. Parts of chapter 3 have been previously published. See Siyuan Yin, "Alternative Forms of Media, ICTs, and Underprivileged Groups in China," *Media, Culture and Society* 40, no. 8 (2018): 1221–36; Siyuan Yin, "Cultural Production in Working-Class Resistance: Labor Activism, Gender Politics, and Solidarities," *Cultural Studies* 34, no. 3 (2019): 418–41. I appreciate the permission to include the materials here.

6. For some selected media reports on Sun Heng, see Haoran Lu, "Sun Heng shibanian wei xingongren er ge" 孙恒十八年为新工人而歌 [Sun Heng singing for new workers for eighteen years], *Jinri toutiao* 今日头条, August 26, 2020, https://www.toutiao.com/article/6865082322044060167/?wid=1688459459669; "Tanfang Picun" 探访皮村 [Visiting Picun village], Zhongguo nongcun wang 中国农村网, December 13, 2021, http://journal.crnews.net/mhsh/2016n/2016ndsyq/915543_20161215111306.html.

7. Lü Tu's book *Zhongguo xin gongren* has played an important role in constructing the identity of the new worker that the MWH aims to cultivate

through its advocacy work. See Tu Lü, *Zhongguo xin gongren* 中国新工人 [Chinese new workers] (Beijing: Fanlü, 2013).

8. T. Lü, *Zhongguo xin gongren.*

9. Raymond Williams, *Marxism and Literature* (Oxford: Oxford University Press, 1977), 17.

10. Lisa Rofel, *Other Modernities: Gendered Yearnings in China after Socialism* (Berkeley: University of California Press, 1999).

11. On compassionate journalism, see Sun, "Indoctrination."

12. For some examples of media reports on MWH, see "Ceng bei biqian de gongyouzhijia" 曾被逼迁的工友之家 [Migrant Workers' Home once being forced to relocate], *Jiemian* 界面新闻, January 15, 2017, https://www.jiemian.com/article/1069399.html; Jing Ding et al., "Zai Beijing pinming dagong de dagongren" 在北京拼命打工的打工人 [Hard-working workers in Beijing], *Liaowang* 瞭望, May 6, 2021, http://lw.xinhuanet.com/2021-05/06/c_139928069.htm.

13. Exceptions are some news reports on Sun Heng and scholar volunteers who advocated for migrant workers' rights.

14. Rucht, "Quadruple 'A.'"

15. Migrant workers are restricted to access public services in cities due to their *hukou* status as rural residents.

16. In 2003, Sun Zhigang, a college student in Guangdong Province, was beaten to death after he was forced into a detention center because he did not provide proof of temporary residency. The incident triggered nationwide public discussions and criticism of the custody and repatriation policy, which was then abolished. The policy was initiated in 1961 to restrict population mobility and lasted till 2003. Since 1990, the policy had been mainly targeting rural migrant workers to regulate their mobility. In 2009, a migrant worker at a construction site was diagnosed with black lung disease. His experience and difficulties in demanding compensation from the company have attracted wide public attention to black lung disease, a typical occupational disease that millions of migrant workers suffer from. In 2010, due to the unbearable working conditions, more than a dozen young migrant workers committed suicide at the Foxconn company. These three events have all attracted media and public attention to migrant workers' suffering in China.

17. For endorsements of the museum, see "Shehui gejie dui dagong wenhua yishu bowuguan jiqi zhongchou huodong de jiyu" 社会各界对打工文化艺术博物馆及其众筹活动的寄语 [Messages from the society to the laboring art museum and its crowdfunding activities], Sohu 搜狐, July 25, 2017, https://www.sohu.com/a/159833947_653202.

18. "Shehui gejie."

19. Stuart Hall, "The Problem of Ideology: Marxism without Guarantees," in *Stuart Hall: Critical Dialogues in Cultural Studies*, 2nd ed., ed. David Morley and Kuan-Hsing Chen (New York: Routledge, 2005), 25-47.

20. Hall, "Problem of Ideology."

21. Duo Xu, vocalist, "Beijing, Beijing" 北京北京 [Beijing, Beijing], by New-Worker Troupe, track 6 on *Laodong yu zunyan* 劳动与尊严 [Labor and dignity], Beijing jingwen chang pian chuanbo 北京京文唱片传播, 2013.

22. Here, I'm using the term "distinction" in the sense developed by Pierre Bourdieu. See Bourdieu, *Distinction*.

23. Heng Sun, vocalist, "Weishenme" 为什么 [Why], by New-Worker Troupe, track 9 on *Wo de jita hui changge* 我的吉他会唱歌 [My guitar knows what to sing], Beijing dadi minyao gouji wenhua yishu chuanbo 北京大地民谣国际文化艺术传播, 2011; Duo Xu, vocalist, "Chengshi de shenghuo" 城市的生活 [Urban life], by New-Worker Troupe, track 2 on *Women de shijie women de mengxiang* 我们的世界 我们的梦想 [Our world our dream], Dalian yinxiang 大连音像, 2008.

24. Ching Kwan Lee, "The 'Revenge of History': Collective Memories and Labor Protests in North-Eastern China," *Ethnography* 1, no. 2 (2000): 217-37, https://doi.org/10.1177/14661380022230741; Qiu, "Social Media."

25. Heng Sun, vocalist, "Biao ge" 彪哥 [Brother Biao], by New-Worker Troupe, track 3 on *Wo de jita hui changge* 我的吉他会唱歌 [My guitar knows what to sing], Beijing dadi minyao gouji wenhua yishu chuanbo 北京大地民谣国际文化艺术传播, 2011.

26. H. Sun, "Biao ge."

27. C. Lee, "Revenge of History," 52; Pun, *Made in China*.

28. Heng Sun, Yuan Sun, Guoliang Jiang, vocalists, "Women de shijie women de mengxiang" 我们的世界我们的梦想 [Our world and our dreams], by New-Worker Troupe, track 1 on *Women de shijie women de mengxiang* 我们的世界 我们的梦想 [Our world our dream], Dalian yinxiang 大连音像, 2008.

29. Shani Orgad, *Media Representation and the Global Imagination* (Malden, MA: Polity Press, 2012).

30. Heng Sun, vocalist, "Tuanjie qilai taogongqian" 团结起来讨工钱 [Unite and ask for arrears wages], by New-Worker Troupe, track 4 on *Laodong yu zunyan* 劳动与尊严 [Labor and dignity], Beijing jingwen chang pian chuanbo 北京京文唱片传播, 2013.

31. "Bu gan le" 不干了 [I quit], music and lyrics by Duo Xu and the New-Worker Troupe, Picun shequ laodongjie wanhui 皮村社区劳动节晚会 [Picun Community Labor Day Gala], Beijing, China, May 1, 2016.

32. Duo Xu, vocalist, "Hei! Renjian" 嘿!人间 [Hey! World], by New-Worker Troupe, track 2 on *Hei! Renjian* 嘿!人间 [Hey! World], Dadi minzhiyao 大地民之谣, 2023.

33. The line "Zhumen jiurou chou, lu you dong si gu" (朱门酒肉臭，路有冻死骨) is from the poem "Zi jing fu fengxian yonghuai wubai zi" (自京赴奉先咏怀五百字). The line "An de guangsha qianwanjian, dabi tianxia hanshi juhuanyan (安得广厦千万间，大庇天下寒士俱欢颜) is from the poem "Maowu wei qiufeng suo poge" (茅屋为秋风所破歌).

34. Jiemian is a multimedia commercial platform established by Shanghai United Media Group. The platform targets middle-class readers with national

and international news, financial analyses, and popular culture. Zhengwu is one of Jiemian's sections, publishing nonfiction and focusing on social issues in contemporary China. Fan Yusu's article "I am Fan Yusu" was first published on Zhengwu. In 2020, Zhengwu was closed due to financial reasons, and the original link is not available. For the repost of the article, see Yusu Fan, "Wo shi Fan Yusu" 我是范雨素 [I am Fan Yusu], Sohu 搜狐, September 13, 2018, https://www.sohu.com/a/253642863_147822.

35. For instance, Li Yanhong and Fan Yingjie's study argues that the "compassionate public" mainly constituted by the middle-class can hardly form solidarity with working-class populations, since their reading stories of suffering simply embodies a form of media consumption. See Yanhong Li and Yingjie Fan, "Yuanchu kunan de zhongjiehu" 远处苦难的中介化 [Mediated distant suffering], *Xinwen yu chuanbo yanjiu* 新闻与传播研究 11 (2019): 55–74. A commentator criticizes the middle-class gaze. Zhongmu, "'Nongmingong sikao haidegeer' de xushi, nandao bushi sichengxiangshi ma?" "农民工思考海德格尔"的叙事，难道不是似曾相识吗? [Isn't the narrative of "migrant workers thinking about Heidegger" familiar?, *Xinjing bao* 新京报, December 8, 2021, https://m.bjnews.com.cn/detail/163893226914032.html.

36. Based on an analysis of visual and audio production by Chinese factory workers, Jack Linchuan Qiu has developed a system for categorizing worker-generated content according to different practices and their implications—namely, whether the actions are collective, whether they adopt advocacy goals, and whether they can lead to empowerment. See Jack Linchuan Qiu, "Locating Worker-Generated Content (WGC) in the World's Factory," in *The Routledge Companion to Labor and Media*, ed. Richard Maxwell (New York: Routledge, 2015): 303–14; Qiu, *Goodbye iSlave*.

37. Atton, "Reassessment"; Atton, *Alternative Media*; Atton, "Alternative Media."

38. In the summer of 2019, I was invited by Prof. Zhang Huiyu to give a talk to the literature group. I selected a topic on feminist movements in the United States and China, introducing some historical and contemporary accounts of women's resistance in the two countries from a comparative perspective. The talk was well received among member workers and several student visitors.

39. See Wei Huang and Manfei Chen, "Fan Yusu huole zhihou" 范雨素火了之后 [After Fan Yusu became popular], Renmin wang 人民网, May 2, 2017, http://culture.people.com.cn/n1/2017/0502/c87423-29247857.html.

40. Huiyu Zhang, "Fachu women de shengyin, gongren wenxue de yiyi yu jiazhi" 发出我们的声音，工人文学的意义与价值 [Expressing our voices, meanings, and value of workers' literature], *Xinhua yuebao* 新华月报 9 (2016): 49.

41. Rodriguez, "Civil Society"; Rodriguez, "Citizens' Media."

42. Hadl, "Alternative Media."

43. Zhixi Hao, "Weiquan fenxiang" 维权分享 [Sharing rights protection], *Picun shequ bao* 皮村社区报, August 5, 2014.

44. Rodriguez, "Citizens' Media."

45. Qiu, "Locating Worker-Generated Content"; Qiu, "Social Media"; Wallis, "Technology and/as Govermentality."

46. Gramsci, *Antonio Gramsci.*

47. B. Meng, *Politics of Chinese Media*; Y. Zhao, "Neoliberal Strategies."

48. Hongmei Li, *Advertising and Consumer Culture in China* (Malden, MA: Polity Press, 2016); Hye-Jin Paek and Zhongdang Pan, "Spreading Global Consumerism: Effects of Mass Media and Advertising on Consumerist Values in China," *Mass Communication and Society* 7, no. 4 (2004): 491–515.

49. See, e.g., Wei Bu, "Shehuizhuyi wenyi de benzhi shi renmin de wenyi" 社会主义文艺的本质是人民的文艺 [The essence of socialist literature and art is people's literature and art], Zhongguo fazhan menhu wang 中国发展门户网, January 20, 2017, http://m.wyzxwk.com/content.php?classid=25&id=376028; "2013 Dagong chunwan juxing" 2013打工春晚举行 [Dagong Spring Festival gala is held in 2013], Hangzhou wang 杭州网, January 28, 2013, https://news.hangzhou.com.cn/shxw/content/2013-01/28/content_4585644.htm; "Bu Wei: Wenhua quanli shi renquan bukefenge de yibufen" 卜卫:文化权利是人权不可分割的一部分 [Bu Wei: Cultural rights are an integral part of human rights], Sohu 搜狐, October 20, 2010, http://news.sohu.com/20101020/n276079282.shtml.

50. Bu, "Shehuizhuyi wenyi."

51. Both official and commercial media have interviewed Zhang Huiyu in their reports on MWH and literature group. See, e.g., "'Fan Yusu men' he tamen de laoshi" "范雨素们"和他们的老师 ["Fan Yusu" and their teachers], Renmin wang 人民网, May 2, 2017, http://cpc.people.com.cn/BIG5/n1/2017/0502/c64387-29249231.html; Shiye Fu, "Zai dushuli, nvgong doushi yinxingren" 在都市里,女工都是隐形人 [Female workers are invisible in cities], *Jiemian xinwen* 界面新闻, December 20, 2017, https://www.jiemian.com/article/1830918.html.

52. Yingdeng Meng, "'Dagong chunwan' yu 'xin gongren wenhua' de chuangzao lujing" "打工春晚"与"新工人文化"的创造路径 ["Dagong Spring Festival gala" and the production of "new-worker culture"], *Wenyi lilun yu piping* 文艺理论与批评 10 (2017): 45–54; Z. Wang, *Finding Women.*

53. Hongzhe Wang, "Kunan yu mengxiang de tuanjie—yidong hulianwang shidai de xingongren wenhua" 苦难与梦想的团结—移动互联时代的新工人文化 [The unity of hardship and dreams: New worker culture in the digital age], *Yishu guangjiao* 艺术广角 4 (2017): 22.

54. Tu Lü, *Zhongguo xin gongren: Wenhua yu mingyun* 中国新工人:文化与命运 [Chinese new workers: Culture and destiny] (Beijing: Fanlü, 2015).

55. Hui Wang, "Liangzhong xinqiongren jiqi weilai—jieji zhengzhi de shuailuo, zaixingcheng yu xinqiongren de zunyan zhengzhi" 两种新穷人及其未来—阶级政治的衰落,再形成与新穷人的尊严政治 [Two types of the new poor and their futures—the fall of class politics, reformation, and the new poor's political dignity], *Kaifang shidai* 开放时代 6 (2014): 59.

56. MWH established Tongxin Primary School (Tongxin xiaoxue; 同心小学)

for migrant workers' children in 2005. It is one of the few schools for migrant workers' children in Beijing.

57. J. Chan and Selden, "China's Rural Migrant Workers"; T. Guo, "Rights in Action"; Sun, "Inequality."

58. Pun and Lu, "Unfinished Proletarianization"; Qiu, "Locating Worker-Generated Content"; Qiu, "Social Media."

59. Thompson, *English Working Class*, 168.

60. Gramsci, *Antonio Gramsci*.

61. Elizabeth J. Perry and Mark Selden, "Introduction: Reform, Conflict and Resistance in Contemporary China," in *Chinese Society: Change, Conflict and Resistance*, ed. Elizabeth J. Perry and Mark Selden (London: Routledge, 2010), 15.

62. Hall, *Hard Road*.

63. Hall, *Hard Road*, 74.

Chapter 4

1. Parts of chapter 4 have been previously published. See Yin, "Alternative Forms of Media"; Yin, "Cultural Production." I am grateful for the permission to include the materials here.

2. Z. Wang, *Finding Women*.

3. Yin, "Re-articulating Feminisms."

4. Yin, "Re-articulating Feminisms."

5. Simidele Dosekun, "For Western Girls Only? Post-feminism as Transnational Culture," *Feminist Media Studies* 15, no. 6 (2015): 960-75; Rosalind Gill, "Postfeminist Media Culture: Elements of a Sensibility," *European Journal of Cultural Studies* 10, no. 2 (2007): 147-66; Angela McRobbie, *The Aftermath of Feminism: Gender, Culture and Social Change* (Thousand Oaks: SAGE, 2009). On postfeminism in China, see, e.g., Anna Iskra, "'Be Soft like Water, Little Woman': Cultivating Postfeminism in Postsocialist China," *Signs: Journal of Women in Culture and Society* 48, no. 3 (2023): 659-82; Sara Xueting Liao, "Wang Hong Fashion Culture and the Postfeminist Time in China," *Fashion Theory* 25, no 5. (2021): 663-85; Fan Yang, "Post-feminism and Chick Flicks in China: Subjects, Discursive Origin and New Gender Norms," *Feminist Media Studies* 23, no. 3 (2019): 1059-74.

6. Gill, "Postfeminist Media Culture."

7. Sarah Banet-Weiser, *Empowered: Popular Feminism and Popular Misogyny* (Durham, NC: Duke University Press, 2018).

8. Banet-Weiser, *Empowered*.

9. Yin, "Re-articulating Feminisms."

10. See, e.g., Briskin and McDermott, *Women Challenging Unions*; Anne-Marie Greene and Gill Kirton, "Advancing Gender Equality: The Role of Women-Only Trade Union Education," *Gender, Work and Organization* 9, no. 1 (2002): 39-59.

11. Pun and Lu, "Unfinished Proletarianization."

12. Hatla Thelle, "Building Their Own Stage: Constructing the New Worker in China," *Journal of Human Rights Practice* 5, no. 2 (2013): 358-79.

13. See, e.g., Siyuan Yin and Yu Sun, "Intersectional Digital Feminism: Assessing the Participation Politics and Impact of the MeToo Movement in China," *Feminist Media Studies* 21, no. 7 (2021): 1176-92, https://doi.org/10.1080/14680777.2020.1837908.

14. Jia Tan, "Digital Masquerading: Feminist Media Activism in China," *Crime, Media, Culture* 13, no. 2 (2017): 171-86; Jia Tan, *Digital Masquerade: Feminist Rights and Queer Media in China* (New York: New York University Press, 2023); Bin Wang and Catherine Driscoll, "Chinese Feminists on Social Media: Articulating Different Voices, Building Strategic Alliances," *Continuum Journal of Media and Cultural Studies* 33, no. 1 (2019): 1-15.

15. Hartmann, "Unhappy Marriage," 24.

16. Combahee River Collective, "(1977) The Combahee River Collective Statement," BlackPast, April 1977, https://www.blackpast.org/african-american-history/combahee-river-collective-statement-1977/.

17. Kimberle Crenshaw, "Demarginalizing the Intersection of Race and Sex: A Black Feminist Critique of Antidiscrimination Doctrine, Feminist Theory and Antiracist Politics," *University of Chicago Legal Forum* 1, no. 8 (1989): 139-67.

18. Kimberle Crenshaw, "Mapping the Margins: Intersectionality, Identity Politics, and Violence against Women of Color," *Stanford Law Review* 43, no. 6 (1991): 1241-99.

19. Patricia Hill Collins, *Intersectionality as Critical Social Theory* (Durham, NC: Duke University Press, 2019).

20. Collins, *Intersectionality*, 50.

21. Angela McRobbie, "Setting Accounts with Subcultures: A Feminist Critique," *Screen Education* 39 (1980): 37-49.

22. McRobbie, "Setting Accounts."

23. MacKinnon, "Feminism," 520.

24. Hartmann, "Unhappy Marriage," 24.

25. Phil Brown and Albert Park, "Education and Poverty in Rural China," *Economics of Education Review* 21, no. 6 (2002): 523-41; Emily Hannum, "Poverty and Basic Education in Rural China: Villages, Households, and Girls' and Boys' Enrollment," *Comparative Education Review* 47, no. 2 (2003): 141-59; Vilma Seeberg, "Girls' Schooling Empowerment in Rural China: Identifying Capabilities and Social Change in the Village," *Comparative Education Review* 58, no. 4 (2014): 678-707.

26. Mies, *Patriarchy*.

27. Yu Duan, vocalist, "Nüren de zibai" 女人的自白 [Women's claims], by Jiu Ye, n.p., 2016.

28. "Nüren de zibai" 女人的自白 [Women's claims], music and lyrics by Jiu

Ye, Picun shequ laodongjie wanhui 皮村社区劳动节晚会 [Picun Community Labor Day Gala], Beijing, China, May 1, 2016.

29. Christopher Klein, "The Strike That Shook America," HISTORY, September 3, 2012, https://www.history.com/news/the-strike-that-shook-america.

30. James Oppenheim, lyricist, "Bread and Roses," written 1911, music by Martha Coleman, composed 1922, http://www.protestsonglyrics.net/Inspirational_Songs/Bread-and-Roses.phtml.

31. These activists and workers are from a migrant-worker NGO, Lüse qiangwei (绿色蔷薇), in Shenzhen, Guangdong Province. The NGO was established in 2015 to provide service and advocate for rights for female migrant workers and migrant children.

32. Jiu Ye, "Shijie you women butong" 世界有我们不同 [Our being makes it a different world], n.p., 2018.

33. Yu Duan, vocalist, "Ertong de huayuan" 儿童的花园 [Children's garden], by Jiu Ye, n.p., 2018.

34. Yin, "Re-articulating Feminisms."

35. The data was collected from Jianjiao's website in 2017. As Jianjiao' website and WeChat account were permanently shut down in 2021, the source is no longer available to retrieve.

36. On LGBTQ activism in China, see, e.g., Hongwei Bao, *Queer Comrades: Gay Identity and* Tongzhi *Activism in Postsocialist China* (Copenhagen: Nias, 2018); Hongwei Bao, *Queer Media in China* (Oxfordshire: Routledge, 2021); Hongwei Bao, "In Queer Memory: Mediating Queer Chinese History in Digital Video Documentaries," *Panoptikum* 29 (2023): 94-114; Stephanie Yingyi Wang, "Unfinished Revolution: An Overview of Three Decades of LGBT Activism in China," *Made in China Journal* 6, no. 1 (2021): 90-95.

37. Carolyn M. Byerly and Karen Ross, *Women and Media: A Critical Introduction* (Malden, MA: Blackwell, 2006), 99-128 passim. See examples in Ananda Mitra, "Voices of the Marginalized on the Internet: Examples from a Website for Women of South Asia," *Journal of Communication* 54, no. 3 (2004): 492-510; Shabnam Virmani, "Women Making Meaning: Telling Stories about Reality in India," *Feminist Media Studies* 1, no. 2 (2001): 233-43.

38. Byerly and Ross, *Women and Media.*

39. On the critique of the middle-class focus of the MeToo movements and Feminist Voices, see Yin and Sun, "Intersectional Digital Feminism"; Yin, "Re-articulating Feminisms."

40. Downing, "Social Movement Media," 346.

41. Rodriguez, "Civil Society"; Rodriguez, "Citizens' Media."

42. On LGBTQ groups, culture, and communities, see, e.g., Bao, *Queer Media*; Lucetta Yip Lo Kam, *Shanghai Lalas: Female* Tongzhi *Communities and Politics in Urban China* (Hong Kong: Hong Kong University Press, 2013); Chongzheng Wei and Wenli Liu, "Coming Out in Mainland China: A National Survey of LGBTQ Students," *Journal of LGBT Youth* 16, no. 2 (2019): 192-219; Boyang

Zhang et al., "Searching for the Rainbow Connection: Regional Development and LGBT Communities in China," *Journal of Contemporary China* 32, no. 140 (2023): 296-318.

43. The data was collected in 2017 from Jianjiao's WeChat account. The source is not available to retrieve since Jianjiao's shut down.

44. Atton, "Alternative Media."

45. See, e.g., Cory L. Armstrong and Jessica Mahone, "#MeToo in Practice: Revisiting Social Media's Influence in Individual Willingness to Mobilize against Sexual Assault," *Feminist Media Studies* 23, no. 1 (2023): 185-98; Kaitlynn Mendes, Jessica Ringrose, and Jessalynn Keller, "#MeToo and the Promise and Pitfalls of Challenging Rape Culture through Digital Feminist Activism," *European Journal of Women's Studies* 25, no. 2 (2018): 236-46; Jing Zeng, "#MeToo as Connective Action: A Study of the Anti-sexual Violence and Anti-sexual Harassment Campaign on Chinese Social Media in 2018," *Journalism Practice* 14, no. 2 (2020): 171-90.

46. On connective actions, see W. Lance Bennett and Alexandra Segerberg, "The Logic of Connective Action: Digital Media and the Personalization of Contentious Politics," *Information, Communication and Society* 15, no. 5 (2012): 739-68; Bennett and Segerberg, *Logic of Connective Action*.

47. Nico Carpentier, Rico Lie, and Jan Servaes, "Community Media—Muting the Democratic Media Discourse?," in *Political Communication*, ed. Philip Seib (London: SAGE, 2008) 16-36.

48. Arne Hintz, "Towards Community and Non-profit Media Legislation in South America: Challenging Media Power through Citizen Participation," in *The International Political Economy of Communication: Media and Power in South America*, ed. Cheryl Martens, Ernesto Vivares, and Robert W. McChesney (London: Palgrave MacMillan, 2014), 46-62; Arne Hintz, "Policy Hacking: Citizen-Based Policymaking and Media Reform," in *Strategies for Media Reform: International Perspectives*, ed. Des Freedman (New York: Fordham University Press, 2016), 223-38.

49. Arne Hintz, "Policy Activism: Advocating, Protesting and Hacking Media Regulation," in *The Routledge Companion to Media and Activism*, ed. Graham Meikle (London: Routledge, 2018), 319-28.

50. Yanping Guo, "Female Projectionists on the Move: Exhibiting Socialist Gender Equality in Rural China (1949-1966)," *Gender and History* 36, no. 2 (2024): 639-56; Yalan Huang, "War on Women: Interlocking Conflicts within *The Vagina Monologues* in China," *Asian Journal of Communication* 26, no. 5 (2016): 466-84.

51. Mies, *Patriarchy*; Z. Wang, *Finding Women*.

Chapter 5

1. Mario Diani, "The Concept of Social Movement," *Sociological Review* 40, no. 1 (1992): 1-25.

2. Della Porta and Diani, *Social Movements*; Mario Diani and Ivano Bison, "Organizations, Coalitions, and Movements," *Theory and Society* 33 (2004): 281–309.

3. Yongshun Cai, *Collective Resistance in China: Why Popular Protests Succeed or Fail* (Stanford: Stanford University Press, 2010); Perry and Selden, "Introduction"; Guobin Yang, *The Power of the Internet in China: Citizen Activism Online* (New York: Columbia University Press, 2009).

4. Anita Chan, "Strikes in China's Export Industries in Comparative Perspective," *China Journal* 65 (January 2011): 227–51, https://doi.org/10.1086/tcj .65.25790556; Xiao Han, "Searching for an Online Space for Feminism? The Chinese Feminist Group Gender Watch Women's Voice and Its Changing Approaches to Online Misogyny," *Feminist Media Studies* 18, no. 4 (2018): 734–49, https://doi.org/10.1080/14680777.2018.1447430; Y. Huang, "War on Women"; Ronggui Huang and Ngai-ming Yip, "Internet and Activism in Urban China: A Case Study of Protests in Xiamen and Panyu," *Journal of Comparative Asian Development* 11, no. 2 (2012) 201–23; Jun Jing, "Environmental Protests in Rural China," in *Chinese Society: Change, Conflict and Resistance*, ed. Elizabeth J. Perry and Mark Selden (New York: Routledge, 2000), 197–214; C. Lee, "Revenge of History"; Tyrene White, "Domination, Resistance and Accomodation in China's One-Child Campaign," in *Chinese Society: Change, Conflict and Resistance*, 3rd ed., ed. Elizabeth J. Perry and Mark Selden (New York: Routledge, 2010), 171–96; G. Yang, *Power of the Internet*; Yin and Sun, "Intersectional Digital Feminism."

5. C. Lee, "Revenge of History."

6. C. Lee, "Revenge of History."

7. R. Huang and Yip, "Internet and Activism."

8. G. Yang, *Power of the Internet.*

9. Zixue Tai, "Networked Resistance: Digital Populism, Online Activism, and Mass Dissent in China," *Popular Communication* 13, no. 2 (2015): 120–31, https://doi.org/10.1080/15405702.2015.1021469; Zixue Tai, "Networked Activism in China," in *Social Networking: Redefining Communication in the Digital Age*, ed. Anastacia Kurylo and Tatyana Dumova (Lanham, MD: Rowman and Littlefield, 2016), 145–60; Zixue Tai, "Social Media and Contentious Action in China," in *The Routledge Companion to Media and Activism*, ed. Graham Meikle (London: Routledge, 2018), 97–107.

10. Christopher Heurlin, *Responsive Authoritarianism in China* (New York: Cambridge University Press, 2016).

11. Cai, *Collective Resistance.*

12. Perry and Selden, "Introduction."

13. Jacka, *Creating a Public Sphere*; Qiusha Ma, *Non-governmental Organizations in Contemporary China: Paving the Way to Civil Society?* (New York: Routledge, 2006).

14. Ma, *Non-governmental Organizations.*

15. Ma, *Non-governmental Organizations*.

16. Jacka, *Creating a Public Sphere*; Ma, *Non-governmental Organizations*; Tony Saich, "Negotiating the State: The Development of Social Organizations in China," *China Quarterly* 161 (March 2000): 124-41; Jing Wang, "NGO2.0 and Social Media Praxis: Activist as Researcher," *Chinese Journal of Communication* 8, no. 1 (2015): 18-41.

17. Saich, "Negotiating the State."

18. Ma, *Non-governmental Organizations*.

19. J. Wang, "NGO2.0," 28.

20. Jacka, *Creating a Public Sphere*.

21. Jacka, *Creating a Public Sphere*.

22. Hui Wang, "Contemporary Chinese Thought and the Question of Modernity," trans. Rebecca E. Karl, *Social Text* 55 (Summer 1998): 33.

23. Jude Howell, "Shall We Dance? Welfarist Incorporation and the Politics of State-Labour NGO Relations," *China Quarterly* 223 (September 2015): 702-23, https://doi.org/10.1017/S0305741015001174; Jude Howell, "NGOs and Civil Society: The Politics of Crafting a Civic Welfare Infrastructure in the Hu-Wen Period," *China Quarterly* 237 (2019): 58-81; Han Zhu and Lu Jun, "The Crackdown on Rights-Advocacy NGOs in Xi's China: Politicizing the Law and Legalizing the Repression," *Journal of Contemporary China* 31, no. 136 (2021): 518-38. https://doi.org/10.1080/10670564.2021.1985829.

24. H. Zhu and Jun, "Crackdown."

25. Jude Howell and Tim Pringle, "Shades of Authoritarianism and State-Labour Relations in China," *British Journal of Industrial Relations* 57, no. 2 (2018): 223-46, https://doi.org/10.1111/bjir.12436; H. Zhu and Jun, "Crackdown."

26. Ma, *Non-governmental Organizations*.

27. H. Zhu and Jun, "Crackdown."

28. The Chinese state first initiated the national project of Building a New Socialist Countryside (Jianshe shehuizhuyi xinonngcun; 建设社会主义新农村) in 2006 to reduce rural poverty and improve rural lives. Subsequently, Xi's administration revived the policy with the slogan "Rejuvenation of villages." Scholars have criticized local governments' continuous demolition and relocation of rural land, community, and resources. See, e.g., Ningning Chen and Lily Kong, "Rural Revitalization in China: Towards Inclusive Geographies of Ruralization," *Dialogues in Human Geography* 12, no. 2 (2022): 213-17; Elena Meyer-Clement, "Rural Urbanization under Xi Jinping: From Rapid Community Building to Steady Urbanization?," *China Information* 34, no. 2 (2020): 187-207.

29. Robert Asen, "Seeking the 'Counter' in Counterpublics," *Communication Theory* 10, no. 4 (2000): 424-46, https://doi.org/10.1111/j.1468-2885.2000.tb00201.x.

30. Asen, "Seeking the 'Counter.'"

31. Asen, "Seeking the 'Counter,'" 437.

32. Nancy Fraser, "Rethinking the Public Sphere: A Contribution to the Critique of Actually Existing Democracy," *Social Text* 25-26 (1990): 56-80.

33. Oskar Negt and Alexander Kluge, *Public Sphere and Experience: Toward an Analysis of the Bourgeois and Proletarian Public Sphere* (Minneapolis: University of Minnesota Press, 1993).

34. Negt and Kluge, *Public Sphere*.

35. Rita Felski, *Beyond Feminist Aesthetics: Feminist Literature and Social Change* (Cambridge, MA: Harvard University Press, 1989). See also Hoda Elsadda, "Arab Women Bloggers: The Emergence of Literary Counterpublics," *Middle East Journal of Culture and Communication* 3, no. 3 (2010): 312-32, https://doi.org/10.1163/187398610X538678; Michael Salter, "Justice and Revenge in Online Counter-Publics: Emerging Responses to Sexual Violence in the Age of Social Media," *Crime, Media, Culture* 9, no. 3 (2013): 225-42, https://doi.org/10.1177/1741659013493918; Ann Travers, "Parallel Subaltern Feminist Counterpublics in Cyberspace," *Sociological Perspectives* 46, no 2. (2003): 223-37, https://doi.org/10.1525/sop.2003.46.2.223.

36. W. Sun, *Subaltern China*.

37. Wanning Sun draws upon Ranajit Guha, Dipesh Chakrabarty, and Gayatri Spivak's discussions on subaltern consciousness. See W. Sun, *Subaltern China*.

38. Fengyan Wang, "Confucian Thinking in Traditional Moral Education: Key Ideas and Fundamental Features," *Journal of Moral Education* 33, no. 4 (2004): 429-47; Ping Li et al., "Deyu as Moral Education in Modern China: Ideological Functions and Transformations," *Journal of Moral Education* 33, no. 4 (2004): 449-64.

39. Qiu, *Goodbye iSlave*, 132.

40. On the role of hometowns in networks' formation among migrant workers, see Jacka, *Rural Women*; Pun, *Made in China*.

41. Jacka, *Rural Women*. The term *dagong* (打工) means "to work," and *mei* (妹) is a colloquial term for "young woman" or "sister." Therefore, *dagongmei* directly translates to "working sisters" or "female laborers." The concept gained attention in the late twentieth and early twenty-first centuries as a reflection of the significant influx of young female workers from rural to urban areas in China, particularly during periods of rapid industrialization and economic development. In both media and popular discussions, the term *dagongmei* is often utilized as a derogatory identity category when referring to young female migrant workers.

42. Lee and Shen, "Anti-solidarity Machine?"

43. Lee and Shen, "Anti-solidarity Machine?"; Carolyn Hsu, "Beyond Civil Society: An Organizational Perspective on State-NGO Relations in the People's Republic of China," *Journal of Civil Society* 6, no. 3 (2010): 259-77.

44. Franceschini, "Labour NGOs."

45. "Beijing gongyouzhijia jianjie" 北京工友之家简介 [Introduction to Beijing

Migrant Workers' Home], Zhongguo fazhan jianbao 中国发展简报, accessed September 11, 2024, https://www.chinadevelopmentbrief.org.cn/company/detail/185.html; "Zhongxuanbu wenhuabu biaozhang fuwu nongmin fuwu jiceng wenhua xianjin jiti" 中宣部文化部表彰服务农民服务基层文化先进集体 [The Publicity Department and the Ministry of Culture commended advanced groups for serving farmers and promoting grassroots culture], Zhonghua renmin gongheguo zhongyang renmin zhengfu 中华人民共和国中央人民政府, December 14, 2015, https://www.gov.cn/jrzg/2005- 12/14/content_126981.htm.

46. Anthony J. Spires, "Contingent Symbiosis and Civil Society in an Authoritarian State: Understanding the Survival of China's Grassroots NGOs," *American Journal of Sociology* 117, no. 1 (2011) 1-45.

47. Spires, "Contingent Symbiosis."

48. MWH's public accounts on WeChat usually have less than one thousand page views for its articles. The number is quite small compared with popular public accounts on WeChat, with over one hundred thousand page views.

49. Qiu, "Social Media."

50. Nick Couldry, *Why Voice Matters: Culture and Politics after Neoliberalism* (Los Angeles: SAGE, 2010).

51. Jo Tacchi, "The Issues of Voice and the Challenges of Listening," *New Media and Society* 14, no. 4 (2012): 652-68.

Conclusion

1. Matt Bolton, "'Democratic Socialism' and the Concept of (Post)Capitalism," *Political Quarterly* 91, no. 2 (2020): 334-42; Richard Wolff, *Understanding Socialism* (New York: Democracy at Work, 2019).

2. hooks, *Feminism Is for Everybody*.

3. Rosemarie Garland-Thomson, "Misfits: A Feminist Materialist Disability Concept," *Hypatia* 26, no. 3 (2011): 597.

4. Combahee River Collective, "Combahee River Collective Statement."

5. Tithi Bhattacharya, ed., *Social Reproduction Theory: Remapping Class, Recentering Oppression* (London: Pluto, 2017); Federici, "Social Reproduction Theory"; MacKinnon, "Feminism"; Mies, *Patriarchy*.

6. On "conjunctural analysis," see Lawrence Grossberg, *We Gotta Get Out of This Place: Popular Conservatism and Postmodern Culture* (New York: Routledge, 1992).

Bibliography

Althusser, Louis. *On Ideology*. 1971; repr., London: Verso Books, 2008.

Anagnost, Ann. "The Corporeal Politics of Quality (*Suzhi*)." *Public Culture* 16, no. 2 (2004): 189-208.

Anderson, Bridget. "Just Another Job? Paying for Domestic Work." *Gender and Development* 9, no. 1 (2001): 25-33.

Armstrong, Cory L., and Jessica Mahone. "#MeToo in Practice: Revisiting Social Media's Influence in Individual Willingness to Mobilize against Sexual Assault." *Feminist Media Studies* 23, no. 1 (2023): 185-98.

Asen, Robert. "Seeking the 'Counter' in Counterpublics." *Communication Theory* 10, no. 4 (2000): 424-46. https://doi.org/10.1111/j.1468-2885.2000.tb00201.x.

Atton, Chris. *Alternative Media*. Thousand Oaks: SAGE, 2002.

Atton, Chris. "Alternative Media." In *Encyclopedia of Social Movement Media*, edited by John D. H. Downing, 15-19. Thousand Oaks: SAGE, 2011.

Atton, Chris. "A Reassessment of the Alternative Press." *Media, Culture and Society* 21, no. 1 (1999): 51-76. https://doi.org/10.1177/016344399021001003.

Atton, Chris. *Routledge Companion to Alternative and Community Media*. New York: Routledge, 2015.

Banet-Weiser, Sarah. *Empowered: Popular Feminism and Popular Misogyny*. Durham, NC: Duke University Press, 2018.

Bao, Hongwei. "In Queer Memory: Mediating Queer Chinese History in Digital Video Documentaries." *Panoptikum* 29 (2023): 94-114.

Bao, Hongwei. *Queer Comrades: Gay Identity and* Tongzhi *Activism in Postsocialist China*. Copenhagen: Nias, 2018.

Bao, Hongwei. *Queer Media in China*. Oxfordshire: Routledge, 2021.

Bartky, Sandra Lee. *Femininity and Domination Studies in the Phenomenology of Oppression*. Oxfordshire: Routledge, 1990.

Battistella, Graziano. "The Human Rights of Migrant Workers: Agenda for NGOs." *International Migration Review* 27, no. 1 (1993): 191-201.

Bauder, Harald. "Foreign Farm Workers in Ontario (Canada): Exclusionary Discourse in the Newsprint Media." *Journal of Peasant Studies* 35, no. 1 (2008): 100-118.

BBC (China edition). "Shenzhen dangju beizhi hushi fushikang shijian" 深圳当局被指忽视富士康事件 [Shenzhen government was criticized of neglecting the Foxconn instance]. May 27, 2010. https://www.bbc.com/zhongwen/trad/world/2010/05/100527_foxconn_shenzhen.

Bennett, W. Lance. "Communicating Global Activism: Some Strengths and Vulnerabilities of Networked Politics." In *Cyberprotest: New Media, Citizens and Social Movements*, edited by Wim van de Donk, Brian D. Loader, Paul G. Nixon, and Dieter Rucht, 109-28. London: Routledge, 2004.

Bennett, W. Lance, and Alexandra Segerberg. "The Logic of Connective Action: Digital Media and the Personalization of Contentious Politics." *Information, Communication and Society* 15, no. 5 (2012): 739-68.

Bennett, W. Lance, and Alexandra Segerberg. *The Logic of Connective Action: Digital Media and the Personalization of Contentious Politics*. London: Cambridge University Press, 2013.

Bhattacharya, Tithi, ed. *Social Reproduction Theory: Remapping Class, Recentering Oppression*. London: Pluto, 2017.

Bickerton, Geoff, and Jane Stinson. "Challenges Facing the Canadian Labour Movement in the Context of Globalization, Unemployment and the Casualization of Labour." In *Labour and the Challenges of Globalization: What Prospects for Transnational Solidarity?*, edited by Andreas Bieler, Ingemar Lindberg, and Devan Pillay, 161-76. London: Pluto, 2008.

Bieler, Andreas, Ingemar Lindberg, and Devan Pillay. "The Future of the Global Working Class: An Introduction." In *Labour and the Challenges of Globalization: What Prospects for Transnational Solidarity?*, edited by Andreas Bieler, Ingemar Lindberg, and Devan Pillay, 1-11. London: Pluto, 2008.

Bieler, Andreas, Ingemar Lindberg, and Devan Pillay, eds. *Labour and the Challenges of Globalization: What Prospects for Transnational Solidarity*. London: Pluto, 2008.

Boal, Augusto. *Theatre of the Oppressed*. Toronto: Pluto, 1979.

Bolton, Matt. "'Democratic Socialism' and the Concept of (Post)Capitalism." *Political Quarterly* 91, no. 2 (2020): 334-42.

Bourdieu, Pierre. *Distinction: A Social Critique of the Judgement of Taste*. London: Routledge, 1984.

Brickner, Rachel K., and Meaghan Dalton. "Organizing Baristas in Halifax Cafes: Precarious Work and Gender and Class Identities in the Millennial Generation." *Critical Sociology* 45, no 4. (2019): 485-500.

Briskin, Linda, and Patricia McDermott, eds. *Women Challenging Unions: Feminism, Democracy, and Militancy.* Toronto: University of Toronto Press, 1993.

Brown, Phil, and Albert Park. "Education and Poverty in Rural China." *Economics of Education Review* 21, no. 6 (2002): 523-41.

Bu Wei. "Shehuizhuyi wenyi de benzhi shi renmin de wenyi" 社会主义文艺的本质是人民的文艺 [The essence of socialist literature and art is people's literature and art]. Zhongguo fazhan menhu wang中国发展门户网, January 20, 2017. http://m.wyzxwk.com/content.php?classid=25&id=376028.

Byerly, Carolyn M., and Karen Ross. *Women and Media: A Critical Introduction.* Malden, MA: Blackwell, 2006.

Cai, Yongshun. *Collective Resistance in China: Why Popular Protests Succeed or Fail.* Stanford: Stanford University Press, 2010.

Cammaerts, Bart, Alice Mattoni, and Patrick McCurdy. Introduction to *Mediation and Protest Movements,* edited by Bart Cammaerts, Alice Mattoni, and Patrick McCurdy, 1-20. Bristol: Intellect, 2013.

Carpentier, Nico, Rico Lie, and Jan Servaes. "Community Media—Muting the Democratic Media Discourse?" In *Political Communication,* edited by Philip Seib, 16-36. London: SAGE, 2008.

Castells, Manuel. *Communication Power.* Oxford: Oxford University Press, 2009.

Castells, Manuel. *Networks of Outrage and Hope-Social Movements in the Internet Age.* Cambridge: Polity, 2012.

Castells, Manuel. *The Rise of the Network Society.* Hoboken: John Wiley and Sons, 1996.

Chan, Anita. "Strikes in China's Export Industries in Comparative Perspective." *China Journal* 65 (January 2011): 227-51. https://doi.org/10.1086/tcj.65.25790556.

Chan, Chris King-chi. "Community-Based Organizations for Migrant Workers' Rights: The Emergence of Labour NGOs in China." *Community Development Journal* 48, no. 1 (2012): 6-22.

Chan, Chris King-chi, and Ngai Pun. "The Making of a New Working Class? A Study of Collective Actions of Migrant Workers in South China." *China Quarterly* 198 (June 2009): 287-303.

Chan, Chris King-chi, Ngai Pun, and Jenny Chan. "The Role of the State, Labour Policy and Migrant Workers' Struggles in Globalized China." *Global Labour Journal* 1, no. 1 (January 2010): 132-51. https://doi.org/10.15173/glj.v1i1.1068.

Chan, Jenny. "Jasic Workers Fight for Union Rights." *New Politics* 17, no. 2 (Winter 2019): 84-89.

Chan, Jenny Wai-Ling. "Chinese Women Workers Organize in the Export Zone." *New Labor Forum* 15, no. 1 (2006): 19-27.

Chan, Jenny, Manjusha Nair, and Chris Rhomberg. "Precarization and Labor Resistance: Canada, the USA, India and China." *Critical Sociology* 45, no. 4-5 (2019): 469-83.

Chan, Jenny, and Mark Selden. "China's Rural Migrant Workers, the State, and Labor Politics." *Critical Asian Studies* 46, no. 4 (2014): 599-620.

Chen, Feng. "Between the State and Labour: The Conflict of Chinese Trade Unions' Double Identity in Market Reform." *China Quarterly* 176 (2003): 1006-28.

Chen, Feng. "China's Road to the Construction of Labor Rights." *Journal of Sociology* 52, no. 1 (2015): 24-38.

Chen, Ningning, and Lily Kong. "Rural Revitalization in China: Towards Inclusive Geographies of Ruralization." *Dialogues in Human Geography* 12, no. 2 (2022): 213-17.

Cheng, Hsin-I. "On Migrant Workers' Social Status in Taiwan: A Critical Analysis of Mainstream News Discourse." *International Journal of Communication* 10 (2016): 2509-28.

China Labor Bulletin. *Migrant Workers and Their Children.* September 2023. https://clb.org.hk/en/content/migrant-workers-and-their-children.

Chun, Jennifer Jihye. "The Contested Politics of Gender and Irregular Employment: Revitalizing the South Korean Democratic Labour Movement." In *Labour and the Challenges of Globalization: What Prospects for Transnational Solidarity?*, edited by Andreas Bieler, Ingemar Lindberg, and Devan Pillay, 23-42. London: Pluto, 2008.

Clawson, Dan. *The Next Upsurge: Labor and the New Social Movements.* Ithaca, NY: Cornell University Press, 2003.

Coleman, Stephen, and Karen Ross. *The Media and the Public: "Them" and "Us" in Media Discourse.* Malden, MA: Wiley-Blackwell, 2010.

Collins, Patricia Hill. *Intersectionality as Critical Social Theory.* Durham, NC: Duke University Press, 2019.

Collins, Patricia Hill. "Some Group Matters: Intersectionality, Situated Standpoints, and Black Feminist Thought." In *A Companion to African-American Philosophy*, edited by Tommy Lee Lott and John Pittman, 205-29. Hoboken: Blackwell, 2003.

Combahee River Collective. "(1977) The Combahee River Collective Statement." BlackPast, April 1977. https://www.blackpast.org/african-american-history/combahee-river-collective-statement-1977/.

Conquergood, Dwight. "Performance Studies: Interventions and Radical Research." *Drama Review* 46, no. 2 (2002): 145-56.

Constable, Nicole. *Maid to Order in Hong Kong: Stories of Migrant Workers.* 2nd ed. Ithaca, NY: Cornell University Press, 2007.

Constable, Nicole. "Migrant Workers and the Many States of Protest in Hong Kong." *Critical Asian Studies* 41, no. 1 (2009): 143-64.

Couldry, Nick. *Why Voice Matters: Culture and Politics after Neoliberalism.* Los Angeles: SAGE, 2010.

Cox, Laurence, and Alf Gunvald Nilsen. *We Make Our Own History: Marxism and Social Movements in the Twilight of Neoliberalism.* London: Pluto, 2014.

Cranford, Cynthia, and Deena Ladd. "Community Unionism: Organising for Fair Employment in Canada." *Just Labour* 3 (Fall 2003): 46-59.

Crenshaw, Kimberle. "Demarginalizing the Intersection of Race and Sex: A Black Feminist Critique of Antidiscrimination Doctrine, Feminist Theory and Antiracist Politics." *University of Chicago Legal Forum* 1, no. 8 (1989): 139-67.

Crenshaw, Kimberle. "Mapping the Margins: Intersectionality, Identity Politics, and Violence against Women of Color." *Stanford Law Review* 43, no. 6 (1991): 1241-99.

Davis, Angela. *Women, Race and Class.* New York: Random House, 1981.

della Porta, Donatella. "Bridging Research on Democracy, Social Movements and Communication." In *Mediation and Protest Movements*, edited by Bart Cammaerts, Alice Mattoni, and Patrick McCurdy, 21-39. Bristol: Intellect, 2013.

della Porta, Donatella, and Mario Diani. *Social Movements: An Introduction.* 2nd ed. Malden, MA: Blackwell, 2006.

della Porta, Donatella, and Elena Pavan. "The Nexus between Media, Communication and Social Movements: Looking Back and the Way Forward." In *The Routledge Companion to Media and Activism*, edited by Graham Meikle, 29-37. London: Routledge, 2018.

Dencik, Lina, and Peter Wilkin. *Worker Resistance and Media: Challenging Global Corporate Power in the 21st Century.* New York: Peter Lang, 2015.

Denzin, Norman K. "Emancipatory Discourses and the Ethics and Politics of Interpretation." In *The SAGE Handbook of Qualitative Research*, edited by Norman K. Denzin and Yvonna S. Lincoln, 933-58. Thousand Oaks: SAGE, 2005.

Denzin, Norman K. *Performance Ethnography: Critical Pedagogy and the Politics of Culture.* Thousand Oaks: SAGE, 2003.

Diani, Mario. "The Concept of Social Movement." *Sociological Review* 40, no. 1 (1992): 1-25.

Diani, Mario, and Ivano Bison. "Organizations, Coalitions, and Movements." *Theory and Society* 33 (2004): 281-309.

Dibben, Pauline. "Trade Union Change, Development and Renewal in Emerging Economies: The Case of Mozambique." *Work, Employment and Society* 24, no. 3 (2010): 468-86.

Dibben, Pauline, and Sara Nadin. "Community Unionism in Africa: The Case of Mozambique." *Industrial Relations* 66, no. 1 (2011): 54-73.

Ding Jing, Mao Wei, Yang Shujun, and Ren Chao. "Zai Beijing pinming dagong de dagongren" 在北京拼命打工的打工人 [Hard-working workers in Beijing]. *Liaowang* 瞭望, May 6, 2021. http://lw.xinhuanet.com/2021-05/06/c_1399 28069.htm.

Dosekun, Simidele. "For Western Girls Only? Post-feminism as Transnational Culture." *Feminist Media Studies* 15, no. 6 (2015): 960-75.

Douglass, Frederick. *My Bondage and Freedom*. 1855; repr., New York: Dover, 1969.

Downing, John D. H. "Looking Back, Looking Ahead: What Has Changed in Social Movement Media since the Internet and Social Media?" In *The Routledge Companion to Media and Activism*, edited by Graham Meikle, 19-28. London: Routledge, 2018.

Downing, John D. H. "Social Movement Media in the Process of Constructive Social Change." In *The Handbook of Development Communication and Social Change*, edited by Karin Gwinn Wilkins, Thomas Tufte, and Rafael Obregon, 331-50. Malden, MA: Wiley-Blackwell, 2014.

Dribbusch, Heiner, and Thorsten Schulten. "German Trade Unions between Neoliberal Restructuring, Social Partnership and Internationalism." In *Labour and the Challenges of Globalization: What Prospects for Transnational Solidarity?*, edited by Andreas Bieler, Ingemar Lindberg, and Devan Pillay, 178-96. London: Pluto, 2008.

Duvisac, Sara. "Reconstituting the Industrial Worker: Precarity in the Indian Auto Sector." *Critical Sociology* 45, no. 4-5 (2019): 533-48.

Economic Policy Institute. *National Survey of Gig Workers Paints a Picture of Poor Working Conditions, Low Pay*. June 2022. https://www.epi.org/publication/gig-worker-survey/.

Elfstrom, Manfred. "Two Steps Forward, One Step Back: Chinese State Reactions to Labour Unrest." *China Quarterly* 240 (2019): 855-79. https://doi.org/10.1017/S0305741019000067.

Elsadda, Hoda. "Arab Women Bloggers: The Emergence of Literary Counterpublics." *Middle East Journal of Culture and Communication* 3, no. 3 (2010): 312-32. https://doi.org/10.1163/187398610X538678.

Eyerman, Ron, and Andrew Jamison. *Music and Social Movements: Mobilizing Traditions in the Twentieth Century*. Cambridge: Cambridge University Press, 1998.

Fan Yusu. "Wo shi Fan Yusu" 我是范雨素 [I am Fan Yusu]. Sohu 搜狐, September 13, 2018. https://www.sohu.com/a/253642863_147822.

Fang Lan. "Zhongyang diaochazu ganfu Shenzhen fushikang" 中央调查组赶赴深圳富士康 [The investigation team of the central government arrived at Foxconn in Shenzhen]. Sina 新浪财经, May 28, 2010. http://finance.sina.com.cn/roll/20100528/13208019636.shtml.

Fanon, Frantz. *Black Skin, White Masks*. New York: Grove Press, 1952.

Federici, Silvia. "Social Reproduction Theory: History, Issues and Present Challenges." *Radical Philosophy* 204 (2019): 55-57.

Feigenbaum, Anna. "Can the Women's Peace Camp Be Televised? Challenging Mainstream Media Coverage of Greenham Common." In *The Routledge Companion to Media and Activism*, edited by Graham Meikle, 47-56. London: Routledge, 2018.

Felski, Rita. *Beyond Feminist Aesthetics: Feminist Literature and Social Change*. Cambridge, MA: Harvard University Press, 1989.

Foucault, Michel. "The Subject and Power." In *Michel Foucault: Beyond Structuralism and Hermeneutics*, edited by Hubert Dreyfus and Paul Rabinow, 208-26. Chicago: University of Chicago Press, 1983.

Franceschini, Ivan. "Labour NGOs in China: A Real Force for Political Change." *China Quarterly* 218 (2014): 474-92.

Fraser, Nancy. "Rethinking the Public Sphere: A Contribution to the Critique of Actually Existing Democracy." *Social Text* 25-26 (1990): 56-80.

Friedman, Eli. *Insurgency Trap: Labor Politics in Postsocialist China*. Ithaca, NY: Cornell University Press, 2014.

Fu, Diana. "A Cage of Voices: Producing and Doing *Dagongmei* in Contemporary China." *Modern China* 35, no. 5 (2009): 527-61.

Fu, Diana. "Disguised Collective Action in China." *Comparative Political Studies* 50, no. 4 (2017): 499-527.

Fu, Diana. *Mobilizing without the Masses: Control and Contention in China*. Cambridge: Cambridge University Press, 2018.

Fu Shiye. "Zai dushuli, nvgong doushi yinxingren" 在都市里，女工都是隐形人 [Female workers are invisible in cities]. *Jiemian xinwen* 界面新闻, December 20, 2017. https://www.jiemian.com/article/1830918.html.

Fuchs, Christian. "Critique of the Political Economy of Informational Capitalism and Social Media." In *Critique, Social Media and the Information Society*, edited by Christian Fuchs and Marisol Sandoval, 48-63. New York: Routledge, 2013.

Fuchs, Christian. *Social Media: A Critical Introduction*. Thousand Oaks: SAGE, 2014.

Fuentes-Bautista, Martha, and Gisela Gil-Egui. "Community Media and the Rearticulation of State-Civil Society Relations in Venezuela." *Communication, Culture and Critique* 4, no. 3 (2011): 250-74.

Gaetano, Arianne M. "Filial Daughters, Modern Women: Migrant Domestic Workers in Post-Mao Beijing." In *On the Move: Women and Rural-to-Urban Migration in Contemporary China*, edited by Arianne M. Gaetano and Tamara Jacka, 41-79. New York: Columbia University Press, 2004.

Garland-Thomson, Rosemarie. "Misfits: A Feminist Materialist Disability Concept." *Hypatia* 26, no. 3 (2011): 591-609.

Gerbaudo, Paolo, and Emiliano Trere. "In Search of the 'We' of Social Media Activism: Introduction to the Special Issue on Social Media and Protest Identities." In "Social Media and Protest Identities," edited by Paolo Gerbaudo and Emiliano Trere. Special issue, *Information, Communication and Society* 18, no. 8 (2015): 865-71.

Ghodsee, Kristen. *Socialist Women's Activism and Global Solidarity during the Cold War*. Durham, NC: Duke University Press, 2019.

Gibson-Graham, J. K. *A Postcapitalist Politics*. Minneapolis: University of Minnesota Press, 2006.

Gilbert, Helen. "Black and White and Re(a)d All over Again: Indigenous Minstrelsy in Contemporary Canadian and Australian Theatre." *Theatre Journal* 55 (2003): 679-98.

Gill, Rosalind. "Postfeminist Media Culture: Elements of a Sensibility." *European Journal of Cultural Studies* 10, no. 2 (2007): 147-66.

Gitlin, Todd. *The Whole World Is Watching: Mass Media in the Making and Unmaking of the New Left*. Berkeley: University of California Press, 1980.

Glenn, Evelyn Nakano. *Issei, Nisei, War Bride: Three Generations of Japanese American Women in Domestic Service*. Philadelphia, PA: Temple University Press, 1986.

Gramsci, Antonio. *Antonio Gramsci: Selections from Political Writings, 1910-1920*. Translated by John Mathews. New York: International Publishers, 1977.

Greene, Anne-Marie, and Gill Kirton. "Advancing Gender Equality: The Role of Women-Only Trade Union Education." *Gender, Work and Organization* 9, no. 1 (2002): 39-59.

Grez, Evelyn Encalada. "Justice for Migrant Farm Workers: Reflections on the Importance of Community Organising." *Relay: A Socialist Project Review* 12 (2006): 23-25.

Grossberg, Lawrence. *We Gotta Get Out of This Place: Popular Conservatism and Postmodern Culture*. New York: Routledge, 1992.

Gumbrell-McCormick, Rebecca, and Richard Hyman. *Trade Unions in Western Europe: Hard Times, Hard Choices*. Cary, NC: Oxford University Press, 2013.

Guo, Taihui. "Rights in Action: The Impact of Chinese Migrant Workers' Resistances on Citizenship Rights." *Journal of Chinese Political Science* 19 (2014): 421-34.

Guo, Yanping. "Female Projectionists on the Move: Exhibiting Socialist Gender Equality in Rural China (1949-1966)." *Gender and History* 36, no. 2 (2024): 639-56.

Hadl, Gabriele. "Alternative Media: Policy Issues." In *Encyclopedia of Social Movement Media*, edited by John D. H. Downing, 33-35. Thousand Oaks: SAGE, 2011.

Hall, Stuart. *The Hard Road to Renewal: Thatcherism and the Crisis of the Left*. London: Verso Books, 1988.

Hall, Stuart. "The Problem of Ideology: Marxism without Guarantees." In *Stuart Hall: Critical Dialogues in Cultural Studies*. 2nd ed., edited by David Morley and Kuan-Hsing Chen, 25-47. New York: Routledge, 2005.

Han, Xiao. "Searching for an Online Space for Feminism? The Chinese Feminist Group Gender Watch Women's Voice and Its Changing Approaches to Online Misogyny." *Feminist Media Studies* 18, no. 4 (2018): 734-49. https://doi.org/10.1080/14680777.2018.1447430.

Hangzhou wang 杭州网. "2013 Dagong chunwan juxing" 2013打工春晚举行 [Dagong Spring Festival gala is held in 2013]. January 28, 2013. https://news .hangzhou.com.cn/shxw/content/2013-01/28/content_4585644.htm.

Hannum, Emily. "Poverty and Basic Education in Rural China: Villages, House-holds, and Girls' and Boys' Enrollment." *Comparative Education Review* 47, no. 2 (2003): 141-59.

Hao Zhixi. "Weiquan fenxiang" 维权分享 [Sharing rights protection]. *Picun shequ bao* 皮村社区报, August 5, 2014.

Harding, Sandra. *Whose Science? Whose Knowledge? Thinking from Women's Lives*. Ithaca, NY: Cornell University Press, 1991.

Harriss-White, Barbara. *India Working Essays on Society and Economy*. Cam-bridge: Cambridge University Press, 2002.

Hartmann, Heidi I. "The Unhappy Marriage of Marxism and Feminism: To-wards a More Progressive Union." *Capital and Class* 3, no. 2 (1979): 1-33.

Harvey, David. *A Brief History of Neoliberalism*. Cary, NC: Oxford University Press, 2006.

Harvey, David. *The Condition of Postmodernity: An Enquiry into the Origins of Cultural Change*. Cambridge, MA: Wiley-Blackwell, 1989.

Harvey, David. "Neoliberalism as Creative Destruction." *Annals of the Ameri-can Academy of Political and Social Science* 610, no. 1 (2007): 22-44.

Harvey, David. "Universal Alienation." *Triple C: Communication, Capitalism and Critique* 16, no. 2 (2018): 424-39.

Heurlin, Christopher. *Responsive Authoritarianism in China*. New York: Cam-bridge University Press, 2016.

Hickel, Jason. *The Divide: A Brief Guide to Global Inequality and Its Solutions*. London: William Heinemann, 2017.

Hintz, Arne. "Policy Activism: Advocating, Protesting and Hacking Media Reg-ulation." In *The Routledge Companion to Media and Activism*, edited by Graham Meikle, 319-28. London: Routledge, 2018.

Hintz, Arne. "Policy Hacking: Citizen-Based Policymaking and Media Reform." In *Strategies for Media Reform: International Perspectives*, edited by Des Freedman, 223-38. New York: Fordham University Press, 2016.

Hintz, Arne. "Towards Community and Non-profit Media Legislation in South America: Challenging Media Power through Citizen Participation." In *The International Political Economy of Communication: Media and Power in South America*, edited by Cheryl Martens, Ernesto Vivares, and Robert W. Mc-Chesney, 46-62. London: Palgrave MacMillan, 2014.

Hong, Ng Sek, and Malcolm Warner. *China's Trade Unions and Management*. London: Palgrave Macmillan, 1998.

hooks, bell. *Feminism Is for Everybody: Passionate Politics*. New York: Routledge, 2000.

Howell, Jude. "NGOs and Civil Society: The Politics of Crafting a Civic Welfare Infrastructure in the Hu-Wen Period." *China Quarterly* 237 (2019): 58-81.

Howell, Jude. "Shall We Dance? Welfarist Incorporation and the Politics of State-Labour NGO Relations." *China Quarterly* 223 (September 2015): 702–23. https://doi.org/10.1017/S0305741015001174.

Howell, Jude, and Tim Pringle. "Shades of Authoritarianism and State-Labour Relations in China." *British Journal of Industrial Relations* 57, no. 2 (2018): 223–46. https://doi.org/10.1111/bjir.12436.

Hsu, Carolyn. "Beyond Civil Society: An Organizational Perspective on State-NGO Relations in the People's Republic of China." *Journal of Civil Society* 6, no. 3 (2010): 259–77.

Hu, Hongwei, Shuang Lu, and Chien-Chung Huang. "The Psychological and Behavioral Outcomes of Migrant and Left-Behind Children in China." *Children and Youth Services Review* 46 (2014): 1–10. https://doi.org/10.1016/j.childyouth.2014.07.021.

Huang, Ronggui, and Ngai-ming Yip. "Internet and Activism in Urban China: A Case Study of Protests in Xiamen and Panyu." *Journal of Comparative Asian Development* 11, no. 2 (2012): 201–23.

Huang, Shirlena, and Brenda S. A. Yeoh. "Maids and Ma'ams in Singapore: Constructing Gender and Nationality in the Transnationalization of Paid Domestic Work." *Geography Research Forum* 18 (1998): 21–48.

Huang Wei and Chen Manfei. "Fan Yusu huole zhihou" 范雨素火了之后 [After Fan Yusu became popular]. Renmin wang 人民网, May 2, 2017. http://culture.people.com.cn/n1/2017/0502/c87423-29247857.html.

Huang, Yalan. "War on Women: Interlocking Conflicts within *The Vagina Monologues* in China." *Asian Journal of Communication* 26, no. 5 (2016): 466–84.

International Labor Organization. Domestic Workers Convention, C189, no. 189. 2011. https://www.ilo.org/dyn/normlex/en/f?p=NORMLEXPUB:12100:0::NO::P12100_ILO_CODE:C189.

International Labor Organization. *Domestic Workers Organize—but Can They Bargain?* February 2015. https://www.ilo.org/publications/domestic-workers-organize-can-they-bargain.

Iskra, Anna. "'Be Soft like Water, Little Woman': Cultivating Postfeminism in Postsocialist China." *Signs: Journal of Women in Culture and Society* 48, no. 3 (2023): 659–82.

Jacka, Tamara. *Creating a Public Sphere: A Case Study of a Rural Women's NGO in Beijing.* Canberra: Australian National University, 2004.

Jacka, Tamara. "Cultivating Citizens: *Suzhi* (Quality) Discourse in the PRC." *Positions Asia Critique* 17, no. 3 (2009): 523–35. https://doi.org/10.1215/10679847-2009-013.

Jacka, Tamara. *Rural Women in Urban China: Gender, Migration, and Social Change.* New York: Routledge, 2006.

Jakobsen, Kjeld, and Alexandre de Freitas Barbosa. "Neoliberal Policies, Labor Market Restructuring and Social Exclusion: Brazil's Working-Class Response." In *Labour and the Challenges of Globalization: What Prospects for*

Transnational Solidarity?, edited by Andreas Bieler, Ingemar Lindberg, and Devan Pillay, 115–30. London: Pluto, 2008.

Jayawardena, Kumari. *Feminism and Nationalism in the Third World*. 1986; repr., London: Verso Books, 2016.

Jiaodian fangtan 焦点访谈. "Didinghua de chuntian" 地丁花的春天 [Didinghua's spring]. January 7, 2016. http://www.cctv1.tv/jiaodianfangtan/3965.html.

Jiemian 界面新闻. "Ceng bei biqian de gongyouzhijia" 曾被逼迁的工友之家 [Migrant Workers' Home once being forced to relocate]. January 15, 2017. https://www.jiemian.com/article/1069399.html.

Jing, Jun. "Environmental Protests in Rural China." In *Chinese Society: Change, Conflict and Resistance*, edited by Elizabeth J. Perry and Mark Selden, 197–214. New York: Routledge, 2000.

Kam, Lucetta Yip Lo. *Shanghai Lalas: Female Tongzhi Communities and Politics in Urban China*. Hong Kong: Hong Kong University Press, 2013.

Kerr, David. "Theater for Development." In *The Handbook of Development Communication and Social Change*, edited by Karin Gwinn Wilkins, Thomas Tufte, and Rafael Obregon, 207–25. Malden, MA: Wiley Blackwell, 2014.

Kipnis, Andrew. "*Suzhi*: A Keyword Approach." *China Quarterly* 186 (2006): 295–313. https://doi.org/10.1017/S0305741006000166.

Klein, Christopher. "The Strike That Shook America." HISTORY, September 3, 2012. https://www.history.com/news/the-strike-that-shook-america.

Laclau, Ernesto, and Chantal Mouffe. *Hegemony and Socialist Strategy: Towards a Radical Democratic Politics*. London: Verso Books, 2014.

Lee, Ching Kwan. *Against the Law: Labor Protests in China's Rustbelt and Sunbelt*. Berkeley: University of California Press, 2007.

Lee, Ching Kwan. "The 'Revenge of History': Collective Memories and Labor Protests in North-Eastern China." *Ethnography* 1, no. 2 (2000): 217–37. https://doi.org/10.1177/14661380022230741.

Lee, Ching Kwan, and Yuan Shen. "The Anti-solidarity Machine? Labor Nongovernmental Organizations in China." In *From Iron Rice Bowl to Informalization: Markets, Workers, and the State in a Changing China*, edited by Sarosh Kuravilla, Ching Kwan Lee, and Mary E. Gallagher, 173–87. Ithaca, NY: ILR Press, 2011.

Lee, Michelle Ye Hee. "Donald Trump's False Comments Connecting Mexican Immigrants and Crime." Washington Post, July 8, 2015. https://www.washingtonpost.com/news/fact-checker/wp/2015/07/08/donald-trumps-false-comments-connecting-mexican-immigrants-and-crime/.

Leung, Parry P. *Labor Activists and the New Working Class in China: Social Movements and Transformation*. New York: Palgrave Macmillan, 2015.

Leymon, Ann Shirley. "Unions and Social Inclusiveness: A Comparison of Changes in Union Member Attitudes." *Labor Studies Journal* 36, no. 3 (2011): 388–407.

Li, Hongmei. *Advertising and Consumer Culture in China*. Malden, MA: Polity Press, 2016.

Li, Ping, Minghua Zhong, Bin Lin, and Hongjuan Zhang. "Deyu as Moral Education in Modern China: Ideological Functions and Transformations." *Journal of Moral Education* 33, no. 4 (2004): 449-64.

Li, Shi. "The Economic Situation of Rural Migrant Workers in China." *China Perspectives* 4 (2010): 4-15. https://doi.org/10.4000/chinaperspectives.5332.

Li Yanhong and Fan Yingjie."Yuanchu kunan de zhongjiehu" 远处苦难的中介化 [Mediated distant suffering]. *Xinwen yu chuanbo yanjiu* 新闻与传播研究 11 (2019): 55-74.

Liang, Zai, Zhongshan Yue, Yuanfei Li, Qiao Li, and Aihua Zhou. "Choices or Constraints: Education of Migrant Children in Urban China." *Population Research and Policy Review* 39 (2020): 671-90.

Liao, Sara Xueting. "Wang Hong Fashion Culture and the Postfeminist Time in China." *Fashion Theory* 25, no 5. (2021): 663-85.

Lin, Chun. *Revolution and Counterrevolution in China: The Paradoxes of Chinese Struggle.* London: Verso Books, 2021.

Liu, Minghui. *Migrants and Cities: Research Report on Recruitment, Employment, and Working Conditions of Domestic Workers in China.* Conditions of Work and Employment Series 92, International Labor Organization. Geneva: International Labor Office, 2017.

Lorde, Audre. "Age, Race, Class and Sex: Women Redefining Difference." In *Campus Wars: Multiculturalism and the Politics of Difference,* edited by John Arthur and Amy Shapiro, 191-98. Boulder, CO: Westview, 1995.

Lu Haoran. "Sun Heng shibanian wei xingongren er ge" 孙恒十八年为新工人而歌 [Sun Heng singing for new workers for eighteen years]. *Jinri toutiao* 今日头条, August 26, 2020. https://www.toutiao.com/article/6865082322044060167/?wid=1688459459669.

Lü Tu. *Zhongguo xin gongren* 中国新工人 [Chinese new workers]. Beijing: Fanlü, 2013.

Lü Tu. *Zhongguo xin gongren: Wenhua yu mingyun* 中国新工人:文化与命运 [Chinese new workers: Culture and destiny]. Beijing: Fanlü, 2015.

Ma, Qiusha. *Non-governmental Organizations in Contemporary China: Paving the Way to Civil Society?* New York: Routledge, 2006.

MacKinnon, Catherine A. "Feminism, Marxism, Method, and the State: An Agenda for Theory." *Signs* 7, no. 3 (1982): 515-44.

Madison, D. Soyini. "Performance, Personal Narratives, and the Politics of Possibilities." In *The Future of Performance Studies: Visions and Revisions,* edited by Otis J. Aggert Festival and Sheron J. Dailey, 276-86. Annandale, VA: National Communication Association, 1998.

Madison, D. Soyini, and Judith Hamera, eds. *The SAGE Handbook of Performance Studies.* Thousand Oaks: SAGE, 2006.

Magowan, Fiona. "Dancing with a Difference: Reconfiguring the Poetic Politics of Aboriginal Ritual as National Spectacle." *Australian Journal of Anthropology* 11, no. 2 (2000): 308-21.

Mahmood, Zaad. "Trade Unions, Politics and Reform in India." *Indian Journal of Industrial Relations* 51, no. 4 (2016): 531-49.

Marcus, George E. "Ethnography in/of the World System: The Emergence of Multi-sited Ethnography." *Annual Review of Anthropology* 24 (1995): 95-117.

Marx, Karl. *Capital: A Critique of Political Economy*. Vol. 1, *The Process of Production of Capital*. 1867; repr., London: Penguin Classics, 1990.

McLell, Mark. "Art as Activism in Japan: The Case of a Good-for-Nothing Kid and Her Pussy." In *The Routledge Companion to Media and Activism*, edited by Graham Meikle, 162-70. London: Routledge, 2018.

McRobbie, Angela. *The Aftermath of Feminism: Gender, Culture and Social Change*. Thousand Oaks: SAGE, 2009.

McRobbie, Angela. "Setting Accounts with Subcultures: A Feminist Critique." *Screen Education* 39 (1980): 37-49.

Meikle, Graham. "Introduction: Making Meanings and Making Trouble." In *The Routledge Companion to Media and Activism*, edited by Graham Meikle, 1-15. London: Routledge, 2018.

Mendes, Kaitlynn, Jessica Ringrose, and Jessalynn Keller. "#MeToo and the Promise and Pitfalls of Challenging Rape Culture through Digital Feminist Activism." *European Journal of Women's Studies* 25, no. 2 (2018): 236-46.

Meng, Bingchun. *The Politics of Chinese Media: Consensus and Contestation*. New York: Palgrave Macmillan, 2018.

Meng, Bingchun, and Yanning Huang. "Patriarchal Capitalism with Chinese Characteristics: Gendered Discourse of 'Double Eleven' Shopping Festival." *Cultural Studies* 31, no. 5 (2017): 659-84. https://doi.org /10.1080/09502386 .2017.1328517.

Meng Yingdeng. "'Dagong chunwan' yu 'xin gongren wenhua' de chuangzao lujing" "打工春晚"与"新工人文化"的创造路径 ["Dagong Spring Festival gala" and the production of "new-worker culture"]. *Wenyi lilun yu piping* 文艺理论与批评 10 (2017): 45-54.

Meyer-Clement, Elena. "Rural Urbanization under Xi Jinping: From Rapid Community Building to Steady Urbanization?" *China Information* 34, no. 2 (2020): 187-207.

Mies, Maria. *Patriarchy and Accumulation on a World Scale: Women in the International Division of Labour*. New York: Zed Books, 2022.

Mills, Mary Beth. "Gender and Inequality in the Global Labor Force." *Annual Review of Anthropology* 32 (2003): 41-62.

Mitra, Ananda. "Voices of the Marginalized on the Internet: Examples from a Website for Women of South Asia." *Journal of Communication* 54, no. 3 (2004): 492-510.

Montgomery, Jessica L. "The Inheritance of Inequality: *Hukou* and Related Barriers to Compulsory Education for China's Migrant Children." *Pacific Rim Law and Policy Journal* 21, no. 3 (2012): 591-622. https://digitalcommons.law .uw.edu/wilj/vol21/iss3/7.

Moors, Annelies, Ray Jureidini, Ferhunde Özbay, and Rima Sabban. "Migrant Domestic Workers: A New Public Presence in the Middle East?" In *Publics, Politics and Participation: Locating the Public Sphere in the Middle East and North Africa*, edited by Seteney Shami, 151-76. New York: Social Science Research Council, 2009.

Mutua, Kagendo, and Beth Blue Swadener. Introduction to *Decolonizing Research in Cross-Cultural Contexts: Critical Personal Narratives*, edited by Kagendo Mutua and Beth Blue Swadener, 1-23. Albany: State University of New York Press, 2004.

National Bureau of Statistics of China. *2022 Annual Report of Rural Migrant Workers*. April 2023. https://www.stats.gov.cn/sj/zxfb/202304/t20230427_1939124.html.

Negt, Oskar, and Alexander Kluge. *Public Sphere and Experience: Toward an Analysis of the Bourgeois and Proletarian Public Sphere*. Minneapolis: University of Minnesota Press, 1993.

Ness, Immanuel. *Southern Insurgency: The Coming of the Global Working Class*. London: Pluto, 2016.

Nowak, Jorg. "Strikes and Labor Unrest in the Automobile Industry in India: The Case of Maruti Suzuki India." *Working USA: The Journal of Labor and Society* 19, no. 3 (2016): 419-36.

Ong, Aihwa. *Neoliberalism as Exception: Mutations in Citizenship and Sovereignty*. Durham, NC: Duke University Press, 2006.

Orgad, Shani. *Media Representation and the Global Imagination*. Malden, MA: Polity Press, 2012.

Paek, Hye-Jin, and Zhongdang Pan. "Spreading Global Consumerism: Effects of Mass Media and Advertising on Consumerist Values in China." *Mass Communication and Society* 7, no. 4 (2004): 491-515.

Pangsapa, Piya. "When Battlefields Become Marketplaces: Migrant Workers and the Role of Civil Society and NGO Activism in Thailand." *International Migration* 53, no. 3 (2015): 124-49.

Perry, Elizabeth J., and Mark Selden. "Introduction: Reform, Conflict and Resistance in Contemporary China." In *Chinese Society: Change, Conflict and Resistance*, edited by Elizabeth J. Perry and Mark Selden, 1-30. London: Routledge, 2010.

Posthuma, Anne, and Dev Nathan. *Labour in Global Production Networks in India*. New Delhi: Oxford University Press, 2010.

Pun, Ngai. *Made in China: Women Factory Workers in a Global Workplace*. Durham, NC: Duke University Press, 2005.

Pun, Ngai, and Huilin Lu. "Unfinished Proletarianization: Self, Anger, and Class Action among the Second Generation of Peasant-Workers in Present-Day China." *Modern China* 36, no. 5 (2010): 493-519.

Qiu, Jack Linchuan. *Goodbye iSlave: A Manifesto for Digital Abolition*. Urbana: University of Illinois Press, 2017.

Qiu, Jack Linchuan. "Locating Worker-Generated Content (WGC) in the World's Factory." In *The Routledge Companion to Labor and Media*, edited by Richard Maxwell, 303-14. New York: Routledge, 2015.

Qiu, Jack Linchuan. *Working-Class Network Society: Communication Technology and the Information Have-less in Urban China*. Cambridge, MA: MIT Press, 2009.

Ramirez, Adriana Paz, and Jennifer Jihye Chun. "Struggling against History: Migrant Farmworker Organizing in British Columbia." In *Unfree Labour? Struggles of Migrant and Immigrant Workers in Canada*, edited by Aziz Choudry and Adrian Smith, 87-104. Oakland, CA: PM Press, 2016.

Rauber, Isabel. "The Globalization of Capital and Its Impact on the World of Formal and Informal Work: Challenges for the Responses from Argentine Unions." In *Labour and the Challenges of Globalization: What Prospects for Transnational Solidarity?*, edited by Andreas Bieler, Ingemar Lindberg, and Deven Pillay, 98-111. London: Pluto, 2008.

Renmin wang 人民网. "'Fan Yusu men' he tamen de laoshi" "范雨素们"和他们的老师 [Fan Yusu and their teachers]. May 2, 2017. http://cpc.people.com.cn/BIG5/n1/2017/0502/c64387-29249231.html.

Rodriguez, Clemencia. "Citizens' Media." In *Encyclopedia of Social Movement Media*, edited by John D. H. Downing, 98-102. Thousand Oaks: SAGE, 2011.

Rodriguez, Clemencia. "Civil Society and Citizens' Media: Peace Architects for the New Millennium." In *Redeveloping Communication for Social Change: Theory, Practice, and Power*, edited by Karin Gwinn Wilkins, 147-162. Lanham, MD: Rowman and Littlefield, 2000.

Rofel, Lisa. *Desiring China: Experiments in Neoliberalism, Sexuality, and Public Culture*. Durham, NC: Duke University Press, 2007.

Rofel, Lisa. *Other Modernities: Gendered Yearnings in China after Socialism*. Berkeley: University of California Press, 1999.

Romero, Mary. *Maid in the U.S.A.* New York: Routledge, 2002.

Rosenthal, Rob, and Richard Flacks. *Playing for Change: Music and Musicians in the Service of Social Movements*. New York: Routledge, 2011.

Rovisco, Maria, and Jonathan Corpus Ong. Introduction to *Taking the Square: Mediated Dissent and Occupations of Public Space*, edited by Maria Rovisco and Jonathan Corpus Ong, 1-12. New York: Rowman and Littlefield, 2016.

Rucht, Dieter. "The Quadruple 'A': Media Strategies of Protest Movements since the 1960s." In *Cyberprotest: New Media, Citizens, and Social Movements*, edited by Wim van de Donk, Brian D. Loader, Paul G. Nixon, and Dieter Rucht, 25-48. London: Routledge, 2004.

Saich, Tony. "Negotiating the State: The Development of Social Organizations in China." *China Quarterly* 161 (March 2000): 124-41.

Salter, Michael. "Justice and Revenge in Online Counter-Publics: Emerging Responses to Sexual Violence in the Age of Social Media." *Crime, Media, Culture* 9, no. 3 (2013): 225-42. https://doi.org/10.1177/1741659013493918.

Scopes, Kim. "Understanding the New Labor Movements in the 'Third World':

The Emergence of Social Movement Unionism." *Critical Sociology* 19, no. 2
(1992): 81-101.

Seeberg, Vilma. "Girls' Schooling Empowerment in Rural China: Identifying
Capabilities and Social Change in the Village." *Comparative Education Review*
58, no. 4 (2014): 678-707.

Shi, Yu, and Francis L. Collins. "Producing Mobility: Visual Narratives of the
Rural Migrant Worker in Chinese Television." *Mobilities* 13, no. 1 (2018):
126-41.

Shin, Hyun Bang. "Economic Transition and Speculative Urbanisation in China:
Gentrification versus Dispossession." *Urban Studies* 53, no. 3 (2016): 471-89.

Shutŏ, Wakana, and Mac Urata. "The Impact of Globalization on Trade Unions:
The Situation in Japan." In *Labour and the Challenges of Globalization: What
Prospects for Transnational Solidarity?*, edited by Andreas Bieler, Ingemar
Lindberg, and Devan Pillay, 139-58. London: Pluto, 2008.

Sodhi, J. S. "Trade Unions in India: Changing Role and Perspective." *Indian
Journal of Industrial Relations* 49, no. 2 (2013): 169-84.

Sohu 搜狐. "Bu Wei: Wenhua quanli shi renquan bukefenge de yibufen" 卜卫:文
化权利是人权不可分割的一部分 [Bu Wei: Cultural rights are an integral part
of human rights]. October 20, 2010. http://news.sohu.com/20101020/
n276079282.shtml.

Sohu 搜狐. "Shehui gejie dui dagong wenhua yishu bowuguan jiqi zhongchou
huodong de jiyu" 社会各界对打工文化艺术博物馆及其众筹活动的寄语 [Mes-
sages from the society to the laboring art museum and its crowdfunding ac-
tivities]. July 25, 2017. https://www.sohu.com/a/159833947_653202.

Song, Weixuan, and Xigang Zhu. "Gentrification in Urban China under Market
Transformation." *International Journal of Urban Sciences* 14, no. 2 (2010):
152-63.

Spencer, Neil H., Ursula Huws, Dag Syrdal, and Kaire Holts. *Work in the European Gig Economy: Research Results from the UK, Sweden, Germany, Austria,
the Netherlands, Switzerland and Italy*. Brussels: Foundation for European
Progressive Studies, 2017.

Spires, Anthony J. "Contingent Symbiosis and Civil Society in an Authoritarian
State: Understanding the Survival of China's Grassroots NGOs." *American
Journal of Sociology* 117, no. 1 (2011): 1-45.

Stahler-Sholk, Richard. "Resisting Neoliberal Homogenization: The Zapatista
Autonomy Movement." *Latin American Perspectives* 34, no. 2 (2007): 48-63.

Sudbury, Julia. "A World without Prisons: Resisting Militarism, Globalized
Punishment, and Empire." *Social Justice* 31, no. 1 (2004): 9-30.

Sun, Wanning. "Indoctrination, Fetishization, and Compassion: Media Con-
struction of the Migrant Women." In *On the Move: Women and Rural-to-
Urban Migration in Contemporary China*, edited by Arianne M. Gaetano and
Tamara Jacka, 109-30. New York: Columbia University Press, 2004.

Sun, Wanning. "Inequality and Culture: A New Pathway to Understand Social

Inequality." In *Unequal China: The Political Economy and Cultural Politics of Inequality*, edited by Wanning Sun and Yingjie Guo, 27-42. New York: Routledge, 2013.

Sun, Wanning. *Maid in China: Media, Morality and the Cultural Politics of Boundaries*. New York: Routledge, 2009.

Sun, Wanning. "Narrating Translocality: *Dagong* Poetry and the Subaltern Imagination." *Mobilities* 5, no. 3 (2010): 291-309.

Sun, Wanning. *Subaltern China: Rural Migrants, Media and Cultural Practices*. London: Rowman and Littlefield, 2014.

Tacchi, Jo. "The Issues of Voice and the Challenges of Listening." *New Media and Society* 14, no. 4 (2012): 652-68.

Tai, Zixue. "Networked Activism in China." In *Social Networking: Redefining Communication in the Digital Age*, edited by Anastacia Kurylo and Tatyana Dumova, 145-60. Lanham, MD: Rowman and Littlefield, 2016.

Tai, Zixue. "Networked Resistance: Digital Populism, Online Activism, and Mass Dissent in China." *Popular Communication* 13, no. 2 (2015): 120-31. https://doi .org/10.1080/15405702.2015.1021469.

Tai, Zixue. "Social Media and Contentious Action in China." In *The Routledge Companion to Media and Activism*, edited by Graham Meikle, 97-107. London: Routledge, 2018.

Tan, Jia. *Digital Masquerade: Feminist Rights and Queer Media in China*. New York: New York University Press, 2023.

Tan, Jia. "Digital Masquerading: Feminist Media Activism in China." *Crime, Media, Culture* 13, no. 2 (2017): 171-86.

Thelle, Hatla. "Building Their Own Stage: Constructing the New Worker in China." *Journal of Human Rights Practice* 5, no. 2 (2013): 358-79.

Thompson, E. P. *The Making of the English Working Class*. New York: Random House, 1966.

Travers, Ann. "Parallel Subaltern Feminist Counterpublics in Cyberspace." *Sociological Perspectives* 46, no 2. (2003): 223-37. https://doi.org/10.1525/sop.2003.46 .2.223.

Tufts, Steven. "World Cities and Union Renewal." *Geography Compass* 1, no. 3 (2007): 673-94.

Unger, Jonathan. *The Transformation of Rural China*. New York: Routledge, 2016. https://doi.org/10.4324/9781315292052. EPUB.

van Crevel, Maghiel. "Misfit: Xu Lizhi and Battlers Poetry (*Dagong Shige*)." *Prism* 16, no. 1 (2019): 85-114.

van Doorn, Niels. "Platform Labor: On the Gendered and Racialized Exploitation of Low-Income Service Work in the 'On-Demand' Economy." *Information, Communication and Society* 20, no. 6 (2017): 898-914.

van Doorn, Niels, Fabian Ferrari, and Mark Graham. "Migration and Migrant Labour in the Gig Economy: An Intervention." *Work, Employment and Society* 37, no. 4 (2023): 1099-111.

Vickers, Tom, and Annie Rutter. "Disposable Labour, Passive Victim, Active Threat: Migrant/Non-migrant Othering in Three British Television Documentaries." *European Journal of Cultural Studies* 21, no. 4 (2018): 486-501.

Virmani, Shabnam. "Women Making Meaning: Telling Stories about Reality in India." *Feminist Media Studies* 1, no. 2 (2001): 233-43.

Walder, Andrew G. *China under Mao: A Revolution Derailed*. Cambridge, MA: Harvard University Press, 2017.

Wallis, Cara. "Technology and/as Govermentality: The Production of Young Rural Women as Low-Tech Laboring Subjects in China." *Communication and Critical/Cultural Studies* 10, no. 4 (2013): 341-58.

Wallis, Cara. *Technomobility in China: Young Migrant Women and Mobile Phones*. New York: New York University Press, 2013.

Wang, Bin, and Catherine Driscoll. "Chinese Feminists on Social Media: Articulating Different Voices, Building Strategic Alliances." *Continuum Journal of Media and Cultural Studies* 33, no. 1 (2019): 1-15.

Wang, Fengyan. "Confucian Thinking in Traditional Moral Education: Key Ideas and Fundamental Features." *Journal of Moral Education* 33, no. 4 (2004): 429-47.

Wang Hongzhe. "Kunan yu mengxiang de tuanjie—yidong hulianwang shidai de xingongren wenhua" 苦难与梦想的团结—移动互联时代的新工人文化 [The unity of hardship and dreams: New worker culture in the digital age]. *Yishu guangjiao* 艺术广角 4 (2017): 22.

Wang, Hui. "Contemporary Chinese Thought and the Question of Modernity." Translated by Rebecca E. Karl. *Social Text* 55 (Summer 1998): 9-44.

Wang, Hui. *The End of the Revolution: China and the Limits of Modernity*. New York: Verso Books, 2011.

Wang Hui. "Liangzhong xinqiongren jiqi weilai—jieji zhengzhi de shuailuo, zaixingcheng yu xinqiongren de zunyan zhengzhi" 两种新穷人及其未来—阶级政治的衰落,再形成与新穷人的尊严政治 [Two types of the new poor and their futures—the fall of class politics, reformation, and the new poor's political dignity]. *Kaifang shidai* 开放时代 6 (2014): 49-70.

Wang, Jing. "NGO2.0 and Social Media Praxis: Activist as Researcher." *Chinese Journal of Communication* 8, no. 1 (2015): 18-41.

Wang, Stephanie Yingyi. "Unfinished Revolution: An Overview of Three Decades of LGBT Activism in China." *Made in China Journal* 6, no. 1 (2021): 90-95.

Wang, Zheng. *Finding Women in the State: A Socialist Feminist Revolution in the People's Republic of China, 1949-1964*. Oakland: University of California Press, 2016.

Warde, Bryan. "Black Male Disproportionality in the Criminal Justice Systems of the USA, Canada, and England: A Comparative Analysis of Incarceration." *Journal of African American Studies* 17, no. 4 (2013): 461-79.

Warner, Malcolm. "Trade Unions in China: In Search of a New Role in the

'Harmonious Society.'" In *Trade Unions in Asia: An Economic and Sociological Analysis*, edited by John Benson and Ying Zhou, 140-56. New York: Routledge, 2008.

Waterman, Peter. "Social-Movement Unionism: A New Union Model for a New World Order?" *Review* 16, no. 3 (Summer 1993): 245-78.

Waterman, Peter. "A Trade Union Internationalism for the 21st Century: Meeting the Challenges from Above, Below and Beyond." In *Labour and the Challenges of Globalization: What Prospects for Transnational Solidarity?*, edited by Andreas Bieler, Ingemar Lindberg, and Devan Pillay, 248-61. London: Pluto, 2008.

Weeks, Kathi. *Constituting Feminist Subjects*. London: Verso Books, 2018.

Wei, Chongzheng, and Wenli Liu. "Coming out in Mainland China: A National Survey of LGBTQ Students." *Journal of LGBT Youth* 16, no. 2 (2019): 192-219.

Weil, David. *The Fissured Workplace: Why Work Became So Bad for So Many and What Can Be Done to Improve It*. Cambridge, MA: Harvard University Press, 2014.

White, Tyrene. "Domination, Resistance and Accomodation in China's One-Child Campaign." In *Chinese Society: Change, Conflict and Resistance*. 3rd ed., edited by Elizabeth J. Perry and Mark Selden, 171-96. New York: Routledge, 2010.

Williams, Raymond. *Marxism and Literature*. Oxford: Oxford University Press, 1977.

Williams, Raymond. *The Long Revolution*. London: Chatto and Windus, 1961.

Wills, Jane, and Melanie Simms. "Building Reciprocal Community Unionism in the UK." *Capital and Class* 28, no. 1 (2004): 59-84.

Winskell, Kate, and Daniel Enger. "Storytelling for Social Change." In *The Handbook of Development Communication and Social Change*, edited by Karin Gwinn Wilkins, Thomas Tufte, and Rafael Obregon, 189-206. Malden, MA: Wiley-Blackwell, 2014.

Wolff, Richard. *Understanding Socialism*. New York: Democracy at Work, 2019.

Workers' Action Center. *Still Working on the Edge: Building Decent Jobs from the Ground Up*. March 2015. https://workersactioncentre.org/wp-content/uploads/2016/07/StillWorkingOnTheEdge-Exec-Summary-web.pdf.

Wood, Ellen. *Empire of Capital*. London: Verso Books, 2005.

Woodcock, Jamie. *The Fight against Platform Capitalism: An Inquiry into the Global Struggles of the Gig Economy*. London: University of Westminster Press, 2021.

Xiao, Yang, and Yanjie Bian. "The Influence of *Hukou* and College Education in China's Labour Market." *Urban Studies* 55, no. 7 (2017): 1504-24.

Xie Stella Yifan and Liyan Qi. "Zhongguo gongchang zaoyu yonggonghuang" 中国工厂遭遇用工荒 [Chinese factories are facing labor shortage]. *Wall Street Journal*, August 28, 2021. https://cn.wsj.com/articles/中国工厂遭遇用工荒.

Xinwen Diaocha 新闻调查. "Didinghua jushe" 地丁花剧社 [Didinghua Theater].

April 22, 2017. https://tv.cctv.com/2017/04/22/VIDEm5u6mbFP33ViLZZZ 84Gc170422.shtml.

Xu, Feng. *Women Migrant Workers in China's Economic Reform.* London: Palgrave Macmillan, 2000.

Xu, Yi. "Labor Non-governmental Organizations in China: Mobilizing Rural Migrant Workers." *Journal of Industrial Relations* 55, no. 2 (2013): 243-59.

Yan, Hairong. "Neoliberal Governmentality and Neohumanism: Organizing *Suzhi*/Value Flow through Labor Recruitment Networks." *Cultural Anthropology* 18, no. 4 (2003): 493-523.

Yan, Hairong. *New Masters, New Servants: Migration, Development, and Women Workers in China.* Durham, NC: Duke University Press, 2008.

Yang, Fan. "Post-feminism and Chick Flicks in China: Subjects, Discursive Origin and New Gender Norms." *Feminist Media Studies* 23, no. 3 (2019): 1059-74.

Yang, Guobin. *The Power of the Internet in China: Citizen Activism Online.* New York: Columbia University Press, 2009.

Yang, Qinran, Yang Liu, and Linchuan Yang. "Commercial Gentrification in China and Its Distribution, Development, and Correlates: The Case of Chengdu." *Frontiers in Environmental Science* 10 (August 2022): 1-15.

Yao Dechao, Lin Zhang, and Weiquan Zou. *Nongcun liudong nüxing chengshi shenghuo fazhan baogao* 农村流动女性城市生活发展报告 [Report on development of rural-to-urban female migrants]. Beijing: Social Sciences Academic Press, 2014.

Yin, Siyuan. "Alternative Forms of Media, ICTs, and Underprivileged Groups in China." *Media, Culture and Society* 40, no. 8 (2018): 1221-36.

Yin, Siyuan. "Cultural Production in Working-Class Resistance: Labor Activism, Gender Politics, and Solidarities." *Cultural Studies* 34, no. 3 (2019): 418-41.

Yin, Siyuan. "'Patriotic Heroes' and 'Foreign Laborers': Politics of Media and Public Discourses on Essential Workers and Migrant Workers in Canada during COVID-19." *International Journal of Communication* (forthcoming).

Yin, Siyuan. "Producing Gendered Migration Narratives in China: A Case Study of *Dagongmei Tongxun* by a Local NGO." *International Journal of Communication* 10 (2016): 4304-23.

Yin, Siyuan. "Re-articulating Feminisms: A Theoretical Critique of Feminist Struggles and Discourse in Historical and Contemporary China." *Cultural Studies* 36, no. 6 (2022): 981-1004.

Yin, Siyuan, and Yu Sun. "Intersectional Digital Feminism: Assessing the Participation Politics and Impact of the MeToo Movement in China." *Feminist Media Studies* 21, no. 7 (2021): 1176-92. https://doi.org/10.1080/14680777 .2020.1837908.

Young, Iris M. "Five Faces of Oppression." *Philosophical Forum* 19, no. 4 (1988): 270-90.

Yu, Au Loong. "The Jasic Mobilisation: A High Tide for the Chinese Labour Movement?" In *Dog Days: Made in China Yearbook 2018*, edited by Ivan Franceschini, Nicholas Loubere, Kevin Lin, Elisa Nesossi, Andrea Pia, and Christian Sorace, 12-16. Canberra: Australian National University Press, 2018.

Zeng, Jing. "#MeToo as Connective Action: A Study of the Anti-sexual Violence and Anti-sexual Harassment Campaign on Chinese Social Media in 2018." *Journalism Practice* 14, no. 2 (2020): 171-90.

Zhang, Boyang, Yuhan You, Guangye He, Fei Yan, and Senhu Wang. "Searching for the Rainbow Connection: Regional Development and LGBT Communities in China." *Journal of Contemporary China* 32, no. 140 (2023): 296-318.

Zhang Huiyu. "Fachu women de shengyin, gongren wenxue de yiyi yu jiazhi" 发出我们的声音，工人文学的意义与价值 [Expressing our voices, meanings, and value of workers' literature]. *Xinhua yuebao* 新华月报 9 (2016): 49.

Zhang, Li. *Strangers in the City: Reconfigurations of Space, Power, and Social Networks within China's Floating Population*. Stanford: Stanford University Press, 2001.

Zhang Ye. "Chengzhongcun wenyi" 城中村文艺 [Art in urban villages]. *Pengpai* 澎湃, March 29, 2018. https://www.thepaper.cn/newsDetail_forward_ 2046443.

Zhao, Yuezhi. *Media, Market, and Democracy in China*. Urbana: University of Illinois Press, 1998.

Zhao, Yuezhi. "Neoliberal Strategies, Socialist Legacies: Communication and State Transformation in China." In *Global Communications: Toward a Transnational Political Economy*, edited by Paula Chakravartty and Yuezhi Zhao, 23-55. Lanham, MD: Rowman and Littlefield, 2008.

Zhao Zhiyong. "Wenhua shijian shouhu diceng quanyi yu zunyan" 文化实践守护底层权益与尊严 [To protect rights and dignity of the underprivileged through cultural practices]. *Refeng xueshu* 热风学术 10 (2016): 159-69.

Zheng, Xiaodong, Yue Zhang, and Wenyu Jiang. "Internal Migration and Depression among Junior High School Students in China: A Comparison between Migrant and Left-Behind Children." *Frontiers in Psychology* 13 (2022): 811617. https://doi.org/10.3389/fpsyg.2022.811617.

Zhongguo fazhan jianbao 中国发展简报. "Beijing gongyouzhijia jianjie" 北京工友之家简介 [Introduction to Beijing Migrant Workers' Home]. Accessed September 11, 2024. https://www.chinadevelopmentbrief.org.cn/company/ detail/185.html.

Zhongguo nongcun wang 中国农村网. "Tanfang Picun" 探访皮村 [Visiting Picun village]. December 13, 2021. http://journal.crnews.net/mhsh/2016n/ 2016ndsyq/915543_20161215111306.html.

Zhonghua renmin gongheguo zhongyang renmin zhengfu 中华人民共和国中央人民政府. "Zhongxuanbu wenhuabu biaozhang fuwu nongmin fuwu jiceng wenhua xianjin jiti" 中宣部文化部表彰服务农民服务基层文化先进集体 [The

Publicity Department and the Ministry of Culture commended advanced groups for serving farmers and promoting grassroots culture]. December 14, 2015. https://www.gov.cn/jrzg/2005- 12/14/content_126981.htm.

Zhongmu. "'Nongmingong sikao haidegeer' de xushi, nandao bushi sichengxiangshi ma?" "农民工思考海德格尔" 的叙事，难道不是似曾相识吗? [Isn't the narrative of "migrant workers thinking about Heidegger" familiar?]. *Xinjing bao* (新京报), December 8, 2021. https://m.bjnews.com.cn/detail/16389322 6914032.html.

Zhou, Min, and Shih-Ding Liu. "Becoming Precarious Playbour: Chinese Migrant Youth on the Kuaishou Video-Sharing Platform." *Economic and Labour Relations Review* 32, no. 3 (2021): 322–40.

Zhou, Shou, and Monit Cheung. "*Hukou* System Effects on Migrant Children's Education in China: Learning from Past Disparities." *International Social Work* 60, no. 6 (2017): 1327–42.

Zhou, Xueguang. *The Logic of Governance in China: An Organizational Approach.* Cambridge: Cambridge University Press, 2022.

Zhu, Han, and Lu Jun. "The Crackdown on Rights-Advocacy NGOs in Xi's China: Politicizing the Law and Legalizing the Repression." *Journal of Contemporary China* 31, no. 136 (2021): 518–38. https://doi.org/10.1080/10670564 .2021.1985829.

Zhu, Pengyu. "Residential Segregation and Employment Outcomes of Rural Migrant Workers in China." *Urban Studies* 53, no. 8 (2015): 1635–56.

Zhu, Ying, Malcolm Warner, and Tongqing Feng. "Employment Relations 'with Chinese Characteristics': The Role of Trade Unions in China." *International Labor Review* 150, no. 102 (2011): 127–43.

Discography

Duan Yu, vocalist. "Ertong de huayuan" 儿童的花园 [Children's garden]. By Jiu Ye. N.p., 2018.

Duan Yu, vocalist. "Nüren de zibai" 女人的自白 [Women's claims]. By Jiu Ye. N.p., 2016.

Jiu Ye. "Shijie you women butong" 世界有我们不同 [Our being makes it a different world]. N.p., 2018.

Oppenheim, James, lyricist. "Bread and Roses." Written 1911, music by Martha Coleman, composed 1922. http://www.protestsonglyrics.net/Inspirational _Songs/Bread-and-Roses.phtml.

Sun Heng, vocalist. "Biao Ge" 彪哥 [Brother Biao]. By New-Worker Troupe. Track 3 on *Wo de jita hui changge* 我的吉他会唱歌 [My guitar knows what to sing]. Beijing dadi minyao gouji wenhua yishu chuanbo 北京大地民谣国际文化艺术传播, 2011.

Sun Heng, vocalist. "Tuanjie qilai taogongqian" 团结起来讨工钱 [Unite and ask for arrears wages]. By New-Worker Troupe. Track 4 on *Laodong yu zunyan* 劳动与尊严 [Labor and dignity]. Beijing jingwen chang pian chuanbo 北京京文唱片传播, 2013.

Sun Heng, vocalist. "Weishenme" 为什么 [Why]. By New-Worker Troupe. Track 9 on *Wo de jita hui changge* 我的吉他会唱歌 [My guitar knows what to sing]. Beijing dadi minyao gouji wenhua yishu chuanbo 北京大地民谣国际文化艺术传播, 2011.

Sun Heng, Sun Yuan, and Jiang Guoliang, vocalists. "Women de shijie women de mengxiang" 我们的世界我们的梦想 [Our world and our dreams]. By New-Worker Troupe. Track 1 on *Women de shijie women de mengxiang* 我们的世界

我们的梦想 [Our world our dream]. Dalian yinxiang 大连音像, 2008.

Xu Duo, vocalist. "Beijing, Beijing" 北京北京 [Beijing, Beijing]. By New-Worker Troupe. Track 6 on *Laodong yu zunyan* 劳动与尊严 [Labor and dignity]. Beijing jingwen chang pian chuanbo 北京京文唱片传播, 2013.

Xu Duo, vocalist. "Chengshi de shenghuo" 城市的生活 [Urban life]. By New-Worker Troupe. Track 2 on *Women de shijie women de mengxiang* 我们的世界我们的梦想 [Our world our dream]. Dalian yinxiang 大连音像, 2008.

Xu Duo, vocalist. "Hei! Renjian" 嘿!人间 [Hey! World]. By New-Worker Troupe. Track 2 on *Hei! Renjian* 嘿!人间 [Hey! World]. Dadi minzhiyao 大地民之谣, 2023.

Index

Page numbers in italics denote figures, and endnotes are indicated by "n" followed by the endnote number.

The authorized representative in the EU for product safety and compliance is:
Mare Nostrum Group B.V.
Mauritskade 21D
1091 GC Amsterdam
The Netherlands
Email address: gpsr@mare-nostrum.co.uk

KVK chamber of commerce number: 96249943

The authorized representative in the EU for product safety and compliance is:
Mare Nostrum Group
B.V Doelen 72
4831 GR Breda
The Netherlands

www.ingramcontent.com/pod-product-compliance
Lightning Source LLC
Chambersburg PA
CBHW030358270326
41926CB00009B/1168